THE BULLY PULPIT

A publication of
the Center for Self-Governance

THE
BULLY PULPIT

The Presidential Leadership of Ronald Reagan

WILLIAM KER MUIR, JR.

ICS PRESS
Institute for Contemporary Studies
San Francisco, California

This book is a publication of the Center for Self-Governance, which is dedicated to the study of self-governing institutions. The Center is affiliated with the Institute for Contemporary Studies, a nonpartisan, nonprofit, public policy research organization. The analyses, conclusions, and opinions expressed in ICS Press publications are those of the authors and not necessarily those of the Institute for Contemporary Studies, the Institute's officers, directors, or others associated with, or funding, its work.

Inquiries should be addressed to ICS Press, Institute for Contemporary Studies, 243 Kearny Street, San Francisco, CA 94108. (415) 981-5353. Fax (415) 986-4878. For book orders and catalog requests call toll-free within the United States: **(800) 326-0263**. Distributed to the trade by National Book Network, Lanham, Maryland.

All photos were taken by White House photographers and appear in this book courtesy of the Ronald Reagan Presidential Library.

Library of Congress Cataloging-in-Publication Data

Muir, William Ker.
   The bully pulpit : the presidential leadership of Ronald Reagan / William Ker Muir, Jr.
      p.   cm.
   Includes bibliographical references and index.
   ISBN 1-55815-167-2 : $22.95
   1. Reagan, Ronald. 2. United States—Politics and government—1981–1989. 3. Political leadership—United States—History—20th century. I. Title.
   E877.M85   1992
973.927'092—dc20   91-42310
                                                                    CIP

To the builders, faculty, staff, and students
of the University of California, Berkeley,
an institution I love

Our conception of ourselves and of each other has always depended on our image of the earth.

When the earth was the World—all the world there was—and the stars were lights in Dante's Heaven, and the ground beneath our feet roofed Hell, we saw ourselves as creatures at the center of the universe, the sole particular concern of God.

And when, centuries later, the earth was no longer the world but a small, wet, spinning planet in the solar system of a minor star off at the edge of an inconsiderable galaxy in the vastnesses of space—when Dante's Heaven foundered and there was no Hell—no Hell, at least, beneath our feet—men began to see themselves not as God-directed actors in the solemn paces of a noble play, but rather as the victims of an idiotic farce where all the rest were victims also and multitudes had perished without meaning.

Now, in this latest generation of mankind, the image may have altered once again. For the first time in all of time men have seen the earth with their own eyes—seen the whole earth in the vast void as even Dante never dreamed of seeing it—seen what whimpering victims could not guess a man might see.

The medieval notion of the earth put man at the center of everything. The scientific notion put him nowhere: beyond the range of sense or reason, lost in absurdity and death. This latest notion may have other consequences. Formed as it was in the eyes of heroic voyagers who were also men, it may remake our lost conception of ourselves. No longer the preposterous player at the center of an unreal stage—no longer that degraded and degrading victim off at the verges of reality and blind with blood—man may discover what he really is.

To see the earth as we now see it, small and blue and beautiful in that eternal silence where it floats, is to see ourselves as riders of the earth together, brothers on that bright loveliness in the unending night—brothers who see now they are truly brothers.

—Archibald MacLeish, Riders on the Earth

There went out a sower to sow: and it came to pass, as he sowed, some fell by the wayside, and the fowls of the air came and devoured it up. And some fell on stony ground, where it had not much earth; and immediately it sprang up, because it had no depth of the earth: but when the sun was up, it was scorched; and because it had no root, it withered away. And some fell among the thorns, and the thorns grew up, and choked it, and it yielded no fruit. And other seed fell on good ground, and did yield fruit that sprang up and increased; and brought forth, some thirty, and some sixty, and some an hundred.

—Mark 4:3–8

Contents

Foreword

Was the American public crazy to elect Ronald Reagan? If one believes the conventional wisdom of political commentary, the answer is clearly yes. But if one considers the changes that took place during Reagan's tenure, one must conclude that most political pundits see the Reagan presidency through spectacles clouded with their own biases.

As William Muir demonstrates, Reagan was a man with a mission—he was determined to deal with the national confusion and pessimism prevalent after the turbulent 1960s and 1970s. Most of all, he wanted to restore the people's capacity for self-reliance and self-government. By listening to the people's grievances and learning about the issues that concerned them, Reagan developed a clear sense of the moral program the nation wanted. Then he devised a strategy for implementing it.

It wasn't a strategy in the usual sense of the word—there weren't clearly defined steps to an end. Instead, Reagan schooled his cabinet, the executive branch staff, and the nation's moral institutions—churches, for example—in his philosophy and sent them out to spread the word. And from his own "bully pulpit," which he carried from coast to coast and around the world, Reagan himself preached resoundingly that self-government could be restored.

If Americans were to accept Reagan's message, they would also have to accept what Alexis de Tocqueville called the burden of freedom: Every individual would have to wrestle with the large philosophical questions of life and do whatever possible to prove that life has purpose, despite its disappointments and failures. Every person would have to take personal responsibility for his or her fate and not depend on the state for protection.

The Reagan we see in these pages seems very like Tocqueville, urging the citizenry to recognize that, although the democratic social condition places a heavy burden on individuals, the spiritual rewards are great. Tocqueville would undoubtedly have applauded Ronald Reagan's achievements and his ability to inspire optimism and generosity in the American people. He would also have been delighted to find Reagan promoting Lao-Tzu's ancient recipe for political success: Govern a great nation as you would cook a small fish; don't overdo it.

Robert B. Hawkins, Jr., President
Institute for Contemporary Studies

Acknowledgments

To all who helped—to Frank Levy, whose skepticism and decency kept this idea from going off the track; to Fred Greenstein, Robert Kagan, Paul Mishkin, Nelson Polsby, and Aaron Wildavsky, whose comments on the manuscript were both supportive and instructive; to two extraordinary teachers, the late George Van Santvoord and Richard Gurney, who demonstrated the meaning of trying; to Robert Lane, who by precept and example taught that the human soul was a proper subject of social science; to Vice President George Bush, gentleman and patriot, who gave me a job and made the book possible; to John Bush and Vic Gold, two encouraging friends; and to my irreverent, funny, honest, adventuresome wife, Pauli—thank you all very much.

Explanation of Citations to Presidential Speeches

The presidential speeches of Ronald Reagan were published in two separate series: a *Weekly Compilation of Presidential Documents* and the annual *Public Papers of the Presidents of the United States: Ronald Reagan*.

The speeches of Reagan's first term (1981–1984) are drawn from the *Public Papers* and are cited in the footnotes as *PP* with the pertinent year, as follows:

PP81   *Public Papers of the Presidents of the United States: Ronald Reagan, 1981* (Washington, D.C.: Government Printing Office, 1982).

PP82:1   *Public Papers of the Presidents of the United States: Ronald Reagan, 1982* (Washington, D.C.: Government Printing Office, 1983), Book 1.

PP82:2   *Public Papers of the Presidents of the United States: Ronald Reagan, 1982* (Washington, D.C.: Government Printing Office, 1983), Book 2.

PP83:1   *Public Papers of the Presidents of the United States: Ronald Reagan, 1983* (Washington, D.C.: Government Printing Office, 1984), Book 1.

PP83:2   *Public Papers of the Presidents of the United States: Ronald Reagan, 1983* (Washington, D.C.: Government Printing Office, 1985), Book 2.

PP84:1   *Public Papers of the Presidents of the United States: Ronald Reagan, 1984* (Washington, D.C.: Government Printing Office, 1986), Book 1.

PP84:2   *Public Papers of the Presidents of the United States: Ronald Reagan, 1984* (Washington, D.C.: Government Printing Office, 1987), Book 2.

The speeches of Reagan's second term (1985–1989) are drawn from the *Weekly Compilations* and are cited in the footnotes as *WC,* along with the pertinent year and volume, as follows:

WC85:21   *Weekly Compilation of Presidential Documents* (Washington, D.C.: Government Printing Office, 1985), vol. 21.
WC86:22   *Weekly Compilation of Presidential Documents* (Washington, D.C.: Government Printing Office, 1986), vol. 22.
WC87:23   *Weekly Compilation of Presidential Documents* (Washington, D.C.: Government Printing Office, 1987), vol. 23.
WC88:24   *Weekly Compilation of Presidential Documents* (Washington, D.C.: Government Printing Office, 1988), vol. 24.
WC89:25   *Weekly Compilation of Presidential Documents* (Washington, D.C.: Government Printing Office, 1989), vol. 25.

THE BULLY PULPIT

Introduction

During his eight years as president, from 1981 to 1989, Ronald Reagan spoke several million words of carefully prepared remarks in public. I wrote this book to explain the process by which those remarks were written and the purposes they were intended to serve. In studying Reagan and his speechwriters, however, I sought insight into more than a particular presidency. My objective was to find general lessons about leadership, ones that people everywhere could apply in their daily lives. A free civilization survives only if it educates its citizens in the skills of leadership. A self-governing society breaks down when its individual members do not know how to take charge of their own circumstances. This book is intended to shed light on the means by which people in any walk of life can exercise leadership effectively in a free society.

But what is leadership? What do leaders do to guide others? What is the key to leading large numbers of free people?

In a nutshell, leadership is the capacity to motivate others. It is what enables officers to evoke courage in their troops; it is what counselors demonstrate when they quicken hope in clients who have thought themselves failures. Leaders speak to the human spirit and explain why it must hold on. When the odds are daunting, when the things we gave our lives to shatter, when we feel alien and apart, leaders revive hope and explain the good of trying. The acts of leaders, writes political scientist James MacGregor Burns, "help release human potentials now locked in ungratified needs and crushed expectations." Or, as the poet Robert Frost once put it, "A [leader] must give his people character."[1]

The tools of leadership are neither fear nor bribery, but thoughts. Leaders express ideas—ideas that explain events, create comradeship, and shape purpose. With articulate thought leaders help others transcend their confusion, loneliness, and despair. A leader's ideas connect people to honorable objectives and inspire them to think purposefully, "What action am I going to take?" instead of submitting hopelessly, "What is going to happen to me?" Since such ideas guide and honor action, they are moral in character. Since they connect distant goals to the practical means of attaining them, they have to be coherent and ring true, or they will not be effective.

When leadership grows to such a scale that leaders can no longer speak directly to those who would follow them, they organize teams to carry their ideas beyond their immediate circle. They develop what I call moral institutions—that is, organizations of individuals disciplined in teaching abstract ideas and in explaining how they can be applied to particular circumstances.

Ronald Wilson Reagan, the forty-first president of the United States, was a leader on such a scale—a national moral leader. He regarded the presidency as a bully pulpit, a place to which Americans looked for hope and from which he was determined to shape the ways they thought about themselves, their society, and their government.[2] And he loved fulfilling that purpose.[3]

Reagan set out a coherent public philosophy, consisting of three fundamental ideas.

The first of those ideas concerned the nature of a free society. The central feature of such a society, said Reagan, is not competition between individuals, but a voluntary and reciprocating association among them. Human beings are one another's partners, capable of combining their strengths and talents and obliged to do so if they are to solve their problems and promote undertakings of significance. The secret of human prosperity in a free society is the art of teaming up.

The second of Reagan's core ideas was that human nature is not perfectible. It consists of a divided self, with hate and love inextricably mixed. Every individual, of whatever culture or status, has both the capacity for cruelty and the free will to overcome the countless temptations to hate and to hurt. No one is an angel, but no one has to be an evil beast.

The third of Reagan's ideas concerned human worth. The ethical measure of individuals, he insisted, is not the consequences of their actions but the magnitude of their efforts to resist their worse selves and uphold their better selves. In other words, what matters about individuals is whether they try to do their best with what they have. Not their material, but their spiritual achievements count: effort is what merits honor.

None of these ideas—concerning social partnership, human imperfectibility, or personal responsibility—was new or radical. Each had deep roots in Western civilized thought. Inspiring others to live by them in the contemporary world, however, required of Reagan both originality and wit.

To spread his ideas to the vast population of America, Reagan developed organizations that could help make his public argument. He first created a presidential speechwriting team. (Chief executives have too much to do to run one-man shows, and so every modern president has enlisted the assistance of numerous men and women, whom they have trained and supervised to perform specialized tasks. Reagan did likewise.) Then he called upon two existing institutions to sow his philosophy in the hearts of the people. One was the presidential cabinet, which accepted the mission of getting his ideas out to particular groups of the populace. The other was the church, with its more universal reach.

Much of my research on the presidential speechwriting process was done in 1983–1985, during the nineteen months I worked on the staff of Vice President George Bush. My job as a vice-presidential speechwriter afforded me the chance to observe the daily routines of presidential speechwriting up close. I also had the opportunity to conduct formal interviews with all the presidential speechwriters working in the White House, and with most of the principal speechwriters for the cabinet secretaries.

PART ONE

RONALD REAGAN'S
BULLY PULPIT

★★★★★★★

A man who once sat at that desk, Theodore Roosevelt, said that the Presidency is a bully pulpit—the pulpit is where the clergyman preaches sermons. It is that. I think this office does offer an opportunity for mobilizing public sentiment behind worthwhile causes. To that extent, there is power that should be used properly and for the right causes that goes with this office.

—Ronald Reagan (1982)

The fact that this book takes the presidency of Ronald Reagan as the raw material for a study of leadership poses a serious problem, one that should be faced right at the outset. Some readers may think that nothing of value can be learned from the Reagan presidency. How, they may wonder, could his presidency be an enlightening or exemplary one if, as some say, he was a lazy, ignorant, and mean-spirited individual? In an institution such as the American presidency, where the organization so often seems to take on the character of the individual managing it, common sense would argue that a person of such character would not be likely to produce a presidency worth studying (except for its bad example).

Numerous intelligent observers of the Reagan presidency have been troubled by this question. Some Europeans, for example, were puzzled by the fact that "even if they did not take Reagan seriously, the American people certainly did; and more important, it was clear that Reagan's two terms in the White House could not, in any reasonable way, be accounted a failure. On the contrary, they had many of the hallmarks of an outstanding success."[1] Yet the evidence supporting the charge of Reagan's personal inadequacies seemed so authoritatively advanced.

But was Reagan really lazy, ignorant, and mean-spirited? What does the evidence actually reveal about his character? Consider three of the more notable books written about Reagan, one by a disenchanted member of his administration, David Stockman; one by a scholar, Garry Wills; and one by a journalist, Lou Cannon.[2] Each had a serious interest in understanding Reagan.

Stockman was director of the Office of Management and Budget in Reagan's first presidential term and, as such, had an office in the White House, attended cabinet meetings, and was a key person in carrying out two of the Reagan administration's earliest legislative priorities—cutting taxes and reducing the federal budget. Because Stockman sharply

7

disagreed with Reagan on economic policy—the president refused to raise taxes and cut defense spending despite the magnitude of the federal budget deficits beginning in 1982—Stockman quit the White House in 1985 and attacked "the Reagan Revolution" in a book he called *The Triumph of Politics*. In it he offered a devastating account of Reagan's character and intelligence.

The scholar, Wills, wrote a biography-like account of Reagan's life, *Reagan's America*. He relied on Stockman's testimony regarding Reagan's first presidential term, but he also drew extensively from other accounts of Reagan's entire life, including his conduct as governor of California (1967–1974). He attempted to sift through all the details of Reagan's public life, going back beyond 1960.

Cannon, a senior White House correspondent for the *Washington Post* throughout the Reagan years, wrote the first substantial biography of the president, *Reagan*. Because Cannon had also covered Reagan's stint as governor of California, his was the only book by a neutral observer who had directly observed Reagan's entire career in elective office.

From these books one might draw the following indictment, consisting of three counts.

First, Reagan was a lazy and incompetent manager of his presidency, a boss who irresponsibly let his subordinates handle the business of the office and who lacked the fortitude to face unpleasant facts and choices. In one telling paragraph, Stockman described Reagan's inattention to the details of managing the presidency. Speaking of the budget that was going to be submitted to Congress in 1981 in the president's name, Stockman marveled, "[Reagan] was letting his fiscal architect [that is, Stockman himself] develop his economic policy revolution for him. He was taking my plan on faith alone." During conferences in which issues were debated, Reagan would idly "scribble some numbers on [a piece of paper]" and then let one of his handlers "step in and tell us to take our arguments to some other ad hoc forum." The president's usual practice, according to Stockman, was to smile and say, "Okay, you fellows work it out."[3]

The president's former budget director made other troubling observations: Reagan allowed his handlers to "keep all the bad news out of the Oval Office"; Reagan was "out of his depth" on issues of great importance; Reagan backed down in the face of forceful subordinates; Reagan lacked the heart "to lead the fight to shrink the American welfare state's giant entitlement programs"; Reagan skipped the kind of crucial detailed work necessary to get beneath the surface of things; Reagan habitually preferred to "reimmerse" himself in flattering constituency correspondence.[4]

Wills echoed Stockman's charge of mental laziness, alleging that Reagan demonstrated similar habits as governor of California: he "temperamentally shied from unpleasant human encounters, and kept himself deliberately removed from the squabbling that was as common in his California administration as it would be in the White House." He was "notoriously light on desk work," instead seeking the limelight and the kind of ceremonial stuff that kept him away from hard choices.[5]

The reporter, Cannon, whose book was the source for much of Wills's commentary on Reagan as governor in California, offered an explanation of Reagan's aversion to detail. Reagan, he surmised, had "a mind which throughout [his] long lifetime had never been exposed to serious challenge."[6]

The second character flaw found in Reagan was stupidity (and ideological rigidity).[7] Stockman recalled Reagan's preparations for the 1980 presidential debates as "miserable . . . filled with woolly platitudes." "[T]he folksy Reader's Digest anecdote" was all that he was capable of understanding; "concepts of any complexity simply did not register"; he would agree to vital decisions of which "he did not have even a dim apprehension."[8] Uncomprehending of reality, unable to analyze the problems set before him, he would not speak; he would not react.

Even more disquieting to Stockman were the times when Reagan did assert himself. Then, the true extent of his stupidity would be revealed. The president would interrupt a discussion with some irrelevant story or other kind of nonsense. "What to do," lamented Stockman about one twenty-minute homily Reagan delivered on economic history and theory, "when your President ignores all the palpable, relevant facts and wanders in circles."[9]

If Stockman described the limits of Reagan's brain, Wills depicted the contents of it. According to Wills, Reagan clung to a picture of an America that never was—a "miniature country of the mind," embedded in a "substitute past" that supposedly would never "really change." The president met proof to the contrary with an "absolute refusal to acknowledge" it. Cannon put it more diplomatically: "Reagan was resistant to information which challenged his preconceptions."[10]

Third, Reagan was accused of having a mean spirit. It was, to be sure, a special kind of mean-spiritedness, for not one of the three authors offered evidence of personal callousness. Quite the contrary: Stockman, for one, was upset because Reagan was "too kind, gentle, and sentimental. . . . He sees the plight of real people before anything else." His sentimentality was a problem, according to Stockman, because "his ideology and philosophy always [took] a back seat when he learn[ed] that some individual human being might be hurt."[11]

Rather, the complaint was that Reagan's policies were cutting back on social programs. Those policies, thought to be unfair to poor people and to minorities, demonstrated a lack of moral imagination. Reagan would not possibly have approved such policies had he had the capacity to empathize. Content to confine himself to the company of the wealthy and the powerful, Reagan was unaware of the afflictions visited on the poor and the powerless by his policies.

To be fair to Reagan, however, all three books contain considerable evidence to rebut these charges. On the question of laziness, Wills and Cannon noted that Reagan "work[ed] hard" at certain tasks. Wills wrote of his commitment to teaching the people, a skill he never tired of improving:

> [He] did not become a skillful debater—as he proved himself against both Robert Kennedy and William F. Buckley even before his presidential debates—merely by good looks. He is a passionate believer in his cause, and one who works hard to present it well. This means that he studies everything he and his government do very closely but from a selective angle, looking first and most intently at what can be done to make the action or ideas as attractive to as many people as possible. . . . [Once he finds] the single strongest claim that [can] be made for [his action or ideas, he does] not tire of repeating it, or lose faith in its efficacy simply because he has become bored with it.[12]

Cannon pointed to Reagan's seriousness of purpose:

> Despite the easy grace and the one-liners, he had always been an overachiever. He mastered his craft. He was serious about his labor union [Reagan was president of the Screen Actors Guild in the 1950s]. He tried to carry out his campaign promises. Comparing him to the last elected Republican president, the Boston *Globe*'s Marty Nolan observed that one difference is "that Reagan sought to be President in order to do something and Nixon sought to be President in order to be something." There is a lot of truth to that.[13]

Such an account of Reagan—as an "overachiever," driven by a desire "to do something"—did not exactly square with the image of an indolent good-for-nothing.[14]

Cannon also disputed the charge that Reagan was a lazy manager. His habit of delegation, he wrote, might seem to stem from lassitude. "However, it was just as legitimately a reflection of his belief in the virtues of cabinet government and of his confidence that he could select able managers to carry out his policies." In fact, both Wills and Cannon respected Reagan's skill in managing a governmental team. His ability to delegate responsibility freed him to pursue his principal purpose, carrying his ideas directly to the people.[15]

Likewise, Cannon disputed the allegation of personal stupidity. "Reagan was neither a rocket scientist nor a stupid man," he wrote.

"Those who dealt with him on a regular basis were impressed with the common sense he displayed in most situations and the uncommonly good judgment he showed at other times." The appearance of stupidity, as Cannon ruefully pointed out, stemmed from a professional habit: "What unnerved reporters who spent considerable time with Reagan . . . was . . . his proclivity for repeating the same memorized answers over and over again in the manner of a man who is saying them for the first time. It was as if someone had hit the 'play' button on a tape cassette recorder." But this capacity to repeat himself in event after event, said Cannon, disguised a mind that "crave[d] discourse, not briefing papers."[16]

Moreover, it concealed an intelligence that was responsive to verified advice. Writing in 1982, Cannon could already see how Reagan in his second year as president was changing his mind about the Soviet Union:

> Reagan had been persuaded, largely by [Secretary of State Alexander] Haig and [National Security Adviser Bill] Clark, that the troubled Russian economy was in decline and that the Soviets were willing to talk seriously about arms reductions. Though ailing Soviet President Leonid Brezhnev quickly rejected Reagan's specific proposal, the Soviets did agree to open talks on nuclear arms reduction in Geneva on June 29 [1982]. Reagan considered this ratification of the advice which had been given him that the Russians, whatever their motives, were willing to deal. Almost imperceptibly, and without acknowledging that it was happening, Reagan was becoming more sophisticated.[17]

Wills went even further. He called Reagan's mind "a very keen intelligence," likening it to the smartness of the Reverend Jesse Jackson, the first serious African-American presidential candidate to seek the Democratic party nomination. (He ran in both 1984 and 1988.)

> Reagan is *not* a do-nothing President. He is making a public *argument*, not merely a grand appearance. This is not just a matter of window-dressing, but of constant analysis and testing *of people's reactions*. He is selling substance, not appearance—just as the advertiser is selling the product, not the slogan. A failure to grasp this has misled those who think that Reagan does not have a good mind. It is not an abstract or speculative mind, nor is it an administrative or a managerial mind. But it is a very keen intelligence [of the kind Jesse Jackson has]. After all, anyone who has spent time with Jesse Jackson knows he has a good mind.[18] (Italics in the original)

Reagan's incisive capacity for "constant analysis and testing of people's reactions" impressed Wills as a special kind of mental keenness, one that made it possible for him to connect his public argument perfectly to the public's most fundamental concerns.

In his backhanded way Stockman conceded as much. It was the president's reflexiveness of intellect, his very sensitivity to the moral concerns of the people and his bone-deep habit of pausing to persuade them to follow his ideas, that surprised and distressed the revolutionary Stockman. Reagan, he lamented, "was a consensus politician, not an ideologue. He had no business trying to make [an economic] revolution because it wasn't in his bones."[19]

The picture of Reagan that Wills and Cannon (and even Stockman) ultimately offered was of a man who cared passionately about, and worked untiringly at, making a public argument. Reagan, they agreed, sought to organize the White House so that the routines of managing the U.S. government were delegated to individuals with whom he was in tune. He sought to conserve his personal energies for making his public argument, changing people's minds, and sowing his philosophy in the hearts of the people. His "very keen intelligence" in articulating that philosophy and making claims for it, his habits of "analysis and testing of people's reactions," his personal conviction, his commitment to accomplishing his goals and leaving something behind that mattered, his ability to "find good people to work for him" and give them credit for their abilities—such was their account of Reagan in the White House.[20]

What we end up with is an enigma: a widely shared impression that Reagan was out of his depth as president, but highly equivocal evidence to support it. In fact, the assertion that the president was lazy, ignorant, and mean-spirited did not really apply to his personal or political competency. Wills and Cannon (and even Stockman) ultimately granted that he worked hard, intelligently, and sincerely on communicating with the people. Rather, the charges against Reagan amounted to an adverse evaluation of the justice of the president's public philosophy and the importance of his devoting so much time to the public assertion of it.

What came of spending so much presidential energy on making a public argument? That question is impossible to answer entirely convincingly, but consider this: Reagan said at the outset of his administration that his purpose was to instill optimism in the American people, and the mood of the people turned optimistic. He said that one of his key goals was to prompt private generosity, and personal philanthropy increased.[21] Was there a connection between intentions and events? When purpose and result so neatly coincide, the most skeptical observer ought to pause before rejecting the possibility of cause and effect.

Now it is time to get on with the story of the bully pulpit of Ronald Reagan. We begin with America's moral condition before his presidency and with the speechwriters he assembled to improve it.

1

★★★★★★★

Freedom and Leadership

Very early in his search [Plato] must have discovered that truth, namely, the truths we call self-evident, compels the mind, and that this coercion, though it needs no violence to be effective, is stronger than persuasion and argument. The trouble with coercion through reason, however, is that only the few are subject to it, so that the problem arises of how to assure that the many, the people who in their very multitude compose the body politic, can be submitted to the same truth.

—Hannah Arendt, Between Past and Future *(1961)*

From the perspective of history, the 235 million Americans alive in 1981, at the beginning of their country's twentieth decade, were well fed, well housed, and well educated.[1] And they thought of themselves as free and self-reliant.

But freedom was an iffy thing. Americans had the liberty to associate with whomever they chose—if anyone chose to associate with them. They could marry whom they wanted, if another would accept them. They could work where they wanted, if other people were willing to pay for their services. They could travel where they wanted, if someone would provide them hospitality once they got there. They were free to discuss everything on earth, if somebody would bother to converse with them. They were even free to take comfort from whatever religion pleased them, if their God was sufficiently pleased by their faith or good works to give them solace. Americans lived free, but they were free on one condition—that they please others. In order to get help, they had to help others. This routine of voluntary give-and-take was epitomized by the marketplace, but it pervaded every aspect of American life. Americans

13

were obliged to return something of value tomorrow if they wanted something of value today.[2]

The contingency of personal freedom shaped the character of Americans. It prompted Americans to care about one another and to cultivate their capacity to walk in others' shoes; for if freedom depended on pleasing others, it was necessary to learn to discern what it was that pleased them. The practices of voluntary give-and-take entangled Americans in the affairs and hopes of their neighbors, making America a tolerant and considerate society.[3] That moral effect was the upside of personal freedom.

But its contingent nature had a second consequence, a downside. Freedom was mentally and emotionally exhausting. Occasional feelings of shortcoming, disappointment, and loneliness were inescapable aspects of the free life. Personal freedom exacted high emotional dues.[4]

In the spring of 1986 several Soviet educators visited the United States to observe practices at a dozen first-rank high schools. Afterward the chief of the delegation commented on the way American students were encouraged to think for themselves. What struck him most forcibly was the heavy responsibility the students assumed for their own work: there was virtually no "mothering" by their teachers. "Of course," he elaborated, "you have to do this because you train them for a tougher life," where they must be more "competitive." In the Soviet Union, in contrast, "we live in an environment that takes care of us from the cradle to the grave, and we tend to be dependent on one another." Then, speaking of the American students, he added, "Their self-reliance is something that we should have more of."[5]

Americans had trouble appreciating—or admitting—just how tough life was in their self-reliant society. Because of the general diffusion of wealth and comfort, they tended to belittle their own hardihood out of the belief that, in the Gershwins' ironic verse in *Porgy and Bess*, "the livin' is easy." In fact, the opposite was the case. Modern times complicated moral life. The one thing that cars, abundant energy, and high technology made easier was the assumption of additional burdens. In earlier days, when an individual could not view people starving in some distant land, or fly fifteen hundred miles to care for an ailing parent, or telephone someone halfway around the world, his circle of obligation was confined, and he was acquitted of extensive responsibilities.[6] Modern technology, by widening people's range of duties, magnified their sense of shortcoming.

Moreover, because of its conditional character, the free life was filled with opportunities to fail—to be divorced, go broke, be lonely or degraded or overcommitted. When disappointment struck—when interpersonal relationships failed, when severe economic fluctuations occurred, when the decisions of others turned sour—the principle of self-reliance led the individual to shoulder the blame personally.

The men and women constituting this free society were highly susceptible to a sense of individual isolation. A century and a half ago the great French observer of democracy in America, Alexis de Tocqueville, warned that the effect of modernity was to strip the individual of his traditional connections to others. Isolated from family and class, he felt "powerless" in the face of forces much larger than himself.[7]

Attention had to be paid to the wear and tear of freedom. If the threads of hope were not continually repaired, they soon unraveled, "delivered up to the ruin of time," in Hannah Arendt's fine phrase.[8] The fabric of a free society had constantly to be backed with understanding. Otherwise, things fell apart.

And things did fall apart seemingly everywhere in the United States during the troubled decades of the 1960s and 1970s. Those were years of significant challenge, anger, and disrespect. There was the civil rights struggle against America's legacy of racial discrimination; there was the antiwar fury over Vietnam and America's intervention in the foreign affairs of other nations; there was experimentation with drugs and new lifestyles. When the writer Joan Didion visited San Francisco in 1967 and saw the countercultural "hippie" community living in the Haight-Ashbury district, she reacted with horror to the ignorance, the wretchedness, and the loveless estrangement of its young inhabitants, the "flower children" of that drug-filled era of revolt:

> We were seeing the desperate attempt of a handful of pathetically unequipped children to create a community in a social vacuum. Once we had seen these children, we could no longer overlook the vacuum, no longer pretend that the society's atomization could be reversed. This was not a traditional generational rebellion. At some point between 1945 and 1967 we had somehow neglected to tell these children the rules of the game we happened to be playing. Maybe we had stopped believing in the rules ourselves, maybe we were having a failure of nerve about the game. Maybe there were just too few people around to do the telling. These were children who grew up cut loose from the web of cousins and great-aunts and family doctors and lifelong neighbors who had traditionally suggested and enforced the society's values. They are children who have moved around a lot, *San Jose, Chula Vista, here.* They are less in rebellion against the society than ignorant of it, able only to feed back certain of its most publicized self-doubts, *Vietnam, Saran Wrap, diet pills, the Bomb.*
>
> They feedback exactly what is given them. Because they do not believe in words—words are for "typeheads" . . . and a thought which needs words is just one more of those ego trips—their only proficient vocabulary is in the society's platitudes. As it happens I

am still committed to the idea that the ability to think for oneself depends upon one's mastery of the language, and I am not optimistic about children who will settle for saying, to indicate that their mother and father do not live together, that they come from "a broken home." They are sixteen, fifteen, fourteen years old, younger all the time, an army of children waiting to be given the words.[9]

Didion saw that the lost flower children of the 1960s had never been told "the rules of the game," had never been encouraged to develop the courage to try to be valuable to others, had not been taught how to think independently, and had not been trained in the arts of association. These lessons, she wrote with sadness, "had somehow [been] neglected"— "at some point between 1945 and 1967."

And after 1967 the neglect went on and American society continued to drift. By 1979 the president of the United States, Jimmy Carter, was so troubled by the confusion and pessimism in the nation that he addressed the nation about his concern:

A majority of our people believe that the next five years will be worse than the past five years. The productivity of American workers is actually dropping. We remember when the phrase "sound as a dollar" was an expression of absolute dependability, until inflation began to shrink our dollar and our savings. There is growing disrespect for government and for churches and for schools. [We have] a system of government that seems incapable of action. [All we see is] paralysis and stagnation and drift. It's a crisis of confidence . . . a growing doubt about the meaning of our own lives and in the loss of unity of purpose for our nation. The symptoms of this crisis are all around us.[10]

What Carter depicted as a crisis of confidence—"a growing doubt about the meaning of our own lives" and "the loss of unity of purpose for our nation"—was the moral consequence of neglecting to renew the ideas of a self-governing people.

There was the ruin of time.

At other points in our history the lessons of freedom had not been neglected. The community made sure that all persons belonging to it heard and mastered "the rules of the game we happened to be playing." In the seventeenth century, in the first English settlements on the American continent, the New Englanders dealt communally with the self-doubts that lurked in their souls. The weekly sermon was a part of their civic life, supplying them with a sense of purpose, educating them in the language and values of self-government, and enveloping their communities in the web of a common sense of things. Sermons provided the rhetoric of freedom.

Ever since, the sermon (along with the pulpit from which it was delivered) has signified the indispensable part ideas play in keeping a free people from falling apart and into despair. In Hawthorne's *The Scarlet Letter,* the language of the Reverend Mr. Dimmesdale resounded throughout colonial Boston. In the powerful opening image of *Moby Dick,* Herman Melville likened the preacher's pulpit to the prow of the ship of state. In a more secular age, President Theodore Roosevelt conceived of the presidency as giving him "a bully pulpit" from which to do the very things Didion said must not be left neglected: to create a community, to suggest society's values, to explain mankind's ways, to challenge the trendy platitudes of the day, to anticipate the individual's self-doubts and give meaning to the battle to overcome them.

To what must the rhetoric of the nation's pulpits speak? Specifically, what were, as Arendt put it, those "truths we call self-evident"? In assessing democracy in America in the nineteenth century, Alexis de Tocqueville asked himself just that question. This was what he concluded:

> There is hardly any human action, however particular it may be, that does not originate in some very general idea men have conceived of the Deity, of his relation to mankind, of the nature of their own souls, and of their duties to their fellow creatures. Nor can anything prevent these ideas from being the common spring from which all the rest emanates.[11]

If Tocqueville was right, if in fact "there [was] hardly any human action . . . that [did] not originate" in our profoundest ideas about human nature, human values, and human society, then the moral pulpits of free nations had to speak to these profound issues. What was "the nature of [our] own souls"? By what measure did we value the efforts of our lives (that is, what "Deity" should we adopt, and what was "his relation to mankind")? What were our "duties to [our] fellow creatures"? Moral leadership consisted of replenishing "the common spring" of the human spirit with frequent, clear, consistent, and convincing answers concerning the human condition, life's purposes, and the procedures by which individuals could properly cope with their frailties and limitations.

The nation did not lack for noise. There were many sources of fragmentary and partisan answers. But most were listened to by only a fraction of the people.

Was there a common moral voice? And from what pulpit might it be heard? One possibility was the president of the United States. After all, one of the powers of the presidency was to speak. It was a uniquely independent power, for the Constitution did not oblige the president to share his pulpit with any other branch of government. His messages to the people did not have to be authorized by Congress, or upheld by the

Supreme Court, or executed by the bureaucracy. The president was free to use the rhetorical prominence of his office to clarify the ideas that animated his people and gave purpose to their actions. The person who sat in the Oval Office could replenish "the common spring from which all the rest emanates"—the spiritual reserves free people drew upon to slake their moral thirst. At least he could if he wanted to—and if he knew how.

In the past some presidents have shied from using this power. Others have incidentally fulfilled the moral need of their people while pursuing their policy goals. What was distinctive about the presidency of Ronald Reagan (1981–1989) was the centrality of its character-shaping purposes. It was organized to achieve a moral revolution—moral in the sense of affecting the animating ideas of the American people, a revolution in the sense of returning the nation to its intellectual starting point.

Its chief objective was to mold the fundamental axioms on which Americans premised their lives. It was "the most important thing we have tried" to do, Reagan wrote his chief of staff, James W. Baker, in 1985:

> You [Baker] have mastered the art of Washington politics, but your roots are still deep in the soil of Texas, and it was there that you learned the fundamental values that you and I share. You know that life can be hard and unpredictable, but you also know that Americans are a people who look forward to the future with optimism. That sense of optimism is the most important thing we have tried to restore to America during the past four years, and it has helped me more than I can ever say to have someone by my side who understands that bedrock faith in our nation's future as well as you do.[12]

To restore optimism, Reagan used the presidency to speak about the self-interest of individuals, their responsibilities to one another, and (most fundamental of all) their very nature. He set out to define a philosophy of freedom, to distinguish it from a philosophy of equality, and to plant it in the soul of the nation.

Virtually all of Reagan's domestic policy achievements either ended in that moral goal or proceeded from it. The cuts in the federal budget, the domestic and international stabilization of the dollar, the reduction of income tax rates, "revenue neutral" tax reform, the increase in voluntarism, the reforms in social policy, the emphasis on excellence in education combined with an insistence on infusing moral values into school curricula, the withdrawal of central government from some of its former regulatory and fiscal responsibilities, the adherence to free trade and resistance to protectionism—all became part of the president's agenda because they reinforced his moral objectives of preparing Americans for the task of living free.

2

★★★★★★★★

Speechwriters in the White House

Why did I get an interest in writing? Power. Writing is a great power.
There were things I felt strongly about, and writing enabled me to
communicate with people for my purposes.

—Anthony R. Dolan (1984)

The White House, where President Reagan and his presidential staff had their offices, is an enclosure. The shut gates and high fences surrounding the White House set the executive apart from the other branches of government. The public is free to enter and depart the Capitol, the home of Congress, and the Supreme Court Building, the summit of the American judiciary. The presidency is a personal institution, however, and the White House is the president's private home, where his family lives and keeps house. And so there are fences and gates that close.

In addition to the family residence, the White House enclosure holds a complex of offices. The working half of the White House is called the Executive Compound. It consists of two buildings, separated by an asphalt alleyway. On the alley's east side is the West Wing, a twentieth-century addition. A low, unprepossessing three-story building, it contains the Oval Office of the president, office space for the vice president, and a set of rooms for a half dozen of the president's closest advisers. It also contains the Press Room, once an indoor swimming pool, but now used to confine the crowd of correspondents covering the White House scene.

West of the alleyway is the Old Executive Office Building (OEOB), a colossal, five-story building of French Renaissance design, as imposing and permanent as a giant granite butte. The OEOB once housed all the diplomatic and military departments of the nation. In the era of the modern presidency it has come to be inhabited by the president's staff, which distributes itself among seven principal offices—the National Security Council, the Domestic Council, the Office of Management and Budget, the Council of Economic Advisers, the science adviser, the Office of Legal Counsel, and the Communications Division.

The staff of the White House, together with the custodians, chauffeurs, mailmen, and cooks for the several employee dining rooms, amount to about seven hundred individuals. Daily these White House personnel pass freely in and out of the compound, there to do the president's work under employment agreements the president can terminate at will.

All persons free of this contractual restraint are prohibited entry into the compound—unless they come as invited guests. (The press is an exception. White House correspondents are admitted to the White House compound but are confined to the White House press secretary's office.) No matter their importance—whether cabinet members, members of Congress, federal judges, civil servants, or private citizens—individuals not in the direct employ of the president need an invitation from someone inside the White House. If they come to see the president, they come as his guests, for an appointed time and on his terms. "Nobody pops in," presidential assistant Martin Anderson once wrote.[1]

Unlike the houses of Congress, where Democrats and Republicans occupy neighboring offices and converse spontaneously with each other, the White House is a quiet and orderly place. Unruly discourse, partisan dialogue, discordant ideas—they make no appearance in the Executive Compound. True, newspapers infiltrate the White House, even opposition ones that advocate alien causes; to an extent, they function as surrogates for real opposition. But they are soundless, speechless surrogates, to be read at will and selectively.

Besides its quietness, White House life has another distinguishing feature—unity. Since the president is the only employer, the White House staff is his personal company. All depend on his say-so for advancement; all can be fired because he no longer needs their services.

Unlike Congress, with its 535 different bosses, or the Supreme Court, with its nine, the White House has but a single paymaster, one person on whom the careers of all the rest depend. "In the general course of human nature," observed Alexander Hamilton back in 1788, "a power over a man's subsistence amounts to a power over his will."[2] In 1965 one of President Lyndon Johnson's close friends called the White House "a court": he was referring to its monarchical character—the power of one individual, the president, over the will of every other man and woman working in the White House.[3]

The vice president is the lonely exception to this state of dependence. Because he is elected to his office, he is his own boss. Having been made the vice president directly by the people, he has no grounds to fear that the president might fire him (although he could be excluded from the White House). If the vice president does not want to, he does not need to take the president's orders. His uniqueness only emphasizes the more general point: The compound is filled with individuals owing their livelihood, advancement, and future prospects to a single paymaster. Like any institution so dominated, the White House necessarily has a Byzantine character: an overtly obsequious order and a subterranean dynamic of individuals vying for the approval of a single boss.

These two features of the White House—intellectual discipline and administrative unity—serve a purpose in the American governmental structure. With authority so widely dispersed among multiple branches and levels of government, the single-mindedness of the president's staff gives the national executive a level of energy sufficient to jolt the republic into acting on matters it might otherwise find impossible to address.

But the United States is a popular democracy, and ultimately all political power is based on popular approval. Any president who forgets his dependence on the people is sure to pay the consequences. The aristocratic Alexis de Tocqueville ruefully observed in 1835, "The people reign in the American political world as the Deity does in the universe. They are the cause and the aim of all things; everything comes from them; and everything is absorbed by them."[4] No American president could long govern without following the people—or convincing them to follow him. He has to have a means of understanding their "cause" and enlightening their "aim." He needs a means of communicating with them.

Of the approximately seven hundred personnel in the compound during the years of the Reagan presidency, more than a hundred concentrated on helping the president write, talk, and listen to the public.

These wordsmiths were located in four White House units. First, there was the Office of the Press Secretary, which dealt with reporters and their responsibility to disclose the president's actions to their readers and viewers.[5]

Then there was an office that prepared the president's "personal messages." Fifteen professional writers and a host of volunteers had the job of writing personalized letters of celebration, inspiration, and condolence to families and groups. Each week this office wrote, on behalf of the president, nearly five thousand such letters and messages. In the eight years of the Reagan presidency 2 million personal communications from the president were sent to individual members of the public. Each one was crafted to convey the president's interpretation of the routines of daily life—the births and relationships, the deeds and deaths—of a free people.

A third unit of presidential communications was the Office of Public Liaison—the educational college of the White House. Its staff daily organized conferences and discussions for groups seeking, or susceptible to, the president's views on matters of public concern. Did American Jews want to know how the president assesses the Middle East? Then Public Liaison would invite 150 members of the American-Israeli Political Action Committee to a day-long conference in the OEOB—with lectures and readings and question-and-answer sessions on the subject. Did the president seek influential support for the democratic resistance in Nicaragua? Public Liaison would invite sympathetic private groups for a diplomatic and military briefing on Central America. Did black businesspeople need information on the economy? Public Liaison would arrange for representatives of the Black Businessman's Conference to attend sessions with officials from the Commerce and Treasury departments (including the secretaries themselves as often as not and even, sometimes, the president). The Office of Public Liaison was a first-rate school of public affairs.

The fourth unit was the Speechwriting Department. Its members crafted the more than half million public words with which the president spoke to the people each year. Oratory was the indispensable means of reaching the larger public. Radio and television served to carry the president's words directly into the homes of American families. Throughout the eight years of his administration, President Reagan spoke regularly each week over nationwide radio.[6] Even more important, another piece of modern technology, the airplane, connected the president personally to the American people. It enabled him to fly to any part of the nation on any day to address an audience.[7] When he was in Washington, airliners would bring audiences to hear him.

The airplane enabled the president to talk in person to thousands of Americans each month and hundreds of thousands each year.[8] Consider its role in the twenty-six public events at which President Reagan spoke in May 1982, a typical month: two gatherings at the World's Fair in Knoxville, Tennessee; a Republican congressional "Salute to President Reagan" dinner in Washington, D.C.; an observance of the National Day of Prayer in the White House; a commencement ceremony at Eureka College (Reagan's alma mater, in Illinois); a Eureka College alumni dinner in Chicago; a conference of midwestern newspaper editors in Chicago; a Chicago YMCA dinner; a gathering of Chicago high school students; the arrival and the state dinner ceremonies at the White House in connection with the visit of President João Figuerido of Brazil; a small business conference in Washington, D.C.; a gathering of farmers in Landenberg, Pennsylvania; a fund-raiser in Philadelphia for Pennsylvania Governor Richard Thornburgh; another Philadelphia fund-raiser for Pennsylvania

Senator John Heinz; the departure ceremony of Australian Prime Minister Malcolm Fraser after a business visit to Washington, D.C.; remarks at the White House regarding the formation of the Statue of Liberty Centennial Commission; ceremonies related to the luncheon and the departure of King Hassan of Morocco; a White House reception for members of the American Retail Federation; a fund-raiser for Howard University in Washington, D.C.; a White House meeting of the representatives of the International Youth Exchange Programs; a gathering of employees of Rockwell International in Downey, California; a California Republican Party fund-raiser in Los Angeles; the Annual Meeting of Legislators of the Mexico–United States Interparliamentary Conference at Santa Barbara, California; and a Memorial Day ceremony at Arlington National Cemetery outside Washington.

In addition to these twenty-six formal speeches delivered in person in May, he broadcast five weekly radio talks on the topics of economic recovery, unemployment, the federal budget, the armed services, and the Western Alliance. He also held five press conferences, each of which the president opened with a personal statement. In all, thanks to modern transportation and telecommunications, there were thirty-six formal occasions on which he spoke that month. All his remarks were prepared in the Speechwriting Department.

Who were the members of Reagan's Speechwriting Department, and what were they like? The department consisted of six writers, backed up by a dozen researchers and secretaries.

During 1984 and 1985, years that were particularly stable and productive for the department, there was little turnover in personnel or change in organization.[9] The department relished the challenges of winning the presidential political campaign and inaugurating a new presidential term.

The chief of the department, the writer who bore the added responsibilities of editing and making assignments, was Bently Elliott. He was central casting's idea of the typical English professor: tweed coat, thinning blonde hair, debonair, equally capable of the bon mot and the caustic remark, an insouciant surface that covered a pleasant vulnerability and a genuine concern for his colleagues.

He had been a television writer and producer for CBS Television from 1970 to 1975 and had not been happy:

> A lot of reporters and producers there had this certain view of the world that I did not share: that the [Vietnam] war was a force for instability in the world; that our own society was riddled with corruption; that we were basically a dishonest society; that Americans and American business people preyed on one another; that people were victims, and not able to control their own destinies; that if there was a problem, it was someone else's fault.[10]

His discomfort with the CBS view of the world caused Elliott to start defining the philosophical differences that separated him from his colleagues.

> Everybody in CBS seemed to regard business as predators. And they deemed corporations as entities unto themselves. It was ironic because CBS was par excellence a corporation that was helping people. You know, they had pioneered in satellite technology; they were breaking news all over the world; they were a very successful corporation, making the world smaller and bringing people together because of their abilities—their considerable abilities—but they never seemed to make the connection to the news they were reporting and the good CBS as a corporation was able to do.
>
> And all of a sudden I was asking myself, "What am I doing here—doing here with all these cantankerous, critical folks who were so assured they were right?" CBS was like being thrown into the lion's den, but it gave me perspective on what I really believed. I felt my philosophy was pretty realistic, and I felt that capitalism had helped to make my world, the world of Americans, better. And I thought we had an obligation to spread the opportunities which the capitalist system offered and to break down barriers which prevented this prosperity and possibility from being shared.

What heartened him was that he was not altogether a solitary figure at CBS.

> I was one of two or three producers in the entire CBS who voted for Nixon. What I found fascinating, however, that among the videotape guys and the messengers and the couriers, that was where the pro-Nixon votes came. McGovern was loved by the elite and privileged who had already made it, and I found it fascinating watching these essentially blue-collar guys, who think about their houses and the horses running at the track and wisecrack and take things in stride. But when McGovern came on, they rose up and hissed and catcalled—screamed—at McGovern. That made a real impression on me.

In 1975 he heard several speeches by presidential candidate Reagan. They made an impression on him, and he soon left CBS to go to Washington.

> I found myself getting enthusiastic about [Reagan]. All along, I guess I found that I was nothing more than an old-fashioned liberal, liberal in the sense of believing in freedom, and I loved the idea of being alive in liberty. I began to think that liberty was a great thing for individuals to be involved in. And I saw that those nations which had liberty were doing better than those that didn't. When government got overly involved in running things, they inevitably gummed

up the works. I found it challenging to be a warrior for my cause, to be on the side of an underdog idea. People were saying that liberalism was dying, and I found it kind of exciting to resist that opinion.

To champion the "underdog idea" of freedom, Elliott became a professional speechwriter, successively working for President Gerald Ford's secretary of the Treasury, William Simon, Texas Representative Mickey Edwards, and U.S. Chamber of Commerce president, Dick Lesher. In April of 1981 he was hired as a presidential speechwriter, and in 1982 he was made director of speechwriting, the chief. His colleagues liked him and his work, both as a writer and an editor. Among his fellow speechwriters, he enjoyed a reputation for being able to write about complicated economic matters with simplicity and elegance.

He also had a deep identification with Reagan.

Speechwriting is all the more important to this particular president because he is so gifted in being able to express his convictions. Those convictions are in his bones. He's very different from businessmen for whom I have written, who talk facts, but have no profound beliefs. I was very surprised by the depth of his values. He believes in the decency of America; the soundness of its mission; the goodness of its people. It is the result of his whole life; of working in the summer; of his jobs on radio, interviewing all sorts of people; of movies; of being kicked at; of living with his own father and dealing with his father's alcoholism. All those experiences worked those values into the core of his being. The newspeople used to underestimate him; and to this day they underestimate the depth of his convictions.

Elliott worked hard to perfect his ability to write the way the president spoke.

What I personally did to sound like Reagan was to spend the three weeks before I went to work for him reading all his speeches and making these sheaves of notes—on war, on blacks, on rhetoric, on the economy—and I just absorbed his way of expressing things. But, of course, where you really learn his style is when he edits you. What the president does is write with the ear first. Where I would say, "England and the United States today negotiated an agreement which will cause $40 billion worth of additional trade," the president will say, "$40 billion of additional trade will result from an agreement made today between England and the U.S." He uses hard words. He concentrates and speaks with great conciseness. There is very little dead language in his style, either in his letters or his messages or his addresses. His stuff is very concisely written. We overwrite for him, whereas he is prone to economize in language. He has a tremendous austerity in style. And little known to others, he loves facts. I think he's that way because he projects so much emotion and gets emotional quite readily, that he can write free of emotion. He will break down, as he did when in the Vietnam Memorial speech we put something in like, "Dear Son, we put you in God's loving arms." But the president has a sense of himself, and he sees himself talking in a matter of fact way to the man in the street. He is very aware when he is talking out of character.

As chief speechwriter Elliott was responsible for recruiting the rest of the speechwriting team. Among his recruits, none was better than Peggy Noonan.

Noonan was tall and blonde, a reincarnated Carole Lombard, with a tart wit that could protect her even in the most captious of literary circles. Like Elliott, she had once worked at CBS, for a while producing Dan Rather's "CBS Evening News." Most of her career with CBS, however, was spent writing, initially at CBS Radio, where she did daily scripts for Charles Osgood and Dallas Townsend and a weekly program called "The World of Religion." When she was moved to CBS Television, she went as a writer of news and documentaries.

Unlike Elliott, Noonan had not felt particularly alien amidst her colleagues at CBS. In part, it was because she was of a different generation. She had not been alive through World War II; Elliott had and remembered the perilous consequences of America's isolationism before that war and (to some extent) the Korean War. As for the Vietnam War, that great generational dividing line, Elliott and Noonan would have stood on opposite sides in the 1970s. As she put it, "I guess you would say I was patriotically anti-war."[11] She also was not as political as Elliott, not as drawn to winning and losing, not as attracted to defining differences between philosophical sides. She was more a truth-teller than an advocate of a cause, more Paul than Saul, more a depicter of the human condition than an improver of it. For her, getting the story right was writing the story whole. She put the matter wryly.

> Life in fact is very much like high school. You remember how good and how disgusting high school life was. Well, life is just like the last year in high school: teenagers; who's most popular, most likely to succeed; there's cheating on the exams; there are remarkable accomplishments on the athletic field and in the classroom. It's true that people's souls grow all the time, but real life, like high school, is surprising and fun—and tacky.

Born in Brooklyn, Noonan had grown up on Long Island and in New Jersey. She had always thought of herself as a writer: "I wrote a poem in the third grade on the meaning of Thanksgiving, and I thought it summed up everything there was to say about Thanksgiving. And my third-grade teacher loved it, and she read it aloud to all the third-grade classes, and I was hooked. Writing was just natural to me.'' She also found reading natural to her.

> Books excited me with the magic of words. Words made dead things alive again. For example, I loved Stephen Vincent Benét's *John Brown's Body*, and I read it over again every year. As a teenager I loved poetry—more than I do now. T. S. Eliot was really important to me. So was Edna St. Vincent Millay and Emily Dickinson. . . . In one sense the most important book I ever read was the biography of the Mayo brothers. It was a children's book, and it had a happy children's ending: ''Then they went and cured disease.'' When I came to the end and there was nothing more to read, I was so sad I wanted to cry. So I went and got another book. I really missed the Mayo brothers.

In the White House she kept on reading, and she kept on writing. She cared deeply about her work, but no speech meant more to her than the one the president gave at Pointe du Hoc in France, above the beaches of Normandy on June 6, 1984. As Noonan told the story, one could almost hear the passion of Emily Dickinson and the cadences of Stephen Vincent Benét and the nobility of the brothers Mayo challenging her to measure up. Let her own words tell the story.

> I wrote the Pointe du Hoc speech. I wanted it to be a knockout. I wanted to hit a big home run on this one. I wanted to sum up the importance of what happened on those Normandy beaches forty years ago, to show its meaning on the long ribbon of history. And I wanted to express the moral dimension of the War, why the West did what it did. And I wanted to talk about the unity of those countrymen who fought on the beaches of Normandy; I only wanted to do it implicitly, to leave an implicit reminder of the value of unity.
>
> I also knew the veterans would be there, and I wanted justice to be done to them. Justice had not been done to them during the war. There were Pointe du Hocs daily then, and there wasn't time. And justice had never been done to them afterwards. These were extraordinary kids, these nineteen-year-old Rangers of 1944, and now they were sixty-year-olds, a little puffy, gray, a little overweight, and I knew they would be there. I wanted to honor them and those that had died beside them as they stormed those cliffs.
>
> I wanted people to have pictures in their mind of what the past had been like. I wanted the president vividly to describe what these men did forty years ago. It's like writing for radio. I wanted people to know, ''These are the boys who took the cliffs,'' and the TV showing those men.

How did she prepare herself to write the Pointe du Hoc remarks? She read numerous books on the Normandy invasion and underlined the passages about Pointe du Hoc. She got pictures of the area so she could see where the president would be speaking and where the graves and cemetery were. She imagined the scene—the weather, the time of day, the audience—and what it might be like walking by his side as he spoke the first few lines of his address.

What came to Noonan was the following:[12]

> We're here to mark that day in history when the Allied armies joined in battle to reclaim this continent to liberty. For four long years, much of Europe had been under a terrible shadow. Free nations had fallen, Jews cried out in the camps, millions cried out for liberation. Europe was enslaved, and the world prayed for its rescue. Here in Normandy the rescue began. Here the Allies stood and fought against tyranny in a giant undertaking unparalleled in human history.
>
> We stand on a lonely, windswept point on the northern shore of France. The air is soft, but forty years ago at this moment, the air was dense with smoke and the cries of men, and the air was filled with the crack of rifle fire and the roar of cannon. At dawn, on the morning of the 6th of June, 1944, 225 Rangers jumped off the British landing craft and ran to the bottom of these cliffs. Their mission was one of the most difficult and daring of the invasion: to climb these sheer and desolate cliffs and take out the enemy guns. The Allies had been told that some of the mightiest of these guns were here and they would be trained on the beaches to stop the Allied advance.
>
> The Rangers looked up and saw the enemy soldiers at the edge of the cliffs, shooting down at them with machine guns and throwing grenades. And the American rangers began to climb. They shot rope ladders over the face of these cliffs and began to pull themselves up. When one Ranger fell, another would take his place. When one rope was cut, a Ranger would grab another and begin his climb again. They climbed, shot back, and held their footing. Soon, one by one, the Rangers pulled themselves over the top, and in seizing the firm land at the top of these cliffs, they began to seize back the continent of Europe. Two hundred and twenty-five came here. After two days of fighting, only ninety could still bear arms.
>
> Behind me is a memorial that symbolizes the Ranger daggers that were thrust into the top of these cliffs. And before me are the men who put them there.
>
> These are the boys of Pointe du Hoc. These are the men who took the cliffs. These are the champions who helped free a continent. These are the heroes who helped end a war.
>
> Gentlemen, I look at you and I think of the words of Stephen Spender's poem. You are men who in your "lives fought for life . . . and left the vivid air signed with your honor."

Then, having recalled the imaginative device that had helped her create the Pointe du Hoc speech, Noonan went on to describe the president's impressions of the ceremony at Pointe du Hoc:

> He [told] me about the Rangers' reaction to it. He told me that they had tears in their eyes. And he told me funny stories about the Rangers. He obviously loved them. One part of the ceremony was

to have some young Rangers climb the cliffs as it had been done forty years ago. But one old Ranger—he was sixty and sixty pounds overweight, and gray-haired—he said he had wanted to climb the cliffs alongside those young fellas. And he did it with them. He threw the hook up and climbed up right along with the youngsters. And when the president told me about him, his eyes just lit up.

You know, it's fascinating around here. I have talked with people about other White Houses. What marks this one is that the people here really love the guy.

There were four other speechwriters.[13] Tony Dolan was an Irishman who smoked cigars and looked like a Boston ward heeler of years past. In fact, he was an intense and sophisticated man. He came from a family he describes as "politically disaffected" Massachusetts Democrats. He went to Yale as an undergraduate and began writing for the *Yale Daily News*. One of his pieces caught the eye of William F. Buckley, the founder of the *National Review* and godfather of the modern conservative movement in the United States. Buckley invited Dolan to write some pieces for the *National Review* and upon Dolan's graduation got him a job as assistant press secretary for Jim Buckley, who was then running for the Senate from New York.

William Buckley was both his "intellectual hero" and his mentor, grooming Dolan to be a political writer. In 1974, after a variety of jobs in and out of politics, Dolan went to Bill Buckley for still more advice. "And he said, 'If you really want to learn to write quickly'—and that had always been a frustration for me as a writer—'go to a daily newspaper.'"[14] So Dolan took a job with a newspaper. He went to work in Connecticut for the *Stamford Advocate*, and during his two years there he uncovered a Mafia connection to the city's police department. Dolan won a Pulitzer prize for his reports.

Dolan then was recommended to Reagan to write for the 1980 presidential campaign. His political astuteness, sense for his opponent's jugular vein, and literary power made themselves clear for all to see. When Reagan entered the White House in 1981, Dolan came too and served his boss the full eight years, the only speechwriter to do so. (He twice took on the duties of chief speechwriter, in the early and late stages of the presidency.) He derived his greatest satisfaction from expressing the themes of anticommunism and antitotalitarianism.

Al Meyer, the eldest of the speechwriters, looked and sounded like an Ivy League law professor: he had a deep, resonant voice, a measured narrative style that inspired confidence in his listeners, and an analytic bent that dissected everything into its carefully separated components. He was not a law professor, but a career military officer, who had served on the staffs of both the National Security Council and of the Joint Chiefs of Staff. He joined the White House Speechwriting Department in 1982 and was the most comfortable of the team in matters of national defense, intellectually and morally. One evening in his office he was talking of the things that had influenced the way he thought about his military career:[15]

> One chapter of Dostoyevsky's *The Grand Inquisitor*—that chapter had me confront the question of the nature of man. At the time I read it, I was doing postgraduate studies on the Soviet system. And here was this chapter. You know, it's set in sixteenth-century Spain, and Christ has come back, and the Inquisitor is interrogating him.
>
> When I read that chapter, I suddenly knew that I had chosen something important to do, by serving in the military. My life and service to freedom was worth it. I had been right. That was my reaction to that chapter.
>
> Fundamentally, *The Grand Inquisitor* is about the concept of freedom. The question was whether man ought to be free to choose or not. Is man weak or strong? The Grand Inquisitor believes that man is inherently weak and always in need for the state to make his decisions for him. That's the most powerful moment in my reading life.

Dana Rohrabacher was a young but veteran member of the Reagan entourage. Befriended by one of the president's earliest political advisers, Lyn Nofziger, Rohrabacher had been hired as an assistant press secretary during the president's abortive run at the Republican nomination in 1976. After that he took an interim job as a reporter and editorialist for an Orange County, California, newspaper until Nofziger needed him for the 1980 campaign. Rohrabacher looked like a brash, southern Californian Andrew Hardy. In fact, he was a well-connected "Reagan hand," known to the California conservative group that had supported Reagan from the beginning of his elective career. By persons less favorably connected to those circles, he was called a True Believer.[16]

The youngest of the six speechwriters was Peter Robinson. One of the student organizers of the conservative political movement at Dartmouth College, possessor of an Oxford degree, and a former speechwriter for Vice President George Bush, Robinson was literate, accurate, and quick-witted and aspired to write like G. K. Chesterton. He most loved inserting into his speeches the anecdotes, humor, and literary allusions that the president relished.

The six speechwriters were not close friends. They worked in separate offices, and they had different literary heroes. But the striking thing about them was that they were persons of letters first, Rohrabacher and Meyer excepted. In a capital city where virtually every speechwriter was a former journalist, only Rohrabacher, among the president's speechwriters, thought of himself as a newspaperman, and even he had written several film scripts. (Dolan, although he had a journalism Pulitzer prize to his credit, never thought of himself as a reporter.)

What distinguished the president's speechwriters was their love of language. Their shop talk was of writers; they could speak easily of the prose styles of F. Scott Fitzgerald and Evelyn Waugh and other lesser and greater masters of the English language.

They believed that language made a difference in the way mankind thought about itself and, therefore, how men treated one another. With its fun, its beauty, and its solace, rhetoric (whether literature or oratory) made men live better lives. Listen to the youthful and mischievous Peter Robinson talking of the writing craft he loved and the craftsman he most loved—Chaucer.[17]

> Chaucer taught me that his end in writing was profoundly Christian. What he wants to do is help the reader save his soul. It struck me, that's not Hemingway's aim. His was a purely secular one, to tell a good story. Reading Chaucer was the first time I understood that all endeavors could be bent to a moral—and, for me, a Christian— end. An artist, reflecting beauty, could help his viewer participate in the joy of creation.
>
> At the same time, Chaucer is a great corrective against Puritanical impulses. There is no straitlaced stuffiness about him. The Miller's Tale—such bawdiness. I went to my Oxford don, and I challenged him, "Is there any point to this beside the fun of it?" "The point of it," he said, "is the fun of it." That was pretty good news. And while he's tough on all the people in his tales, all the portraits are drawn with such compassion that you forgive them and feel sorry for them— in the end. I took Chaucer's standard as my standard. Here he was writing about the thirteenth century. That was a pretty miserable century—illness, wars, plagues—but his spirit was soaring.
>
> In the Prioress, the Mother Superior, Chaucer drew a woman who, in Chesterton's phrase, failed: "the incomplete submission of a great lady." Try as she might to live up to her vows, she could not quite forsake the world. Wonderful.

Moreover, they felt a mutual respect for each other's craftsmanship and dedication. They were good, but there was no star system. It was a group that functioned ensemble. Peggy Noonan spoke for them all with her comment: "This is a first-rate speechwriting staff. It just is. It's a good staff. It's populated by people who have lots of things to do. The high points of their lives will not be their years in the White House."

At the outset of this chapter we spoke of the "unity" of the White House, a discipline that stemmed from the president's unchecked power to fire (or promote) every employee in it. In the Executive Compound the chief executive was the undisputed boss, and virtually everybody wanted to please the boss. In no office was that desire to please more intense than in the Speechwriting Department. As Dolan put it, because speechwriters were "creative people," they thirsted for appreciation. The Reagan speechwriters also had a clear vision of how to please the president because, before entering the White House, he had written so much himself, good stuff that had inspired them. The speechwriters—and especially Elliott who, as chief speechwriter, edited their drafts—were in tune with the president in the first place and wanted to please him in the second place.

They admired the president's professional writing abilities and responded readily to the slightest personal editing he gave their speeches. His presence was felt in the Speechwriting Department through countless additional cues—the resonance of his old speeches, his careful performance of their new speeches, and, most of all, his encouragement. That encouragement did not come through frequent personal presence in the speechwriters' offices; it was more subtle. His care in preparation to give a speech, his flawless delivery, his evident joy in the concise expression of an idea or a story, his leaving the speechwriters' drafts alone without nitpicking editing, and, above all, his willingness to go public with their words—these were the things that told the speechwriters that he was not afraid to let them do their best, and so they did their best.

3

★★★★★★★

The Speechwriting Process

*You know, on the White House, I admit I had a lot of preconceptions of
what it would be like, and the White House experience has reinforced a
very strong perception I have that most clichés are true, and people have
reputations for reasons. I found that so with CBS: most clichés about
CBS turned out to be true. When I went there, I thought I would pierce
the layer and get to the reality, but the reality was the layer. All clichés
about the White House are true. I had been told about the Byzantine politics
of the West Wing—and it's true; that there would be cheap jockeying for
this and that—all true; that there'd be some sleazy backstabbing in the
White House—true; and that some people are here to serve their country
and its people—and that's true.*

—Peggy Noonan (1984)

The routine by which speeches were written and edited in the Reagan
White House was straightforward, the process simple to describe. The
chief speechwriter assigned an event to himself or to one of his colleagues,
who prepared a first draft and handed it over to the chief for editing.
Thereafter, the speech was circulated for comments—both from within
the White House and from all relevant executive agencies. Responding
to their suggestions, the speechwriter wrote a second draft, which was
then forwarded to the president for his changes and approval.

The routine was as uncomplicated as that. Each speech proceeded
through these six steps: assignment, drafting, editing, circulation, revision
within the Speechwriting Department, and revision by the president
himself. Behind the White House gates speechwriting happened much
as it would happen anywhere else—in business, in clubs, in the family.

Chalk one up for Peggy Noonan's observation in the epigraph for this chapter: "the reality was the layer."

Still, these procedures had several distinctive features.

First, the speechwriters in the Reagan White House never specialized in particular subjects. It was true that each of them had personal preferences, each had areas of special knowledge, and each was reputed to be handier with some kinds of events than with others. But none of these factors determined who won a particular assignment. For example, Al Meyer, the former military officer, always hankered to discuss national defense, and he was good at it. Chief speechwriter Bently Elliott, however, was just as likely to assign a national security speech to someone else and put Meyer to work on a domestic topic of which he had little knowledge. Much like the judiciary's tradition against specialization, the procedure of rotating topics met three primary needs: to keep all the writers enthusiastic and informed, to free the process of overdependence on any one individual, and to keep the speeches rhetorically fresh.

Second, the circulation of draft speeches within the White House and agencies frequently produced contention. People were interested in what the president was going to say because his speeches had the force of policy within the executive branch. Presidential speeches gave the government direction, and the energies they set in motion could accelerate or stymie the objectives (and careers) of officials who really cared about their responsibilities. Within the quiet and unity of the presidency, the circulation of a draft speech aroused strong-willed individuals. Those who knew what mattered in government converged on speeches.

Third, amidst whatever contention their drafts provoked, the speechwriters dominated. After all, they had written the words that precipitated the turmoil in the first place. They had framed the issues and structured the content. Those to whom the drafts were circulated were asked for their reactions, and in responding they tended to focus their criticisms at the margins. Their practice was to urge only those changes touching their particular responsibilities, to concentrate on altering only what was critical to their jobs. As Rohrabacher, the lifelong Reaganaut, observed, "80 percent of what we write is spoken by the president without change."[1]

Fourth, the speechwriter dominated because in the typical controversy the numerous officials to whom the draft was circulated would clash with one another. It was the speechwriter who adjudicated their disagreements, who was "the referee among warring factions."[2] Whenever those opposed to the draft were united in their views, the speechwriter might have to be more accommodating. But usually there was conflicting advice, leaving the author in the catbird seat. "Most of the time," said Rohrabacher, "whether or not you use their material is up to you—and, of course, the president."[3] Speechwriters had to defend the choices they made, but around the negotiating table they were always the ones who made the first judgment.

Fifth, even in a presidency as intellectually unified as Reagan's, the range of disagreement over a speech could be surprisingly wide. Where you stand depends on where you sit, the saying goes, and specialized responsibilities caused individuals to see things differently. In contrast to the shorter-term perspective of administration officials, for example, agencies tended to look indifferently at the next election, and their memories stretched back decades. Peter Robinson ruefully told about an encounter with the Environmental Protection Agency (EPA) in 1985.

> I remember calling up the EPA and asking for a list of "our" accomplishments. After a long wait, they sent back a list of accomplishments, 1976 to 1981 [years when Jimmy Carter was president]. I went through the ceiling, I was so mad. After letting them know, I waited—and waited. Finally, I got something more, which took the list through 1981. I just gave up after that.[4]

A skeptic might say that the Reagan administration had so emasculated the EPA that there were no achievements in the environmental area to list. But that is precisely the point. What career specialists thought was a shameful record and beneath notice, political people attached to the Reagan White House deemed a cause for honor. Conflicts of perspective happened all the time.

There were other kinds of conflict: between electoral and policy concerns, between domestic and diplomatic considerations, and, above all, between rhetorical and policy objectives. Matters of technique caused disagreements, too. The length of a speech, the preparation of visual exhibits, the need for a quotable aside to catch media attention really mattered to some members of the president's staff but were mere nits to others. Amidst this vortex of controversy, personal ambitions would swirl.

Finally, the president mattered. For one thing, the speechwriters anticipated his likes and dislikes. For another thing, he had the last word: no one disputed his right to make a revision or resolve a disagreement his way. Moreover, he left his speechwriters feeling that they mattered and that they were entrusted by him with "the conscience of the presidency" (in the words of Al Meyer).[5]

What was striking about the speechwriting process was the minimal influence of the media. True, the speechwriters gave attention to the crafting of the one sentence that television might be expected to put on the evening news or that newspapers might pick up for a lead to their stories. Equally true, the threat of exposure of gaffes and misrepresentation led to accuracy. But the majority of speeches were never covered, and even with those that were, the limits of space and time allowed the media to report little more than a fraction of a speech. What the reporters would not report, they could not influence, Rohrabacher pointed out:

> Reagan's average major speech is around fifteen up to twenty-five minutes, depending on the audience's laughter and applause. That's somewhere between ten and twelve pages. One segment of the speech is newsworthy because in it you're talking about policy. The rest is rhetorical and of not much use except to the audience itself. That part contains his philosophy, his fundamental ideas.

The immediate audience, with its anticipated reactions, was usually the principal consideration in the writer's mind. Who the audience would be was determined by factors internal to the administration and outside the control of the media.

To illustrate the speechwriting process and the influence of audience, let us take a second look at the speech at Pointe du Hoc, discussed in the last chapter. Recall that the speech was to be delivered in Europe on June 6, 1984, the fortieth anniversary of D-Day, from the cliffs of French Normandy, overlooking the beaches where the Allies invaded Hitler's Europe. The immediate audience was to consist of veterans of that invasion and local French dignitaries. The American television networks were expected to give some live coverage to the event, although how much could not be known ahead of time. The setting was going to be international, the occasion was a commemoration of brave men, and the audience would be expecting something reflective and philosophical.

As we know, Elliott designated Noonan to do the D-Day speech because of her ardent desire to write it. In composing the draft for circulation, she worked in a solitary way, consulting with no one, doing her own research, and selecting the central themes herself: the presence of evil in the human condition (what she called "the moral dimension of the war")[6] and the need and capacity of individuals to ally with each other to compensate for their individual powerlessness.

When her draft went to Elliott for editing, he liked it. Noonan spoke of her working relationship with the chief of the Speechwriting Department: "Normally Ben Elliott goes over a speech first. He edits more heavily with some than with others. He usually stops when I get irritated. He does not like to override anyone. And I note his reactions: when his color rises, I back down. But Ben makes my speeches better when it's a political speech."

The Pointe du Hoc speech was tonal, not political, and Noonan's draft required virtually no editing before it was circulated for agency review. Noonan described what happened:

The speech circulated widely after it went out of this office, and I have to tell you it was controversial. One reason was that a woman wrote it. I have to tell you I have learned about the military and how they think over in Defense. . . . And the idea that a woman wrote the speech and that I had never seen combat upset them beyond belief. Cliques tried to tear it apart, and I saw that what they were doing was without the intention of being helpful.

But besides personal prejudice, there were other reasons for the objections to the speech. Noonan mentioned them. "There were the advance men. It was an eleven-minute speech, and the advance men only wanted a six-minute speech. They said the networks wouldn't show more than six minutes, or they would lose their audience. It turned out the networks gave it an hour, and they would have taken a much longer speech."

Throughout the fight over the speech, however, Noonan maintained control of it. Her adversaries might have felt that the phrase "maintained control" understated the passion with which she defended the integrity of her draft.

So I resisted, and I resisted pretty well—with others' help, I may say. I went berserk. I went to Elliott, and I went to [Richard] Darman [deputy chief of staff, to whom the Speechwriting Department was immediately responsible], and I said, "Do you realize what those fools are doing to my speech?"

Changes were made, and compromises were struck. But Noonan remained at the center of the negotiating process. "Eventually they did cut the speech. Darman and [Michael] Deaver [presidential assistant with final say over all advance arrangements] made some cuts, from eleven minutes to eight. It was too bad, because they cut out some good stuff. Most things are better shorter, but this one wasn't."

At last, the revised draft was ready to send to the president. Noonan described some of her apprehensions about this final stage of the speechwriting process.

Now, the president knew it was an important speech, and usually with important speeches, he really marks them up. New paragraphs, deletions, additions all over the place. But with this speech he didn't change at all. I was really disappointed. I thought he hadn't read it. But it turned out he had, and he had liked it. And he prepared for it beautifully.[7]

Pointe du Hoc was a ceremonial speech, philosophical in purpose, tonal in nature, addressed to the common sense of the American people.

Now, compare what happened in the case of a policy speech to the National League of Cities, where the audience consisted of local political officials who were knowledgeable and keen to hear details of presidential actions of vital significance to them.

The National League of Cities met annually in convention in Washington, D.C. In 1984 the league invited the president to address it, and the president accepted. The several thousand mayors and city officials were expected to be at worst a hostile audience (or at best an apprehensive one), not believing that the Reagan administration wanted to keep in place previous policies of fiscal support. They expected the president to tell them what his specific programs were going to be. Had he talked evocatively, as he had at Pointe du Hoc, he would have surprised and disappointed them. The president's senior staff knew what the league's expectations were likely to be. As a matter of fact, they had coveted the league's invitation precisely because it was an opportunity to define the administration's urban policy as it was being developed in the agencies (notably Transportation, Treasury, and Housing and Urban Development). They gave specific instructions to the Speechwriting Department about the content of the remarks—to list "our" urban policy proposals. The specific instructions for the National League of Cities speech contrasted with the discretion initially given the speechwriters regarding Pointe du Hoc.

There were other differences as well. Television would not be giving live coverage to the League of Cities event, nor would the speech get more than the briefest mention on the evening news. Among the print journalists, however, it would likely receive front-page treatment in the *New York Times* and the *Washington Post*, the so-called serious press.

The chief assigned the speech to Al Meyer, the former military officer, who had never before written a speech on urban matters. His knowledge of American cities was minimal, and he knew virtually nothing about past or current federal policy toward them. He started from scratch.

Instead of going off by himself and reading books as the literary Noonan had done with Pointe du Hoc, Meyer did what came naturally to him. He used the phone and spoke to government experts. He had always run down topics that way. "I'm not an urban specialist," said Meyer with a touch of understatement, "so I went out and asked the urban specialists, 'What is our urban policy?' . . . Well, it almost seemed that none of them had ever been asked that before, but their answers consisted of little chips of various pieces. And there were lots of pieces: New Federalism, block grants for sewers, mass transit, hospitals, and so on."[8]

And the more he listened to what they told him, the less satisfactory he found their point of view. In fact, Meyer was deeply bothered by what he heard; the pieces of the "policy" did not cohere, and, worse, they all boiled down to the federal government bankrolling city programs, and little else. Meyer remarked: "If that were our policy, to give out money to the cities, then the Democrats would always outbid us. That could not be our urban policy, and especially in an election year when the Democrats could outpromise us without qualms."[9]

Meyer had quickly become aware that the urban experts he consulted were not looking at things from the same vantage point as the president. So when Meyer sat down to put words on paper, he found himself acting independently of the instructions given him by the senior staff.

> Well, the more I thought about it, the more convinced I was that we needed a better, more comprehensive definition. Sooner or later, I came up with an outline, and since no one had ever defined it that way, it stood as the Reagan "urban policy." But it was a definition under which the Republicans could do better than the Democrats.

As Meyer saw it, he was driven by his task to address the big questions. He had to speak about the meaning of things.

> What is it that will bring people to want to live in cities? What is it that will incline corporations to want to build in cities, particularly in northern cities? Well, in part, it's mass transit, and in part it's New Federalism, which places decision-making authority at lower levels of government and lets people there have responsibility. But in part it's safe streets, less crime, less drugs, better schools, and improvement of all of education. It's a feeling of neighborhood, with all the traditional values of neighbor helping neighbor, of a feeling of togetherness and belonging, values we Republicans are always talking about.

It was important that Meyer wrote with the specific audience of the National League of Cities in mind. It forced him to understand the feelings of the mayors and responsible local officials—their pride, their honor, the apprehensions they felt in their work. If he were to overcome their suspicions, he had to give expression to their feelings and connect them to the president's philosophy. For in Meyer's mind it was philosophy that provided people with a scale of meaning, a definition of "progress," and a context in which individuals could see how their individual actions connected and added up to something whole and more noble than its parts. It was philosophy that would make them go energetically, if they were to go at all, in a new direction.

Thus, despite his initial ignorance of urban policy and despite instructions from above to write of concrete proposals, Meyer found that he had drafted a philosophical speech. When it was eventually circulated to the agencies and his ideas were exposed to the review process, each specialized department made objections to this sentence or that paragraph, but none rejected the outline that Meyer had originated. A number of little changes were made, but the philosophy stayed—and, thus, it became the Reagan "urban policy" because Meyer, having written the initial draft, maintained the dominant position in the process.

What was the nature of the outline that stayed intact? What Meyer did was to structure the speech around four principles. In doing so, he used specific policies to illustrate those principles. Here was the core of his handiwork, the heart of the president's remarks to the League of Cities:

> We should be confident. We are the same people who put our ambitions and skills to work and built the best cities in the world. . . . Now, I know that success will not come easy. It'll take great effort and patience. But it can and will be done. Rebuilding cities begins with economic growth, and I believe our economic recovery is the most important urban renewal program in America today. . . .
>
> The second key to success is a renewed emphasis on federalism. We believe that when it comes to running cities local officials can do a better job from city hall than bureaucrats can from Washington. [Applause] You tempt me to quit right here. [Laughter] . . .
>
> Public-private partnerships are the third important key for sparking economic opportunity and development of urban areas. . . .
>
> The fourth and final key to a stronger, more prosperous, and stable urban America is a strengthening of basic values through renewal of community life. People coming together in a spirit of neighborhood is what makes cities worth living in. It's what keeps businesses and attracts new ones. And it's what keeps faith with the fine traditions of the past while enabling us to build the future with confidence. Shakespeare said, "The people are the cities." And if our cities can create thriving neighborhoods that offer excellence in education, efficiency and affordability, safety on—but drugs and crime off—our streets, then they can become great centers of growth, diversity, and excitement, filled with sound, colors, warmth, and delight. . . .
>
> The spirit of renewal is the American spirit, and we see that spirit everywhere we look, from the healthy rise in corporate and private giving to thousands of exciting private sector initiatives, and from neighbors helping neighbors to a welcome return to our basic values.[10]

"Economic growth" (which meant lower income tax rates), reduced federal government responsibility, "public-private partnerships" (which meant increased private charity), and increased volunteer neighborhood organization—those were not the concrete proposals of federal agencies. Those were the philosophical principles of the president, as formulated in "the conscience of the presidency"—the Speechwriting Department.

With obvious relish, Meyer smiled as he observed of his success:

> It illustrates that the bottom line is the spoken word. The president forces the government to treat with broad issues in a comprehensive way—if he does it right. From his position as president, whether it's urban policy or relations with West European allies, he forces the whole government to focus on that issue.

Tony Dolan—the formidable, cigar-chomping, Boston Irishman from Yale, whose hero and mentor was William F. Buckley—spoke of politics this way:

> Some think that speechwriting is an adjunct to what the candidate [or official] does, and for that reason campaigns and government budgeting always starve it. They think that what governing is about are meetings, conferences, phone calls, rules, and decisions. That's wrong. I would argue that ideas are the stuff of politics. Ideas are the great moving forces of history. If you acknowledge that, then not only do you make speechwriting important, you make it your most important management tool you have. Ronald Reagan knows how important his speeches are. Not only do they provide a statement of purpose for the government, it is through his speeches that managers understand where they're going. And especially is that important in our form of government, where we do not have a parliamentary majority. Here you have to mobilize public opinion to make the government work in the direction the president wants, and Ronald Reagan—or any president, for that matter—does that through his speeches.[11]

Full of intensity, Dolan paid attention to ideas. He was suspicious of people, whether they were members of the public or managers of government, until he had discerned their fundamental assumptions about human nature, society, and personal values. He phoned people who had written things he liked and encouraged them to write more. He wrote articles himself. He planted philosophy in a presidential speech, fumed if it were ever weeded out for some technical reason, and replanted it so fiercely and repeatedly in future speeches that he wore resistance down or got the support of the president himself to insert it.

He shared with Noonan a love for the written word. When he talked of the great events of history, he spoke of books. Authors were his heroes, Whittaker Chambers (a disillusioned former Communist of the 1930s) a saint, Chambers's autobiography, *Witness*, a testament.

He was a scintillating speechwriter—controversial, acerbic, and proud of his craftsmanship—and he set an example of courage and persistence that his fellow speechwriters gladly followed. They all could recall how, once, determined to prevent last-minute changes in a speech written for a presidential visit to Europe, Dolan had paid his own way to France just so he could personally fend off changes suggested by the president's inner circle.

By example and precept, he inspired his colleagues to fight for what they knew was right for the president. If it took "go[ing] berserk" to save the philosophical heart from being cut out of a speech, he stirred his fellow writers to do it. Diplomatic but fiercely committed, Dolan stood sentry against others' efforts to load the president's speeches with the stuff of "meetings, conferences, phone calls, rules, and decisions"—the stuff that Dolan felt was the detritus of politics.

A passion for ideas pervaded the speechwriting process of the Reagan White House. And it abided there because Dolan and each of his speechwriting colleagues knew they were writing for a president with whom they were in tune—because Reagan was as deeply convinced as they were that "ideas are the stuff of politics."

4

★★★★★★★

The Bully Pulpit

*Franklin Delano Roosevelt . . . and John Kennedy, that bright spirit,
and Teddy Roosevelt . . . all loved the Presidency, loved the bully pulpit
of the office. . . . So do I.*

—*Ronald Reagan (1984)*

The speechwriters were proud of the special bond between them and
Reagan, who had entrusted them with the job of animating the "conscience of the presidency." Their sense of mission was almost palpable.
In their minds the Speechwriting Department was the soul of the
administration, appointed to provide both the government and the
people with a direction for their energies. Reagan's writers were not
embarrassed about asserting the importance of their place in the White
House. They were convinced that "speeches [were] where it's at in
this administration."[1]

They were animated not only by their sense of place, but also by
their sense of time. Their reading of the past confirmed the importance
of presidential rhetoric in shaping the way Americans thought about
themselves. The people in their private and public lives drew purpose
and hope from the language of great presidents, who linked, as Peter
Robinson put it, "what is going on in America to what is America's
purpose" and thereby "elevated the people's magnanimity, made them
less selfish, and broadened their notion of their self-interest."[2] Presidential
speech making, like good literature, had a moral function.

The best language of former presidencies had been woven into the
ribbon of history. The Speechwriting Department in the Reagan White

43

House aspired to perform its craft in a way worthy to gain a place on that same ribbon.

Peggy Noonan talked about past presidents: "When I first came here [to the White House], I was quite taken with Theodore Roosevelt and his notion of the presidency, and I wrote with Theodore Roosevelt in mind, or at least my image of him as an ebullient, feisty character."[3] From 1901 to 1909 Teddy Roosevelt enlivened the presidency with his energy. He was an irrepressible speaker, and it is said that he was the first to describe the presidency as a bully pulpit.[4] Noonan went on to say:

> You know the derivation of the phrase "bully pulpit"? Teddy Roosevelt invented it. It's one of his formulations. "Bully" was one of his favorite adjectives—it was his favorite favorable adjective. It meant terrific. "Bully pulpit" meant a place from which one could influence more minds at one time than from any other lectern.

Teddy Roosevelt was only thirty-nine years old in 1901, when he succeeded to the presidency after William McKinley (1897–1901) was assassinated. As president, Roosevelt traveled more extensively throughout the United States than any previous chief executive. And everywhere he went, he gave talks. He spoke with a nearly irresistible sincerity.

There was much to speak about; the turn of the century was not without its tumult. Industrial strikes disturbed the land: the coal mines, for example, were struck for seven long months in 1902. Domestically, there were financial abuses in the private sector, and the presence of poverty in an increasingly prosperous America was being condemned as a national scandal. Internationally, there dimly appeared signs of breakdown in the diplomatic arrangements that had secured the long truce of the nineteenth century. The Russo-Japanese War (1904–1905) was a big war, testing Great Britain's capacity as the world's peacekeeper.

Interestingly, much of what President Roosevelt said during these important years would disappoint the present-day reader. The bulk of his remarks shed little light on the great events of his era; the imagery of his rhetoric was meager; and his principles were surprisingly shallow.[5] Yet, once in a while, he hit a home run. Consider a speech in 1906, in which Roosevelt spoke to journalists of the dangers of unbalanced and inflated reporting of America's shortcomings:

> The material problems that face us today are not such as they were in [President George] Washington's time, but the underlying facts of human nature are the same now as they were then. Under altered external form we war with the same tendencies toward evil that were evident in Washington's time, and are helped by the same tendencies for good. It is about some of these that I wish to say a word today.

In Bunyan's "Pilgrim's Progress" you may recall the description of the Man with the Muck-Rake, the man who could look no way but downward, with the muck-rake in his hand, who was offered a celestial crown for his muck-rake, but who would neither look up nor regard the crown he was offered, but continued to rake to himself the filth of the floor.

In "Pilgrim's Progress" the Man with the Muck-Rake is set forth as the example of him whose vision is fixed on carnal instead of on spiritual things. Yet he also typifies the man who in this life consistently refuses to see aught that is lofty, and fixes his eyes with solemn intentness only on that which is vile and debasing. Now, it is very necessary that we should not flinch from seeing what is vile and debasing. There is filth on the floor, and it must be scraped up with the muck-rake; and there are times and places where this service is the most needed of all the services that can be performed. But the man who never does anything else, who never thinks or speaks or writes save of his feats with the muck-rake, speedily becomes, not a help to society, not an incitement to good, but one of the most potent forces for evil.[6]

To any Reagan writer, that would have been exemplary presidential rhetoric. Chief speechwriter Elliott would have appreciated Roosevelt's chiding the press for its excesses. Dolan would have been gratified that political discourse had been enriched with a word like "muckraker." Noonan would have applauded the explicitness of the axiom regarding humanity's unchanging nature, with its eternal "tendencies toward evil [and] for good." Robinson would have smiled at Roosevelt's happy invocation of John Bunyan. Although eight decades separated Teddy Roosevelt from the Reagan White House of the 1980s, his buoyancy and fearlessness (as the speechwriters imagined his ebullience and stout heart) touched them.

The Speechwriting Department of Ronald Reagan was also influenced by two more recent presidents: Teddy Roosevelt's nephew, Franklin Delano Roosevelt (1933–1945), and "that bright spirit," John Fitzgerald Kennedy (1961–1963).

Franklin Roosevelt entered the White House as the thirty-second president. At that time deep economic depression was touching virtually everybody, and despair and anger had fallen upon the land. He was inaugurated amidst cruel times. Then, twelve years later, when he died in office, the only president ever to win four consecutive terms, war had come, and he had commanded the largest American military force in history, deploying it against the Axis nations of Germany, Italy, and Japan on two fronts, Western Europe and the Pacific. These two events—the Great Depression and World War II—evoked some of the most memorable presidential oratory in our nation's history.

Virtually all of Franklin Roosevelt's speeches had the verve and substance of his uncle Theodore's best efforts.

In a time of depression and disappointment, his speeches were spiced with fun. He loved to parry criticism with mordant irony, and his everyday images captivated his supporters. Take, as an example, his "sick man" metaphor from a 1936 campaign speech, with which he rebutted opposition claims that his administration had gone too far in regulating private business, dragging the economy down.

> Today, for the first time in seven years the banker, the storekeeper, the small factory owner, the industrialist can all sit back and enjoy the company of their own ledgers. They are in the black. That is where we want them to be; that is where our policies aim them to be; that is where we intend them to be in the future.
>
> Some of these people really forget how sick they were. I have their fever charts. I know how the knees of all of our rugged individualists were trembling four years ago and how their hearts fluttered. They came to Washington in great numbers. Washington did not look like a dangerous bureaucracy to them then. Oh, no! It looked like an emergency hospital. All of the distinguished patients wanted two things—a quick hypodermic to end the pain and a course of treatment to cure the disease. They wanted them in a hurry; we gave them both. And now most of the patients seem to be doing very nicely. Some of them are even well enough to throw their crutches at the doctor.[7]

That was fun.

But it was Roosevelt's first inaugural address that established a standard of technical excellence by which the Reagan speechwriters were always measuring their own handiwork. They admired the cadences of Roosevelt's first official words, and they respected the eloquence with which he evoked hope and restored self-confidence:

> I am certain that my fellow Americans expect that on my induction into the presidency I will address them with a candor and a decision which the present situation of our nation impels. This is preeminently the time to speak the truth, the whole truth, frankly and boldly. Nor need we shrink from honestly facing conditions in our country today. This great nation will endure as it has endured, will revive and will prosper.
>
> So, first of all, let me assert my firm belief that the only thing we have to fear is fear itself—nameless, unreasoning, unjustified terror which paralyzes needed efforts to convert retreat into advance.[8]

Moreover, the Reagan speechwriters were moved by the imagery with which Roosevelt depicted the material conditions of the time:

Our common difficulties . . . concern, thank God, only material things. Values have shrunken to fantastic levels; taxes have risen; our ability to pay has fallen; government of all kinds is faced by serious curtailment of income; the means of exchange are frozen in the currents of trade; the withered leaves of industrial enterprise lie on every side; farmers find no markets for their produce; the savings of many years in thousands of families are gone.

More, important, a host of unemployed citizens face the grim problem of existence, and an equally great number toil with little return. Only a foolish optimist can deny the dark realities of the moment.

Finally, Reagan's speechwriters were stimulated by the combativeness of FDR, depicting his political opponents as the incompetent adherents "of an outworn tradition":

Faced by failure of credit, they have proposed only the lending of more money. Stripped of the lure of profit by which to induce our people to follow their false leadership, they have resorted to exhortations, pleading tearfully for restored confidence. They know only the rules of a generation of self-seekers. They have no vision, and when there is no vision the people perish.

Those were words of battle to take your hat off to.

As craftsmen, Reagan's writers credited the style for its rhetorical brilliance. As for substance, however, Roosevelt's political philosophy was the near opposite of the public philosophy of the Reagan presidency. Roosevelt's premise that business was an ignoble calling and that working for profit usually led to "callous and selfish wrongdoing" goaded the Reagan writers into their best efforts to dispute it (see Chapter Twelve).

A third historical presence on the ribbon of American history was President John F. Kennedy. Toward him the speechwriters reacted ambivalently. On the one hand, they felt his rhetoric was flawed by its exaggeration, its overpromise, its youthful and imprudent exuberance. His first inaugural, for example, filled the speechwriters with rue. In the interest of the rounded phrase Kennedy's rhetoric overpromised: "Man holds in his mortal hands the power to abolish all forms of human poverty and all forms of human life." "Let every nation know, whether it wishes us well or ill, that we shall pay any price, bear any burden, meet any hardship, support any friend, oppose any foe to assure the survival and the success of liberty." "Let all our neighbors know that we shall join with them to oppose aggression or subversion anywhere in the Americas. And let every other power know that this hemisphere intends to remain the master of its own house." "To that world assembly of sovereign states, the United Nations, our last best hope in an age where the instruments of war have far outpaced the instruments of peace, we renew our pledge of support—to prevent it from becoming merely a forum for invective— to strengthen its shield of the new and the weak—and to enlarge the area in which its writ may run.'' And, of course, the famous and ambiguous phrase, ''And so, my fellow Americans—ask not what your country can do for you—ask what you can do for your country.''[9] These phrases— irresponsible and lacking austerity—were examples of what was to be avoided. ''If you can talk with crowds and keep your virtue,'' Rudyard Kipling said. The verdict of the speechwriters was that some of President Kennedy's rhetoric had flunked that antidemagogic test miserably.

On the other hand, they genuinely admired the unpretentiousness, charm, and wit that poured forth in Kennedy's daily, often spontaneous appearances before the public. At such times he touched both the hearts *and* the minds of Americans. Against the remembered Kennedy as a man of character and joy, the speechwriters measured their own boss. They did not find him lacking, and they wrote to reveal those same comfortable virtues in Reagan.

The speechwriters also had a worst case, an example to shun. All six mentioned Jimmy Carter, the president who had preceded Ronald Reagan, as especially inept.

The philosophical Dolan thought Carter lacked a coherent public philosophy. Former army officer Meyer thought Carter neglected the importance of hope in leading others: ''Jimmy Carter's mistake was to convince us that we were losers.'' The populist Noonan thought he trivialized the people's concerns. Even worse by her standards, he lacked poetry.

> He did not try to be good. Whenever [his speechwriters] inserted anything that was a little abstract, that was a little poetic, the president, just like a little engineer, would cut it out. He did not understand the need for metaphor and the fun stuff that people relate to. Carter would never have tolerated, much less come up with, a metaphor like Lincoln's, ''A house divided against itself cannot stand.'' He would have said this speech is not about houses, it's not about real estate, and snip, it would be out of there.[10]

Note how Noonan compared Carter to Abraham Lincoln. Lincoln's presence was felt in every department in the White House, but nowhere more fully than in the Speechwriting Department. All the Reagan speechwriters agreed: Lincoln was apart, without equal, the president who best used his office to write the creed of freedom on the American soul. Where the six writers admired FDR's style and looked to his rhetoric for its technique, they drew their inspiration from Lincoln. He elevated their purposes. He challenged them to tackle the fundamental questions on the minds of the people and address them with dignity.

The speechwriters evoked President Lincoln recurrently. The youthful and devout Robinson discussed the relationship of religion and politics in American history.

> Religion legitimates our system of government. The United States political philosophy stands at the intersection of religion and politics. Lincoln said as much in the second inaugural. What he says, when one comes down to it, is that there was one overarching issue, Could men own other men? And the religious answer—not the economic, not the material answer—was, ''No.''[11]

Lincoln's second inaugural was spiritual and philosophical. It spoke of the sinfulness and magnanimity of the human soul, of the brotherhood that bonded mankind, and of the ways men and women were to live their lives to fulfill their covenant with God. Listen to the words with which Lincoln addressed the partisans of both the Union and the Confederacy as they continued to war with one another in 1865.

> Neither party expected for the war the magnitude or the duration which it has already attained. Neither anticipated that the cause of the conflict might cease with or even before the conflict itself should cease. Each looked for an easier triumph and a result less fundamental and astounding. Both read the same Bible and pray to the same God, and each invokes His aid against the other.
>
> It may seem strange that any men should dare to ask a just God's assistance in wringing their bread from the sweat of other men's faces, but let us judge not that we be not judged. The prayers of both could not be answered. That of neither has been answered fully. The Almighty has His own purposes. ''Woe unto the world because of offenses! for it must needs be that offenses come; but woe to that man by whom the offense cometh.''
>
> If we shall suppose that American slavery is one of those offenses which, in the providence of God, must needs come, but which, having continued through His appointed time, He now wills to remove, and that He gives to both North and South this terrible war as the woe due to those by whom the offense came, shall we discern therein any departure from those divine attributes which the believers in a living God always ascribe to Him? Fondly do we hope, fervently do we pray, that this mighty scourge of war may speedily pass away.
>
> Yet, if God wills that it continue until all the wealth piled by the bondsman's 250 years of unrequited toil shall be sunk, and until every drop of blood drawn with the lash shall be paid by another drawn with the sword, as was said 3,000 years ago, so still it must be said, ''The judgments of the Lord are true and righteous altogether.''
>
> With malice toward none, with charity for all, with firmness in the right as God gives us to see the right, let us strive on to finish the work we are in, to bind up the nation's wounds, to care for him who shall have borne the battle and for his widow and his orphan—to do all which may achieve and cherish a just and lasting peace among ourselves and with all nations.[12]

"With malice toward none, with charity for all": that was the Bully Pulpit at its most sublime.[13]

History made a difference. Even the artless examples of failed presidents warned of the dangers of presidential utterances being incoherent, banal, or mindless of the inadvertent expectations they could arouse.

History also offered positive examples and taught a transcendently important lesson—that worthy ideas, powerfully and clearly expressed, caused Americans to be more decent people. To utter the nation's most fundamental ideas repeatedly, to apply principles consistently to actions, to govern with philosophy—these constituted the indispensable responsibilities of the American presidency. Repetition and reinforcement of the American public philosophy were fatiguing duties, but, by connecting to history, the Reagan writers renewed their energies to perform them vigorously.

Even in a White House as full of memory as Reagan's, however, nothing would have happened without the president's encouragement. Many presidents have occupied the White House, employed speechwriters, and addressed the nation. Few have been remembered for formulating a memorable public philosophy.

Presidents are not complete masters of their fate, but they enjoy great influence. They command the attention of those they employ. To the extent that they select talented personnel, teach them well, and inspire their best efforts, presidents are potent creatures.

So it was with Reagan and the speechwriters he employed. Each member of his team of writers acknowledged Reagan's role as a master stylist. In the manner of his early speeches, they wrote likewise.

His style was so distinctive that, as speechwriter replaced speechwriter, the difference was hardly detectable. His philosophy was so clear and his argument so articulate that his speechwriters were challenged to be clear and articulate in how they justified things. His public presentation of himself was so artful that they knew their handiwork would not be wasted. His calm delighted them, his jokes amused them, and his personal anecdotes gladdened them. They were disciplined by his understatement, intrigued by his improvisations, and pleased by his pleasure in their work. They knew he liked general ideas and the building of an argument.

In short, they loved the reasonableness of this nice man and the niceness of this man of reason. And they appreciated that he connected them (to repeat Robinson's words) "to what is America's purpose."

PART TWO

THE IDEAS OF FREEDOM

*The fit between Ronald Reagan's language and the American people is
indeed a tight one. And I understand what you meant by describing
Reagan's power as "primal": like a rock in the Morvan, like plain
truth, like the wilderness of Nevada.*

—François Mitterrand (1986)

Two great values vie to dominate the American mind. One is freedom,
the other equality. The former requires each citizen to take personal
responsibility and expects much in the way of social and technical skills,
human understanding, and individual courage. The latter, in its most
mundane form, tends to speak of collective responsibility and to oblige
the state to watch over the fate of those constituting the society under
its sway. Freedom gives scope to human flaws and virtue; in the name
of equality some Americans would restrict the expression of both.[1]

One hundred and fifty years ago Alexis de Tocqueville noted this
rivalry of political philosophies in the United States and observed the
human willingness to surrender personal liberty for a degrading form of
equality unless educated otherwise:

> There exists . . . in the human heart a depraved taste for equality,
> which impels the weak to attempt to lower the powerful to their own
> level and reduces men to prefer equality in slavery to inequality with
> freedom. Not that those nations whose social condition is democratic
> naturally despise liberty; on the contrary, they have an instinctive
> love of it. But liberty is not the chief and constant object of their desires;
> equality is their idol; they make rapid and sudden efforts to obtain
> liberty and, if they miss their aim, resign themselves to their dis-
> appointment; but nothing can satisfy them without equality, and they
> would rather perish than lose it.[2]

The central event of political life in modern times has been the rivalry
between liberty and material equality, between self-government and
paternalistic government, between the contingency of the free life and
the certitudes of the submissive one. If human liberty is to prevail as "the
chief and constant object" of Americans' desires, it must have a powerful champion. To the presidency and its bully pulpit falls the task of
fortifying the meaning of moral freedom and the spiritual importance of
being the masters of our own souls. It is the presidency that can educate

the democracy, that can speak the language of freedom with all the eloquence and statesmanship at its command, and that can replenish "the common [philosophical] spring from which all the rest emanates."[3] The presidency of Ronald Reagan sought to execute that task, aspiring to do it with exceptional skill. It set out to formulate three axioms of freedom as answers to the fundamental questions: What is human society? What is human nature? What is the measure of the good life?

The next four chapters examine those axioms as they evolved over the eight years of the Reagan presidency.

5

Partnership: Defining Human Society

Society . . . is a partnership in all science; a partnership in all art; a partnership in every virtue, and in all perfection. And as the ends of such a partnership cannot be obtained in many generations, it becomes a partnership not only between those who are living, but between those who are living, those who are dead, and those who are to be born.

—*Edmund Burke,* Reflections on the Revolution in France *(1790)*

Peggy Noonan was explaining why Reagan's story-telling and metaphorical gifts were so important to his leadership: "The likening of one thing to another is a way of trying to convey a realistic picture of what is going on and calling for the need to face up to it."[1] It was her belief that one of the responsibilities of the chief executive was to teach the American people about their society and to show them how to prosper in it. By offering an understandable explanation of events, by providing society with what sociologists call a "controlling definition of the situation," a president can help Americans decide how they ought to behave toward each other. His influence on their personal decisions depends heavily on his gift of metaphor. By likening things to one another, by using the familiar to interpret the unknown and the abstract, a president can teach the citizenry "what [is] going on" in their society, enabling them more accurately to anticipate the actions and reactions of strangers.

In any era the greatest danger to community morale is misleading metaphors: they prompt people to act inappropriately and cause things to fall apart. Altering bad analogies is key to the nation's bettering itself. That meant Noonan's first duty as a presidential speechwriter was to identify any problematic metaphors then dominant among the people and replace them with more accurate ones.

When Reagan entered the White House in 1981, was there a single metaphor dominating American society? Yes. It was that life was a footrace, in which each American was pitted against other Americans in a winner-take-all competition. Recall its most powerful expression in President Lyndon Johnson's 1965 commencement address at Howard University in Washington, D.C.: "You do not take a person who for years had been hobbled by chains and liberate him, bring him to the starting line of a race, and then say, 'You are free to compete with all the others,' and still justly believe that you have been completely fair."[2] That passage appeared in a speech given by Johnson to a predominantly African-American faculty and student body. He was referring to the civil rights of African Americans, a group that had been long hobbled by the laws of slavery and Jim Crow segregation. Bigotry and racial discrimination—the hateful legacy of slavery—had bedeviled American society for more than three centuries. In 1965 one of the principal objectives of the Johnson presidency was to rally the federal government to help overcome the force of that legacy. At the time that Johnson spoke at Howard, his presidency had already succeeded in getting Congress to pass the Civil Rights Act of 1964 and the Voting Rights Act of 1965. It had also set in place the administrative means to compel compliance with that pair of measures. The Howard University speech was intended to provide the justification for the prominent role the federal government was beginning to assume in civil rights matters. The Johnson speechwriting team developed the metaphor of the footrace to signify the government's responsibility for securing the civil rights of African Americans.

The metaphor, however, raised a question: If life was like a footrace, who were going to be the winners and losers in the head-to-head competition it implied? Contemplating this awkward topic, Johnson and his speechwriters committed the national government to preventing all persons previously hobbled by chains from losing ever again. In the words of the Howard University speech, the federal government was obliged to achieve "not just equality as a right and a theory, but equality as a fact and as a result."[3]

Powerful metaphors—and the footrace metaphor turned out to be very powerful—take on a life of their own, notwithstanding the designs of their inventors. Hardly was the image of the footrace uttered than it resonated in the schools and colleges throughout the land. It rang true to African Americans, and it also sounded right to the members of the baby-boom generation, an age group so populous that it had to push its way into overcrowded circumstances at every stage of its growing up. To these young adults the footrace notion captured their feelings of being resented and unneeded, and they embraced it.

The Johnson administration did not anticipate either the extreme popularity or the fertile implications of the footrace image. The three succeeding presidential administrations of Nixon, Ford, and Carter (1969–1981) failed to dispute it, and so it increased in authority, becoming the controlling definition of the era.

Picturing human society as a footrace was not a wholly new coinage in American political rhetoric, but President Johnson's version was novel in its stark competitiveness. The import of the metaphor cannot be overstated, for it turned out to have five invidious implications.[4]

For one thing, it depicted a society in which there were countless losers. With only a few prizes for an ever-growing number of entrants, existence became an increasingly vicious interpersonal competition, a life-and-death struggle of all against all—a virtual civil war, in which many were defeated by the strength and wisdom of their own countrymen. The race being conceived as a zero-sum game, the speedier, braver, and more intelligent the competition, the more inevitable was the people's defeat.

Second, the competition was isolating and cutthroat, evoking individualism in its narrowest sense. Compassion was impractical: to stop and pick up a fallen competitor meant losing the race. Love was against the rules: coalescing and cooperating together in groups were forbidden by the laws of the competition.

The third implication was this: if life was a winner-take-all footrace, yet some of the individual competitors were not being treated fairly, then fairness required that some official be designated to give a head start to those who for so long had been running in chains. The only acceptable handicapper was the state—that is, the national government in Washington, D.C.

Fourth, if removing the chains from those that had been hobbled and giving them a head start did not end up achieving equal results, if, despite help, history's previous losers continued to lose, then the fault was in society, in "you," the winners of the American footrace in the unfair past. After all, you—or your ancestors—probably won previous contests because your competition had to run in chains. The accusatory implication of the footrace metaphor even made thinkable the remedy of the state punitively impeding some entrants so that they would not win, despite the fact that history was not their fault.[5] It would be fair to hobble the swift because the rules of the race deemed that it must end in a dead heat, with each contestant equal as a fact and as a result.

Fifth, in a world likened to a footrace, logically there should be no volunteers helping the slow and the fallen; no one other than government officials ought to help the slow, or dole food out to the lowly, or give rest to the fatigued. If, despite the logic that no private citizen should help, some did lend a kindly hand to heal others' pain, they were seen as either fools or hypocrites. Moreover, their presence as private volunteers signified that the state was not doing its job right, that it had not done enough or been sufficiently compassionate. The existence of charity meant that the handicapper-in-charge was somehow messing up.

Now, the point of this discussion is not to blame President Johnson for likening American life to cutthroat competition and dishonoring voluntarism. Doubtless, one of the principal motives behind his legislative program was fairness. Unquestionably, many of the consequences of the Great Society legislation were helpful. And, very likely, Johnson's purpose in creating the footrace metaphor was actually to encourage private charity.

Rather, the point is that metaphors can escape the control of their creators and run away in unexpected directions. This was especially true of the footrace metaphor. Irrespective of Johnson's intentions, it caused some Americans, especially young adults, to believe that theirs was a society in which individuals detached themselves from one another's fate and competed remorselessly.

Moreover, these five inadvertent implications echoed the modern world's most powerful single testament to material equality. Recall the metaphor with which Karl Marx and Friedrich Engels concluded *The Communist Manifesto:* "The proletarians have nothing to lose but their chains. They have a world to win."[6] Like Marx's manifesto, Johnson's metaphor depicted a society in which a privileged class was waging a "more or less veiled civil war" against a shackled and helpless class. In order to win their group struggle, the shackled underdogs were encouraged to focus their hatred and envy on their oppressors and to destroy them. Interpreted that way, the footrace metaphor was a call for viciousness.

Even with a more benign interpretation, the analogy of life to a competitive footrace was incoherent. As Garry Wills, the classicist-turned-commentator, observed, "the metaphor is a mess."[7] What made it so was that the outcome of the footrace was "fixed." The race had to end in a dead heat, and if everyone knew that ahead of time, why should anyone want to run it? Little wonder that many Americans, like the flower children described by Joan Didion, were confused by the rules of the game, if the rules were as senseless as these appeared.

Despite its viciousness and incoherence, the footrace metaphor became the political platitude of the age. Partisans of different stripes embraced it. To some it signified that equality was in the saddle of events; to others it countenanced personal greed. To defuse the misleading implications of this inherited image, President Reagan and his speechwriters developed an alternative picture of American society—the metaphor of "partnership."[8]

Partnership was voluntary, its roots set in the constitutional right to assemble and the frontier habits of moving on. The analogy of partnership supplied American individualism with a social context. It implied a basis for cooperation, which was prompted by self-interest but fortified over time by gratitude and mutual respect. It stood for the primacy of personal freedom as powerfully as Johnson's footrace represented the primacy of equality.

The metaphor of partnership provided a consoling contrast to the image of the solitary, self-absorbed, long-distance runner. At the same time, it had less invasive implications than other possible metaphors, such as "house" or "family" (like Lincoln's "house divided" or FDR's "new deal" in the household's ongoing pinochle game). Partnership instructed a society in what to do when trouble struck. "Team up," it said. "The strength and wisdom of others are advantages, not threats. The secret of a free society is association, and the secret of association is exchange, give-and-take." It taught that giving fair weight was the central rule of sustaining teamwork.

The state was not denied a place in the partnership metaphor, but it was not elevated to the dominating know-it-all role the racecourse metaphor conferred upon it. As a mere potential partner, the state was relegated to being one among many alternative entities with which individuals were free to connect. And like any other liaison, a public-private partnership could be dissolved if either party to it found it nonbeneficial.

The metaphor of partnership also taught the critical distinction between self-sufficiency and self-reliance. Self-sufficiency meant that the individual had to bear all his burdens in solitude; self-sufficient persons avoided relationships and stood aloof from the fate of others. Self-reliance meant no such thing; self-reliant individuals enlisted the assistance of others to solve problems and in turn committed themselves to return (or pass on) the favors when the time came to repay.

Reagan and his administration made *partnership* their motto. They stamped it on their laws (the Job Training Partnership Act), imprinted it on their programs (the Private Sector–Public School Partnership, the Child-Safety Partnership, Public–Private Partnerships for Fair Housing), and proclaimed it to individuals and groups in the president's countless public and personalized messages.[9]

The president's elaborations on the theme of partnership were applied in virtually every public context. At times his imagery was exquisite, as in the story of the mountaineers in his address to the Japanese Diet on November 11, 1983. One can hardly conceive political metaphor more deftly drawn as he spoke of the connected destinies of Japan and the United States.

Our two nations may spring from separate pasts, we may live at opposite sides of the earth, but we have been brought together by our indomitable spirit of determination, our love of liberty, and devotion to progress. We are like climbers who begin their ascent from opposite ends of the mountain. The harder we try, the higher we climb, and the closer we come together—until that moment we reach the peak and we are as one.

It happened last month. One American and two Japanese groups began climbing Mount Everest—the Japanese from the side of Nepal and the Americans from the side of Tibet. The conditions were so difficult and dangerous that before it ended two Japanese climbers tragically lost their lives. But before that tragedy, those brave climbers all met and shook hands just under the summit. And then, together, they climbed to the top to share that magnificent moment of triumph.

Good and dear friends of Japan, if those mountaineers could join hands at the top of the world, imagine how high our combined 350 million citizens can climb, if all of us work together as powerful partners for the cause of good.[10]

The metaphor of the mountaineers reminded its audiences of several features of partnerships. Partners need not be uniform or conform to a single way of doing things (they could have "opposite" starting points and negotiate different terrain). Their very differences might combine to strengthen the partnership beyond a mere aggregate of the efforts of its individual members; the unique strength of one partner could compensate for the frailties and limits of others—and vice versa.

Nor did partnership preclude the existence of civilized rivalry between partners. Friendly and fulfilling competition between partners was the central subject of a toast the president offered to Japanese Prime Minister Zenko Suzuki at a state dinner in 1981:

We have become principal trading partners and chief competitors. There's a legend in Japan about two villages separated by a river, and on moonlit nights a man from one town would come out and sing. And his voice would resound farther and farther, floating out across the river. And then it happened one night another voice was heard, and the second was fully as rich as the first. And when the original singer heard it, he realized he was faced with a strong rival, and he sang and sang at the top of his voice. And the singing grew more and more beautiful as each singer found depths to his talent that he hadn't known were there.

Well, Japan and America are like those singers. We each seek great achievements, and the standards we set for each other are marks of excellence. And yet we do not exhaust ourselves in the contest, but rather pursue our respective goals as friends and allies.[11]

Stimulated by their friendly competition, the two singers exercised their artistry and improved themselves beyond their previous achievements. Because their contest was subject to reasonable traditions and agreeable rules, it did not wear them down. The common experience of each doing his best ripened their mutual respect and, in fact, the contest itself caused them to become true friends and allies—genuine partners.

Once a free society was likened to a partnership and not a brute competition, the meaning of things changed. The most important effect was the favorable light the metaphor cast on economic freedom: If American life were really only a vicious footrace, then economic freedom would be nothing more than an instrument of that brutal competition and the marketplace an arena where the remorseless and the greedy exploited the needy and the decent. But if society was a partnership, then the marketplace assumed another aspect. It could be seen as an enabler of countless acts of voluntary cooperation between supplier and customer. In short, the partnership concept made markets stand out as places where individuals found partners and made arrangements of mutual assistance. The marketplace was seen as benign, enlivening, and full of second chances—an institution in which competition rewarded those who could best *help* others.

In his speeches Reagan regularly set the marketplace in this perspective. In addressing the issue of international competitiveness, he asked whether foreign participation in the American economy was good news or bad. Speaking to his radio audience, Reagan noted:

> Part of the difficulty in accepting the good news about trade is in our words. We too often talk about trade while using the vocabulary of war. In war, for one side to win, the other must lose. But commerce is not warfare. Trade is an economic alliance that benefits both countries. There are no losers, only winners.[12]

In other words, free enterprise was not a state of bitter rivalry and brutish conquest. It was a form of human cooperation. The marketplace was nothing less than institutionalized mutual assistance between persons with certain needs and those with the means to fill them.[13]

Moreover, the partnership metaphor explained how commerce fostered empathy and a desire for excellence in those who participated in it. Jobs in the private sector civilized those who performed them and reinforced kindly, moral habits. The metaphor made sense of why America's founding fathers gloried in the notion of creating a "commercial republic."[14] Commerce made people good, and a commercial republic was a community made decent by the reciprocating habits engendered by its form of social organization.

The metaphor of partnership was designed to have a second consequence—to help Americans see the countless acts of voluntary cooperation occurring in their society. It provided context and meaning to such everyday events as philanthropy, spontaneous acts of charity, community service, mutual benefit societies, and religious organizations. Kiwanis, Rotary, Boys' Clubs of America, Campfire, the Knights of Columbus, the Grange, Hadassah, the Disabled American Veterans, the Order of AHEPA, the Business and Professional Women of America, the union hall, the Bible study group, LULAC, the Holy Name Society—all these voluntary organizations were filtered out of mind by the metaphor of the footrace. Those "thousand points of light" (to borrow an image from Reagan's successor as president, George Bush) were extinguished in the metaphor depicting society as an arena of brutal private competition, in which the sole source of compassion was the government.[15]

Reagan elaborated the metaphor of partnership in connection with his effort to spur voluntarism. Partnership was the key concept in the political philosophy with which he justified the use of private initiatives to solve the nation's social problems. In August 1981, seven months after Reagan entered the White House, he began a campaign to promote private charity. One of his goals was to remind Americans of the importance of voluntarism. It was a complicated and diffuse undertaking, one that required the president's sustained effort.

And sustain that effort he did. In his first thirty-two months as president, "Mr. Reagan featured the subject of private-sector initiatives in more than eighty-four separate speeches, public appearances, proclamations, or similar events, an average rate of nearly one per week."[16] He used virtually every such occasion to speak of the notion of partnership. Typical was his announcement of the formation of the White House Task Force on Private-Sector Initiatives: "Its purpose will be to promote private sector leadership and responsibility for solving public needs, and to recommend ways of fostering greater public-private partnerships . . . and . . . to enlarge the social responsibility of our citizens."[17]

Throughout the public campaign for voluntarism Reagan and his speechwriters developed three themes. The first was that in human nature there exists an instinct for altruism. In developing this theme the president frequently repeated a story from his days as governor of California. A severe Pacific storm had struck the California coast and threatened to wash away some beachfront homes. In the emergency several hundred teenagers had worked to save them. A local television newscaster questioned one of the young rescue workers about why he had gone to help:

No, he didn't live in one of those homes he was trying to save; yes, he was cold and tired. And the newscaster finally wanted to know, well, why were he and his friends doing this? And he stopped for a minute, then he answered, and the answer was so poignant and tells us something so true about ourselves that it should be printed on a billboard. He said, "Well, I guess it's the first time we ever felt like we were needed."[18]

The inherent need to be needed: That was why civility among humans was possible. That individuals desired to live meaningful lives was the key to cooperation and the antidote to envy and hate. The need to do unselfish deeds was part of the individual personality, but it had to be exercised or it would atrophy. Use it, or lose it—that was the truth that needed to be printed on a billboard and affirmed from the bully pulpit of the presidency.

Reagan's second theme was that voluntary organizations, which provided outlets for these unselfish instincts, were fragile. Government endangered them. The unintended consequence of an overly ambitious public policy was to supplant voluntarism, warned the president. He illustrated the theme with a number of stories, like this one:

> I can tell you of an example when I was Governor. In our neighboring State of Oregon, up in Portland, Oregon, people like yourselves in the business community, dealing with the very real problem of high school dropouts, had formed an organization that was tremendously successful in preventing and reducing this rate of dropout. And then the Federal Government adopted a program, and one of the first places they dropped in on was Portland, Oregon. And the first task was to drive that private organization out of business and take over, and they weren't nearly as successful as the private group had been.[19]

Subtle dangers lay in the good intentions and patronizing instincts of democratic government. Prompted by the need to win the people's votes and capacitated with the coercive power to tax, the state tended to enlarge itself into more and more spheres of activity. By trying to do too much, however, it ended up displacing the voluntary associations that had been contributing solutions. Thereafter, the former volunteers would disperse and grow apart. When they did, a vicious circle set in: in the absence of their know-how and energy, problems would become larger, and the state would have to grow even more, which would discourage even further volunteers, and so on, and so on.

The final theme of Reagan's voluntarist philosophy was this: with the disappearance of voluntary organizations, the balance of power between the people and their government would be upset. Here was the president talking to the nation's police chiefs on that subject: "Government interference in our lives tends to discourage creativity and enterprise . . . and preempt those mitigating institutions like family, neighborhood, church, and schools—organizations that act as both a buffer and a bridge between the individual and the naked power of the state."[20]

How did voluntary associations buffer the individual from the naked power of government? And how did they bridge the distance between the individual and the state? First, consider the buffer. The president made his point with a story:

> There was a federal program where they paid students who would be given jobs in the school doing work that needed to be done, washing the blackboards and all that sort of thing, after school was over. And then they came in and found that some of the students weren't juvenile delinquents, and therefore they were fired. They couldn't have those jobs. Now, if anyone can think of a better temptation for a kid to go out and break a window simply to get back on the job and get paid, I don't know what it would be. No reward for those who were doing what they should do; plenty of reward for those who weren't.[21]

His point was a moral one. He was speaking of the danger of government programs designed to help the needy. In ameliorating the unavoidable lot of an unhappy few, the state tempted many others to choose a similar lot for themselves. The good intentions of the federal program to give juvenile delinquents a paying job functioned as an incentive for students who weren't juvenile delinquents to become ones. "Public charity," Tocqueville's term for needs-based public policy, defeated its own purposes when these morally hazardous effects offset its good intentions. Thus, government tempted its people to debase themselves.[22]

Private charity, by contrast, could (and often did) discriminate between the needy who were deserving and those who were not. Nongovernmental organizations saved their help for enterprising individuals who wanted to escape their dependent status. Conversely, private charity withheld assistance from those thought not to be trying to become independent. Thus, private charity could avoid creating the moral hazards that public charity produced. (The check against private charities abusing their flexibility was their pluralism. Even though one charity might discriminate unreasonably, deserving citizens could go to alternative sources of help.)

When private associations were preempted by governmental programs, public charity was left the lone source of help. But public charity had to operate by rigid procedures, ones that discouraged bureaucrats from making the kinds of subtle character-based distinctions private organizations were permitted to make. In the long run, that meant that public charity treated all its applicants as if they were "bad apples." The deserving poor were treated as badly as the undeserving and so were demoralized by a system of charity that regarded them with deep suspicion. Without alternative sources of temporary help, however, that is, without a buffer to keep them separate from the state, they had no recourse but to submit to the governmental practices that demeaned them.

The extinction of voluntary associations had a second consequence. It left the bulk of ordinary citizens a stark choice: if they wanted an outlet for their need to help others, they had either to enter the government or give up their aspiration to lend a helping hand. If any decided on government service, they had to accept the ways of the state. If others chose to stay in private life, the lack of philanthropic organizations would leave them without a bridge to transport themselves out of their daily business routines into a wider sphere of community affairs. Either way, the citizenry ended up turning their destinies over to the state. As a result, the danger of tyranny increased—not a brutal tyranny, but an enervating, administrative tyranny that constantly interfered with individuals' innermost aspirations to live honorably. Under the weight of an officious and distant state, they would despair and, eventually, surrender.

In summing up the connection between a robust voluntarism and real liberty, Tony Dolan remarked:

> Progress in our nation is what the people do, not what the government does for them. The principal heresy of our century is the notion that politics is the salvation of our time. . . . Real progress is what we do in our economic lives, our religious lives, our cultural lives, in small towns, in what Tocqueville liked to call its intermediate institutions. That's what Reagan is talking about all the time. Those mediating institutions are what are so important. Our ability to associate, that's what fascinated Tocqueville, and that's what's important and progressive about this country. State power eviscerates all that. State power is like running a superhighway through a small town. It disturbs the ecology, as the saying goes.[23]

Dolan's reference to Alexis de Tocqueville was no accident. It reflected the powerful influence of the author of *Democracy in America* on the Reagan White House. In fact, if one were to look for the ultimate source of the partnership metaphor, it would be Tocqueville's deep respect for the skill of Americans to team up. Reagan's public philosophy echoed Tocqueville's personal sentiments.

When Tocqueville came to the United States in 1831, he was struck by the difference between his French countrymen and the Americans. In the United States of that time neighbor helped neighbor in raising barns, providing protection against fires, and conducting the bulk of the public business. Tocqueville examined the origins and effects of these habits of teamwork—which he attributed to "the principle of association":

In no country in the world has the principle of association been more successfully used or applied to a greater multitude of objects than in America. . . . If a stoppage occurs in a thoroughfare and the circulation of vehicles is hindered, the neighbors immediately form themselves into a deliberative body; and this extemporaneous assembly gives rise to an executive power which remedies the inconvenience before anybody has thought of recurring to a pre-existing authority superior to that of the persons immediately concerned.[24]

Five years after writing these sentiments, he published the second volume of *Democracy in America*, in which he returned to the topic of teamwork. He noted the particular significance of voluntarism to a free society. One of its effects was political: volunteer associations did much of the public business, thereby fending off the tendency of democratic governments to grow in size and responsibilities.

Americans of all ages, all conditions, and all dispositions constantly form associations. They have not only commercial and manufacturing companies, in which all take part, but associations of a thousand other kinds, religious, moral, serious, futile, general or restricted, enormous or diminutive. The Americans make associations to give entertainments, to found seminaries, to build inns, to construct churches, to diffuse books, to send missionaries to the antipodes; in this manner they found hospitals, prisons, and schools. If it is proposed to inculcate some truth or to foster some feeling by the encouragement of a great example, they form a society. Wherever at the head of some new undertaking you see the government in France, or a man of rank in England, in the United States you will be sure to find an association.[25]

Tocqueville thus warned his fellow Frenchmen against an overreliance on government. It would be a better thing for them, he said, to emulate the United States, where private citizens were doing good work outside the apparatus of government.

In addition to making limited government possible, voluntary associations shaped the character of the volunteers themselves. Their practice of voluntarism made them feel capable of self-reliance. It taught them how to be one another's partners; it made them knowledgeable, proud, public-spirited, and most important of all, caring.

An overactive government preempted private charitable organizations and extinguished this important source of moral improvement: "All the governments of Europe have, in our time, singularly improved the science of administration: they do more things, and they do everything with more order, more celerity, and at less expense; they seem to be constantly enriched by all the experience of which they have stripped private persons."[26] That image, of government stripping private individuals of personal exposure to the conditions of their fellow creatures, exactly expressed Reagan's notion of the moral hazards of an overzealous government. Like Tocqueville, the Reagan administration worried lest a vicious circle would result from making public beneficiaries more dependent and submissive than they had to be and rendering private persons less compassionate and informed than they ought to be.

Tocqueville put it precisely: "The more [the state] stands in the place of associations, the more will individuals, losing the notion of combining together, require its assistance." That premise underlay his cry from the heart:

> Nothing, in my opinion, is more deserving of our attention than the intellectual and moral associations of America. The political and industrial associations of that country strike us forcibly; but the others elude our observation, or if we discover them, we understand them imperfectly because we have hardly seen anything of the kind. It must be acknowledged, however, that they are as necessary to the American people as the former, and perhaps more so. In democratic countries the science of association is the mother of science; the progress of all the rest depends upon the progress it has made.
>
> Among the laws that rule human societies there is one which seems to be more precise and clear than all others. If men are to remain civilized or to become so, the art of associating together must grow and improve in the same ratio in which the equality of conditions is increased.[27]

The Reagan presidency took Tocqueville's admonition seriously, to cultivate the people's art of associating together. Bently Elliott expressed the speechwriters' sense of mission:

> It's funny: the newspeople have always underestimated the importance the president places on voluntarism, but voluntarism ties people within communities together. . . . The feeling that "my" community is tangible is just as important and meaningful in New York in the 1980s as it was last century. The humaneness of Ronald Reagan brings the feeling of humaneness out in us.[28]

To evoke human decency the speechwriters elaborated on the metaphor of partnership, for it expressed the central theme that the people should try to be virtuous. It also served to redefine human compassion: it asserted that the social conscience of the nation was manifested, not in the magnitude of the federal budget, but rather in the hours and money private individuals personally contributed to needy causes.

Reagan took infinite pains to honor the private generosity of the people. He was especially concerned that Americans appreciate the full extent of their personal compassion and the importance of their personal benevolence. Here was Reagan, speaking at the close of his second term, paying one last tribute to the people's social conscience:

> I've heard a lot about this being the era of greed, usually from those who really mean that taxes are too low and government is too small. I wish these critics would explain how it is that in the past 8 years, during this supposed era of greed, charitable giving has risen to record heights in our nation—last year, in cash alone, $94.7 billion. . . . By the way, I suspect that a dollar that comes from our churches and synagogues goes farther to help those in need than one that comes from the Government. And I don't mean just because the Government's overhead is higher. No, it's that the state's power is, at its root, the power to coerce, for example, to demand taxes. The power of the church is the power of love. And that makes all the difference.[29]

With the partnership metaphor highlighting the importance of private effort, Reagan could persuasively teach a key principle of his public philosophy: the highest responsibility of government was to act with restraint, so as not to use the state's "power to coerce" to do damage to the people's "power of love." That was the point of the president's warning in his final State of the Union address: "As an ancient Chinese philosopher, Lao-tzu, said: 'Govern a great nation as you would cook a small fish: do not overdo it.' "[30]

The domestic problems on which the presidency of Lyndon Johnson had focused in the 1960s—racial bigotry and severe inequality—did not go away simply because the Reagan presidency substituted the image of partnership for the footrace metaphor. Rhetorical devices did not cause real social problems to disappear, especially ones with roots three hundred years deep in American society. At the same time, Reagan and his speechwriting team were sure that bigotry and inequality would only worsen if the government crafted its programs so crudely that they stifled personal generosity and a voluntary spirit of teamwork. In their minds no democratic society could long remain generous and good if the bulk of its members were socially ignorant and lacked compassion.

6

★★★★★★★

Imperfectibility: Defining
Human Nature

But we must never forget that no government schemes are going to perfect man. We know that living in this world means dealing with what philosophers call the phenomenology of evil or, as theologians would put it, the doctrine of sin. There is sin and evil in the world, and we're enjoined by Scripture and the Lord Jesus to oppose it with all our might.

—Ronald Reagan (1983)

If teaming up was the way to cope with problems, what caused the problems in the first place? Why were men and women bigoted and cruel? What caused them to be greedy and disloyal, faithless and dishonest? To what extent could they be counted on? What explained their capacity for love and sacrifice and generosity? What made them tick?

All these questions may be summed up in the more abstract question, What is human nature? The answer to that question is the foundation on which all philosophy is built. It is the first earthly question.

Someone once said that all political questions revolve around whether Thomas Hobbes (1588–1679) or Jean-Jacques Rousseau (1712–1778) was right. Is man inherently bad, but ennobled by civilization (as Hobbes insisted), or is he inherently good, but corrupted by civilization (as Rousseau saw things)? As we shall see, Reagan and his speechwriting team focused a good part of their attention on that issue. It was the very seed—the starting point—of the moral message they sought to sow.

In the latter half of the 1970s the author Richard Reeves journeyed through America, talking with more than 180 newspaper publishers, academics, lawyers, community leaders, writers, policemen, clergy, pollsters, and politicians. Repeatedly he was told, "The old values are being destroyed."[1] When he asked what was destroying them, the usual answer was "Freud." Seeking an explanation, Reeves called on Harvard sociologist David Reisman, who had (in Reeves's words) "written perceptively about the impact of Freud and psychology in general on American behavior and ethics." Reeves reported Reisman's response:

> "Let it all hang out" and other idiocies have been elevated to values by the popularizers of psychology. . . . When Freud appeared, we didn't have the intellectual ballast to deal with his ideas. We went overboard from the beginning. So it would be more correct to say that it was not Freud, but misinterpretations of Freud, which have had profound impact in the United States.

On the basis of his own investigations, Reeves concurred:

> The suggestion that people somehow were not responsible for their own behavior, that they were somehow controlled by mysterious forces—unconscious or psychological (or sexual!) forces in the analysis of Sigmund Freud, and economic imperatives in the analysis of Karl Marx . . . had essentially been absorbed into the experiences and character of Americans. . . . The personality for this melange of ideas, information and disinformation, "values" and "life-styles" was the Viennese doctor with a goatee and pince-nez glasses, "Freud."[2]

Reeves wondered, would the idea that people were not personally responsible for their actions, that mysterious and invincible forces victimized them, destroy America's values?[3] Would these misinterpretations of Freud subvert what Joan Didion earlier had called "the rules of the game"?

If Reeves was right that a misinterpreted Freud exerted such an influence on the American character, what did Freud actually say? Freud wrote prolifically and with a breathtaking figurative power. His professional life extended over six decades. He was constantly revising his conclusions and extending them in new directions. One reason so many misinterpreted his work was that he came to reject many fragments of his earlier work and left them behind on the cutting-room floor.

To understand how susceptible Freud was to misinterpretation, I propose we concentrate on what he said in his last writings, the lectures he composed in his final decade as an addendum to his earlier *General Introduction to Psycho-Analysis*. Elsewhere, Freud made similar points more cautiously or made different points (and even contradictory ones). But it is vital to understand what Freud did write that led others to misinterpret him, to turn him into what Reeves called "Freud."

In those *New Introductory Lectures*, Freud expressed confidence that he had discovered the structure of human nature. His basic premise was that mind dominated body: thought governed action. But if that were so, what was the well-spring of that thought? Freud said the source of thought was the id. The id was like a chamber that contained the two fuels of life, the energies called libido (or sexual energy) and aggression (or destructive energy). Within this chamber the two fuels would combine and combust (Freud never explained where the spark came from), sending their unintelligent energies surging from the depths of the id. Through a mechanics that Freud never clarified, these energies, in seeking escape, drove the body into action, and this bodily action relieved the accumulating pressures within. No sooner were these internal stresses relaxed, however, than the next surges of energy would begin to well up, and the cycle of surge, compression, expression, and relaxation would repeat itself. Freud's vision of the id was of human energies impulsively exploding outward and making connections to things in the external world. "Instinctual cathexes seeking discharge—that, in our view, is all the id contains," said Freud (Lecture 31).[4]

Not all the id's energies ended up driving the body's actions in the outer world. Some were repressed. The agent of this repression was the ego. It sat atop the id, like a governor managing a system of valves, blocking some energies and giving outlet to others. The ego controlled the outlets of energy so that the individual's actions would be prudent ones, conforming to the desires of the external world. "On behalf of the id, the ego controls the path of access to motility, but it interpolates between desire and action the procrastinating factor of thought," said Freud (Lecture 31).

The ego, however, was not the complete master within its own realm. It often deferred to the advice of an agent working behind (or above) the scenes. Freud called this adviser the superego. The superego, however, functioned as the trustee of a bygone generation, charged with the responsibility of preserving the past—or at least a distorted and taboo-ridden version of it. The superego badgered the ego to adapt the energies of the id not to a contemporary reality, but to an anachronistic one. The superego's countermanding of the ego's directions raised havoc with human nature, confusing it, paralyzing it, and leading it erratically. "The super-ego seems to have made a one-sided selection and to have chosen the harshness and severity of the parents, their preventive and primitive functions" (Lecture 31).

Freud called his mechanistic image of the origins of thought his "science" of human nature (Lecture 35). But this version of science inevitably implied two extraordinarily important conclusions: first, human nature was perfectible; second, human nature lacked moral freedom.

First, Freud's so-called science, in asserting that there was an earthly explanation of every human action, implied that there was an earthly cause for every human flaw. If there was something wrong with an individual, there had to be a blameworthy factor somewhere external to that individual. If a person was unhappy, the cause of that unhappiness was anachronistic parents (their influence was mediated by the officious and interfering superego). Cast blame; point the finger at somebody else; rebuke and eliminate the external corrupting forces. Then the ego would reign, and life would be pleasant. Freud's science was about improvement, but it provided no theoretical basis for defining the limits to that improvement. Theoretically, it posited an indefinitely improvable human nature. Individuals, in other words, were capable of perfection, because all their imperfections were theoretically due to external factors that could be eliminated.

Second, science, with its goal of providing a comprehensive and exclusive explanation of human behavior in terms of earthly factors, ended up rejecting moral freedom. The determinism of Freud's theory contrasted sharply with the religious theory of Freud's day, which emphasized personal responsibility. Freudianism was a reaction against religion. Freud rejected the notion of the autonomous will inherent in religion.

With its trinity of superego, ego, and id, Freud's theories bore a resemblance to the religious trinity of conscience, soul, and sin. In fact, these trinities were radically different. The conscience was kind; the superego somewhat cruel (Lecture 31). The soul was healed and redeemed by serving others; the ego was damaged and wasted by having to please others. Sin was purposeful and inflicted knowing injury upon others; the id was naive, blameless, and unintelligent, knowing "no values, no good and evil, no morality." The conscience served to guide the pilgrim forward to a better future; the superego pointed mankind backward to his primitive and childish ways. The defeat of sin led to the greater glory of man; conquering the id's untamed passions turned individuals into social conformists (Lecture 31).

Freud never tried to cover up his differences with religion. He declared war on it. "Religion is a really serious enemy" of science, said Freud. It inspired men to pursue unrealistic ethical standards, consoled them when things backfired as a result, and made them resist submitting to "the inevitable" (Lecture 35). Religion—the instrument of anachronism—had to be defeated by the modern men of science.

But the scientific perspective with which Freud displaced religion was affected with a senselessness. There was no room for autonomous human reason to work its effects. Men were never masters of their own futures. "Dark, unfeeling, and unloving powers determine human destiny," said Freud (Lecture 35). Individuals were powerless in the face of these unintelligent and insurmountable forces. Thus, Freud, by embracing a dictatorial determinism, denied man's freedom to choose.

In these final lectures Freud seemed to collapse material and moral forces into one historical necessity. His language caused others to dismiss the difference between matters of circumstance and matters of choice, between the forces beyond humankind's control and those within it, between conditions like windstorms, disease, and economic cycles, on the one hand, and those intentional assaults of humans upon humans, on the other. Science denied that individuals bore responsibility for their purposeful choices to bully, brutalize, and butcher.

Freud's logic of scientific determinism was so compelling that adherents were unable to draw a distinction between accident and murder. With the denial of personal moral freedom, human crime, while distressing, came to be morally indistinguishable from any other factor contributing to man's fate. Just as it would be silly science to denounce as immoral a drought or a band of locusts, so for Freud it was theoretically insupportable to condemn human cruelty. Of the imprisonment and genocide of millions of Russian farmers and other "counterrevolutionaries" by Joseph Stalin and his collaborators, Freud (given his premises) could only say: "At a time when great nations are declaring that they expect to find their salvation solely from a steadfast adherence to Christian piety, the upheaval in Russia—in spite of all its distressing features—seems to bring a promise of a better future" (Lecture 35).

The point was that, by denying that people were free to resist and transcend the "unfeeling, and unloving powers [that] determine human destiny," Freud dwarfed the significance of having one's freedom, even one's life, taken away.

In denying moral freedom any theoretical support, Freud made it likely that those who followed his theories would throw out a crucial notion connected to individual responsibility—the concept of evil. Before Freud's time evil had a special meaning. It meant doing intentional and unnecessary injury to the freedom of another. When the intellectual heirs of Freud denied that men were free, the notion of evil became an anachronism and dropped from the moral vernacular. Its disappearance, however, left what Joan Didion called a vacuum, and it constituted a semantic loss of great importance. It left men silent in the face of human brutality. Since individuals were without moral choice and lacked the purposefulness to conquer the temptation to hate and hurt, they had no claim to dignity. Lacking a basis for worthiness, they had no claim to primacy over the state.

The Reagan presidency sought to fill that moral vacuum and reinvigorate the assumption of individual responsibility. Its principal

instrument in this regard was the word "evil," which it hoped to restore
to the national discourse, thereby affirming moral freedom.

On March 8, 1983, the president paid a brief visit to Orlando, Florida.
In between remarks to a group of educators and an appearance at a
Republican fund-raiser, he squeezed in a talk to the National Association of Evangelicals, a convention of 2,000 politically moderate Baptists
and Methodists.[5] His appearance received virtually no national media
coverage that day; his speech announced no new policy; his remarks were
made to an audience with little political clout. Yet, of all the speeches
the president was to make in his two terms, none was more important
rhetorically. It became known as the "evil empire" speech, but the
reference was not just to a popular movie. The president was talking about
the larger notion of evil—about man's choice to do, or refrain from doing,
purposeful and unnecessary injury to the freedom of others.

> But we must never forget that no government schemes are going to
> perfect man. We know that living in this world means dealing with
> what philosophers call the phenomenology of evil or, as theologians
> would put it, the doctrine of sin. There is sin and evil in the world,
> and we're enjoined by Scripture and the Lord Jesus to oppose it with
> all our might.[6]

He spoke of the recurring presence of evil in American history.

> Our nation, too, has a legacy of evil with which it must deal. The
> glory of this land has been its capacity for transcending the moral evil
> of our past. For example, the long struggle of minority citizens for
> equal rights, once a source of disunity and civil war, is now a point
> of pride for all Americans. We must never go back. There is no
> room for racism, anti-Semitism, or other forms of ethnic and racial
> hatred in this country. I know that you've been horrified, as have
> I, by the resurgence of some hate groups in our midst. The command-
> ment given us is clear and simple: "Thou shalt love they neighbor
> as thyself."

Groups that focused the hate of their members so as to injure others were,
in a word, evil, and they deserved to be denounced as such and opposed.
    He then spoke of the Soviet regime and its systematic preaching
of hatred and aggression in the name of "class war." Communism had
subordinated morality to the interests of class war, calling everything
moral that "is necessary for the annihilation of the old, exploiting social
order and for uniting the proletariat." The Soviet Communist regime was,

in short, a hate group and its leaders functioned to incite and "focus" the hateful impulses of their adherents on innocent victims.

> Let us be aware that while they preach the supremacy of the state, declare its omnipotence over individual man, and predict its eventual domination over all people on the Earth, they are *the focus of evil* in the modern world. It was C. S. Lewis who, in his unforgettable *Screwtape Letters*, wrote: "The greatest evil is not done now in those sordid 'dens of crime' that Dickens loved to paint. It is not even done in concentration and labor camps. In those we see its final result. But it is conceived and ordered (moved, seconded, carried, and minuted) in clean, carpeted, warmed, and well-lighted offices, by quiet men with white collars and cut fingernails and smooth-shaven cheeks who do not need to raise their voice." (Italics mine)

What ought to have been the proper reaction to these quiet practitioners of evil, who would of their own will have crushed the moral freedom of others? The president responded:

> If history teaches anything, it teaches that simple-minded appeasement or wishful thinking about our adversaries is folly. It means the betrayal of our past, the squandering of our freedom. So I urge you to speak out against those who would place the United States in a position of military and moral inferiority. . . .

And then before that assembly of two thousand ministers he summarized his two major points. First, he reiterated the religious understanding of human nature: that it was not perfectible, that there existed in the soul of every man "aggressive impulses," and that "the temptation of pride" to deny them weakened the very strength necessary to struggle with them:

> You know, I've always believed that old Screwtape reserved his best efforts for those of you in the church. So, in your discussions of the nuclear freeze proposals [which Reagan vigorously opposed], I urge you to beware the temptation of pride—the temptation of blithely declaring yourselves above it all and labeling both sides equally at fault, to ignore the fact of history and the aggressive impulses of an evil empire, to simply call the arms race a giant misunderstanding and thereby remove yourself from the struggle between right and wrong and good and evil.

"The aggressive impulses of an evil empire": with that powerful phrase he waged war against those who would deny that each individual was everlastingly flawed, and everlastingly responsible for combating those flaws.[7]

Next, he spoke to the consequences of believing that the individual lacks the moral freedom to struggle against the impulse to hate and hurt.

> The real crisis we face today is a spiritual one; at root, it is a test of moral will and faith. Whittaker Chambers, the man whose own

religious conversion made him a witness to one of the terrible traumas of our time, the Hiss-Chambers case, wrote that the crisis of the Western World exists to the degree in which the West is indifferent to God, the degree to which it collaborates in Communism's attempt to make man stand alone without God. And then he said, for Marxism-Leninism is actually the second oldest faith, first proclaimed in the Garden of Eden with the words of temptation, "Ye shall be as gods." The Western World can answer this challenge, he wrote, "but only provided that its faith in God and the freedom he enjoins is as great as communism's faith in Man." I believe we shall rise to the challenge. I believe that communism is another sad, bizarre chapter in human history whose last pages even now are being written. I believe this because the source of our strength in the quest for human freedom is not material, but spiritual. And because it knows no limitation, it must terrify and ultimately triumph over those who would enslave their fellow man.

The evil empire speech directly addressed the issues raised by Freud in his *New Introductory Lectures*: Did men have to submit to the "dark, unfeeling, and unloving" facts of slavery, racism, anti-Semitism, the concentration camps, and the gulag, as Freud decreed, or did they have the moral freedom to oppose those evils?

Was humanity's only way to avoid bloody anarchy the meek submission to state-imposed enslavement (as Freud insisted), or was history writ large with the successful struggles of free people to deal with—to defeat—hatred and cruelty?

Was the injunction to stop hating unrealistic (as Freud maintained), or had it inspired men to be better than their worst impulses?

Were totalitarian leaders who glamorized evil and focused the impulses to hate and destroy really destined to rule (as Freud conceded), or did those tyrants, by pandering to men's evil impulses, leave their countries enervated and enfeebled and their citizenries unfit for anything but enslavement?

To appreciate the rhetorical power of the Orlando talk, one must understand that President Reagan had expressed many of the same ideas on earlier occasions. He had even used the words "empire" and "evil." Only a year before, he had called the Soviet Union "a huge empire ruled by an elite that holds all power and privilege."[8] And speaking before the British Parliament in June 1982 about the totalitarian forces in the world seeking "subversion and conflict around the globe to further their barbarous assault on the human spirit, he had asked: "What, then, is our course? Must civilization perish in a hail of fiery atoms? Must freedom wither in a quiet, deadening accommodation with totalitarian evil?"[9] But the words "empire" and "evil" did not then explode into the consciousness of the American people as they would in Orlando.

Tony Dolan explained how the words later got into the talk to the Evangelicals:

> The phrase, "evil empire," had originally been in the British Parliament speech, and it was there to the last minute when some of the boys took it out. But I kept coming back to it, and eventually I wore them down, and when it appeared in the Evangelicals speech, they said, "So what? It's an unimportant speech to an unimportant constituency." And the rest is history.[10]

"The boys" was a term Dolan used to describe those members of the president's staff who he felt had no understanding of the intellectual significance of the presidency. They were the kind who thought (as Dolan put it) "that what governing is about are meetings, conferences, phone calls, rules, and decisions." They were the ones who disagreed with Dolan's first principle, that "ideas are the stuff of politics . . . , the great moving forces of history."

Dolan explained that he added the "evil empire" phrase as a followup to the "focus of evil" line in the Orlando speech. When it was likened to *Star Wars* (some even called it "the Darth Vader speech"), he welcomed the reaction, recognizing that it was, like other fantasies, "a healthy expression of reality."

> Kids know there is evil in the world, and no matter how many nice words we use to buffer ourselves from that insight, the reality is that there's evil, and that it has to be fought against. So, when we go back to Normandy to talk to General Bradley's boys about the evil forces they overcame in France [in World War II], no kid is going to be confused by someone trying to raise the question, "Well, what did we do with the Indians?" They are not going to be troubled with what I would call epistemological paralysis.

"Epistemological paralysis" was Dolan's description of the moral uncertainty, the anomie, that tended to arrest decisive action. The lack of language to make important distinctions undermined strong convictions. Dolan continued:

> General Bradley's boys . . . know that no matter how flawed you may be, you have the right to defend yourself against evil people. The point is that in the free world we acknowledge our shortcomings, and seek to do our best the next time, to do better. In the Soviet Union they say their shortcomings are part of the revolutionary process and try to justify them.

"The secret," Dolan said, "is to give the world a cliché, a semantic infiltration."

Now and forever the Soviet Union is an evil empire. . . . The Soviet
Union itself can't let go of it. It torments them; so they say it
themselves. I found that also with the Mafia in Connecticut. The
human conscience is such that evil acts bother people, and I've found
that if you let the bad guys talk, they'll get preoccupied with trying
to rebut it, and in the end they concede it. You know, the Soviets
know the importance of words. That's why they have coined phrases
like Wars of National Liberation and the People's Republics. The Evil
Empire is one of the few semantic victories the West has won. . . . In
history it has always been thus. It was Churchill's rhetoric which made
a difference in the World War. People respond to the truth. With "evil
empire," people said, "That's right. Cut out all the bull. The emperor
has no clothes." Who was it that said "brood of vipers"? Christ. He
did the same thing, with those hypocritical scribes. He just did it.

Dolan talked of the institutional forces within the presidency itself
that moved presidents to speak of such profound subjects as the sinful
nature of man and the moral effect of political systems on character.
According to Dolan, the office itself impelled its incumbents to instruct
a confused world in why liberal democracy was morally superior to
totalitarianism: "When you go to the world and you urge on the expansion of democracies, the importance of holding elections, you think about
the reasons justifying what you urge."

He spoke admiringly of his boss, who had used the presidential
pulpit to such powerful effect.

People say that the president is the great communicator. He's not.
He's the great rhetorician. He uses words. He uses logic. There is
substance in every paragraph. His arguments flow from one point
to the next. And he uses anecdotes and statistics to back them up.
He has a philosophy. He develops it. And he adheres to it. As I said,
the Reagan speechwriters' major function is to plagiarize the
president's old speeches and give them back to him to say.[11]

What difference did it make that Reagan and his speechwriting team
reinfused American discourse with "the phenomenology of evil"? What
happened when he voiced the doctrine of sin, when he warranted to the
American people that mankind was incapable of ever devising a social
order that was going to perfect mankind, that there was evil in every soul—
desire, hate, jealousy, viciousness, pride—and there always would be?

Defining human nature as imperfectible did what Dolan thought
it would do. It built self-confidence. It prevented "paralysis" in the face
of evil. It allowed Americans to say, "Nobody's perfect," and to get on
with life without drowning in self-accusation. It permitted them to defend
themselves against the violence of others without disfiguring their vision

with "the beam in [their] own eye"—without the self-flagellation that results from being too attentive to one's own shortcomings or too eager to blame oneself for everything that has gone wrong in the lives of others. That was an important step in the maturing of American social thought.

Second, it reconnected Americans to their own heritage and made their political and economic institutions understandable. American democracy and all the personal freedoms it permitted were founded on the doctrine of sin. Reagan frequently quoted Lincoln's justification for our system of self-government: "No man is good enough to govern another man without that other's consent."[12] Man's imperfectibility was the self-evident truth on which the Founding Fathers had based their invention of checks and restraints on the central government. Knowing there was no way to remove evil from the human soul, they confined the dominion over which any one individual could exercise coercive power. The words of *Federalist* 51—and the complexity and frustration of the political system implied therein—came to make sense in the light of the phenomenology of evil.

> If men were angels, no government would be necessary. If angels were to govern men, neither external nor internal controls on government would be necessary. In framing a government which is to be administered by men over men, the great difficulty lies in this: you must first enable the government to control the governed; and in the next place oblige it to control itself.[13]

That is to say, the American tradition was to treat man's temptations to cruelty and avidity not as something to root out (because that was not humanly possible), but as something to cope with—by providing a political and economic system of checks and balances, of legal rights, and of market alternatives.

Third, recognizing man's imperfectibility helped Americans understand the moral difference between free and totalitarian societies. The tyrant's vision of perfectibility invariably excused the slaughter of men and women today in the name of purifying humankind tomorrow. In contrast, the recognition of man's flawed nature led to tolerance and personal freedom.[14]

Fourth, it caused the people, and the American governments it elected, to be on guard against the moral hazards of good intentions. It reminded those who would enter politics that the soul is always in the midst of internal combat—the never-ending struggle between its noble and ignoble sides, between its highest aspirations and its meanest temptations. The best that could be done was to strengthen each man and woman's resolve to be responsible. The worst thing that could be done was to tempt them to give in to their temptations.

And fifth, the fact that human nature was not perfect and never perfectible honored humankind. With our flawed and transient natures, what a civilization we humans had built. Despite our unavoidable imperfections, we had built a civilization that reinforced our resolve to transcend them. We humans were truly the salt of the earth, the trustees of a providential fact, discovering and constantly rediscovering (in the words of the American poet Archibald MacLeish) that ''we [are] riders of the earth together, brothers on that bright loveliness in the unending night—brothers who *see* now they are truly brothers.''[15]

7

★★★★★★★

Values of the Spirit: Defining the Good Life

For my own part, I doubt whether man can ever support at the same time complete religious independence and entire political freedom. And I am inclined to think that if faith be wanting in him, he must be subject; and if he be free, he must believe.

—Alexis de Tocqueville (1840)

American philosophy was early identified with the notions of pragmatism. In 1840, for example, Alexis de Tocqueville said that the philosophical method of the Americans was "to accept tradition only as a means of information, and existing facts only as a lesson to be used in doing otherwise and doing better; . . . [and] to tend to results without being bound by means."[1]

This pragmatic concern with results promoted scientific inquiry and technological improvement. But it served less well as a system of ethics. In its answers to the two pressing questions of moral philosophy—"What should I do?" and "What have I counted for?"—it was at once vague and heartlessly severe.

Its vagueness was obvious. It admonished an individual to do "otherwise" and do "better," but it specified neither what "better" was nor the cost of achieving it. To those drawn to pragmatism as a philosophy, its vagueness may have been part of its attraction, representing as it did an openness to experience and a high estimation of the capacity of human creativity to react to practical problems.

Pragmatism's severity was less obvious and largely unintended. Pragmatism emphasized results. That did not preclude pragmatists from

81

evaluating the honesty of the means by which results were obtained. Nor did it blind men like John Dewey (1859–1952) and William James (1842–1910) to the possibly invidious ethical consequences of pragmatism.[2] Yet the logic of pragmatism presupposed that all failure was avoidable.[3] In that sense pragmatism was unreasonably optimistic and therefore tended to inflate ethical standards to perfectionist levels. In every situation there was good waiting to be discovered and defects to be corrected. "Improvement" was the moral end, and every situation was improvable. This optimistic outlook had a paradoxical ethical effect. In light of the inevitability of progress, every failure to make an advance was implicitly blameworthy.

By its silence on the subject of failure, pragmatism dismissed the importance of well-intentioned efforts that failed to improve things. People who did not succeed in rectifying the defect or trouble in the situation did not count. Good intentions, brave efforts, sincerity, tough odds simply fell outside the assumptions of pragmatic moral philosophy. Pragmatism insisted on asking about the palpable consequences of action and inaction: "Did the individual *do* better?" That was the pragmatic ethical question, for an ethic of consequentialism was indifferent to both motive and circumstance. But when events beyond an individual's control resisted his or her attempts to do better, should those attempts not count?

Few people will deny that a pragmatic (or consequentialist) standard may be justified in judging certain areas of human activity. The German scholar Max Weber (1864–1920), for example, thought that actions of the state should be judged by the effects produced by the use (or nonuse) of its coercive powers. He saw pragmatism (he called it the "ethic of responsibility") as one of two choices available to the politician: either the politician could live by an ethic of principle, which made motives the proper measure of his political acts; or he could choose the ethic of responsibility, which would judge such acts by their real consequences. In the realm of politics, Weber insisted, the only acceptable standard was the latter, the consequentialist one. "He who lets himself in for politics, that is, for power and force as means, contracts with diabolical powers, and for his action it is *not* true that good can follow only from good and evil only from evil, but that often the opposite is true. Anyone who fails to see this is a political infant."[4] Weber's point was that anyone entering politics must be held to the most demanding standards of skill, circumspection, and prudence in using the diabolical powers of coercion. Motive and circumstance were both poor excuses for the evil and untoward results of the clumsy practice of coercion.

The holocausts inflicted on innocents by the political leaders of the twentieth century have convinced many that Weber was right. It affronts the moral sense to exonerate brutal tyrants because they proclaim high motives. Likewise, for those in political authority with the power to prevent the tyranny of others, faintheartedness in resisting brutality and slaughter seems morally execrable, no matter the nonviolent scruples behind their inaction. In the area of politics, an ethic of consequentialism had much to commend it.

But pragmatism had shortcomings as a standard by which to measure the lives of ordinary persons. It was too severe. Pragmatism ignored the fact that nonpolitical people did not exercise "force and power as means." Rather, in the contingent world they inhabited, they often lacked the politician's "diabolical powers" on which their survival, not to mention their success, depended.

For the countless victims of the holocausts of modern times, for example, pragmatism was clearly inapplicable. They had no means to prevent the atrocities inflicted on them. They had no power to do better. If pragmatic standards were the measure of the good life, the unconscionable irony would be that the prisoners who died in concentration camps were due no honor. No matter that they were caring and decent and brave in facing death, pragmatism was indifferent to those who achieved no results. In the moral context of the Nazi stalag and the Soviet gulag, the optimism of pragmatism, along with its inevitable materialism, seemed profoundly inappropriate.[5]

There were occasions when an American president considered the shortcomings of pragmatism as an ethical system. Most often it was in his ceremonial role as chief of state, when, like a clergyman, he was expected to speak of tragedy and console a grieving nation. No time was more moving than the annual day of remembrance of the victims of the World War II Holocaust. Held in Washington during Yom Kippur in the spring of each year, the Holocaust services brought to the nation's capital hundreds of Jewish survivors of the Nazi death camps. Reagan spoke to them in each of his first three years as president. On one such occasion in 1982 he took up the moral question, how do we measure the lives of those who were killed?

He told of five young victims—a painter, a singer, a poet, a linguist, and a fifteen-year-old boy who wanted to be a writer and left behind a diary about his love of reading. Of these five youths the president said, "We can only wonder what [they] might have created for us."

Although their lives had been cut short before they were able to accomplish results that would have measured up to pragmatic standards, Reagan pointed out that they had more than lived up to spiritual standards through their "heroism and dignity in the face of adversity." And he quoted the words of an Auschwitz survivor:

> We who lived in concentration camps can remember the men who walked through the huts comforting others, giving away their last

piece of bread. They may have been few in number, but they offer sufficient proof that everything can be taken from a man but one thing: The last of the human freedoms—to choose one's attitude in any given set of circumstances, to choose one's own way.[6]

The measure of the good life, according to the president, was not achievement in the material world, but triumph in the spiritual realm. The decision not to cower but to comfort fellow prisoners, not to steal but to sacrifice, not to wallow in pity but to walk in pride, not to hate but to love: these decisions mark the good life.

What the president was referring to was the decisive ethical importance of trying to be decent in the midst of pain and suffering. Hard times expose spiritual values to view.

No president worth his salt has ever governed without recurrent and serious setbacks. Reagan was no exception: the assassination attempt on his life in 1981, the unexpected downturn of the economy in 1982, the destruction of the Marine Corps barracks in Beirut in 1983, the tragedy of the space shuttle *Challenger* in 1986, the bungling of the Iran-Contra affair in 1986 and 1987. These bitterly disappointing events of failure and misfortune, I would suggest, were the very moments not only when the people scrutinized the president's reactions most intently but when he exerted the most influence on their own standards of moral value and self-esteem.

Why? Because we are all at one time or another failures. We all suffer setbacks. Our companies get into trouble. Our clients lose. Our marriages collapse. Our children become mentally ill, and we cannot seem to comfort them. Our responsibilities conflict. We let up at the wrong moment and flub. When a president confronts the failed results of his own best efforts, he sits down right alongside the rest of us, in the same leaky boat. We watch him and learn from him. In hard times Americans come to understand what the president really values, more so than we could ever have known by watching him in moments of prosperity. If the president teaches well, if he signifies in his reactions to adversity that the human spirit is what counts, he not only teaches us that simple consequentialism is an unsatisfying value, but reinforces our confidence in our own spiritual values. He plays out his own existence on the public stage, and we see that his effort makes a subtle difference. In making the brave effort, he heartens his countrymen to adopt the same ethical measure for themselves. What is most significant, he refutes the severity of consequentialism; he confirms the value of trying and thereby enlarges the self-respect of those who choose to try ''in any given set of circumstances.''

Not always, but often with astonishing effect, Reagan used the bully pulpit not to hide failure but to redeem it with spiritual meaning.[7] In April

1984, for example, presidential candidates might have been expected to consolidate their hard-core supporters by focusing on the national good fortune. The Baptist Fundamentalists were then meeting in Washington for their annual convention, and the White House staff expected the president to speak on social issues of concern to the Baptist leadership, such as abortion, pornography, and school prayer.

Reagan, however, had other plans. He had earlier received a letter from a Marine Corps chaplain, Lt. Comdr. Arnold Resnicoff, who had been on duty that morning in October 1983 when terrorists destroyed the barracks of the American marines posted to Lebanon to keep the peace there. The chaplain was a rabbi, and he described with vividness the devastation and the marines' reaction to it.

The president had forwarded the letter to the Speechwriting Department with a note asking the writers to prepare a few introductory remarks. He was planning to read the entire letter to the Baptist Fundamentalists.[8] Virtually no one in the White House thought the letter appropriate to the occasion, and several members of the staff registered their objections. The Baptist clergy would be expecting a different topic, one closer to their social concerns. Besides, the letter was about one of the administration's failures; it would only recall a disappointing policy, one that was best kept out of the public's mind.

Nonetheless, the president insisted, and it was done. He read the entire letter at the Baptist gathering. By conventional standards the speech was no great triumph. The subject took the Fundamentalists by surprise; it was not what they thought they were going to hear.[9] The applause appeared strained; hecklers in the audience upset the pacing of the delivery; the press coverage was indifferent.

But consider the effect of Rabbi Resnicoff's letter on the two thousand clergy, keeping in mind that the professional responsibility of each of them was to give spiritual consolation from their pulpits and sanctuaries to their own congregations. The president read the entire letter, concluding with these words of Rabbi Resnicoff:

> That October day in Beirut I saw men reach heroic heights—indeed, heights of physical endurance and courage, to be sure, but heights of sacrifice, of compassion, of kindness, and of simple human decency as well, and even if the admission might bring a blush to the cheeks of a few marines, heights of love.
>
> Long ago the rabbis offered one interpretation of the Biblical verse which tells us that we're created in the image of God. It does not refer to physical likeness, they explained, but to spiritual potential. We have within us the power to reflect as God's creatures the highest values of our creator. As God is forgiving and merciful, so can we be; as He is caring and kind, so must we strive to be; as He is filled with love, so must we be.

Because of the actions I witnessed during that hell in Beirut, I glimpsed at least a fleeting image of heaven, for in the hearts and hands of men who chose to act as brothers, I glimpsed God's hand as well. I did not stand alone to face a world forsaken by God. I felt I was part of one created with infinite care and wonderful awesome potential.[10]

Amid memories of carnage and failed policy, the president led the Baptist ministers to contemplate "the highest values of our creator." In reading the letter he magnified two thousandfold the effects of the rabbi's lesson. Yes, free men and women had to deal with circumstances not always of their own choosing, but it was always up to them "to choose their attitude" and to decide whether to reflect the courage, mercy, and caring of a loving God. In responding to those choices, free persons took control of their own destinies. That the marines in Beirut tried "to act as brothers" conferred on them divine worth, a dignity meriting the honor of their community.

Ordinary men and women understood that message—farmers struggling to keep their farms, families coping with a troubled member, jobless workers wondering whether they could learn new skills and start again, isolated folk frightened to live in their crime-ridden neighborhoods, individuals degraded by smart alecks. They knew that they could measure up on the scale of values they shared with their president. They knew that they, like the president, gained dignity by the way they exercised their last freedom—"to choose one's own way." They knew that although they had been created in the image of God, they were not gods themselves; that to live honorably it was enough that they had battled the temptation to quit, to hate, and to hurt. That was the moral result that counted, and by that standard they, too, could stand tall and be honored— and find new depths to their courage.

Seated in her office in the Old Executive Office Building one winter morning in 1984, Peggy Noonan looked like a child of Ireland, a bit untamed, ardent, soulful, even a little haunted. She was speaking of the purposes of her boss, another child of Ireland, the president for whom she had worked less than a year. She described him with a certitude based, not on close acquaintance with him, but on faith verified by experience. He had been her boss for nearly a year, and he had behaved consistently and dependably. She "knew" him. "He is trying," she said, "to return certain freedoms to the people and return a certain attitude towards freedom. That idea is that we all were born into this world, and pretty much have got to figure out why we're here and what we want to do. Government cannot do that for you."[11]

What was that attitude toward freedom? It was that from the moment we were born into this world, we had to discern our own reasons for persisting in it. The burden of freedom was that each individual had to be his own philosopher and govern himself accordingly. Each individual had to think through the big questions for himself: "Who am I?" and "Why am I here?" "The drama of man," as Noonan put it, was that individuals had to engraft their soul with purpose. It was in the shadow of such self-made purposes that the events of our lives took on importance. Would we matter? That was the question with which free men and women were magnificently obsessed.

Tocqueville was intrigued by the way the democratic social condition, which had liberated Americans from inherited status, seemed to magnify the burden of being one's own philosopher: "In most of the operations of the mind each American appeals only to the individual effort of his own understanding."[12] In wrestling with the baffling questions surrounding existence, each American sought to enlarge the capacity of his own understanding. Freedom motivated him to search out the philosophies of others and borrow the pieces that made sense. Likewise, he sorted through the popular culture—as he found it in the church, media, schools, and the like—listening for ideas to enhance his store of notions about human purpose. This extended process of discovering a philosophy and imprinting the soul with it was highly personal and individualistic, yet since the bulk of the elements of his philosophy were drawn from the common culture, there tended to be a philosophical resemblance between the content of his soul and that of other Americans.

The president had an opportunity to add content to that popular culture. That, according to Noonan, was what excited Reagan about his job. And it was what animated Noonan about hers. She borrowed from Abraham Lincoln's first inaugural address to speak of the president's importance in creating a human community with memory: "[The president's] speeches—the ones I called tonal in character—touch the larger mystic chord of memory. They speak to why we are here. . . . Those speeches speak to the drama of man. They look at life with a broader point of view. They provide a context for life."[13]

What the president could provide was an enrichment of the people's philosophical choices with which they could piece together the context for their lives.

Two important effects flowed from this infusion of spiritual values. First, spiritual values transformed feelings of failure into feelings of worthiness. They altered the meanings of American accomplishments.[14]

Consider Willie Loman, in Arthur Miller's *Death of a Salesman*. As a salesman, trying to fill the needs of others, he worked unremittingly. He was a good neighbor and a good husband. He raised two sons as best he knew how. He hurt no one intentionally or without remorse. He never stole. He paid his debts. Willie Loman was a decent man. Yet at the end of his life, when he took his own moral measure, he found himself worthless. "A man must count for something," he cried, but he had no results to count. On a pragmatic ethical scale, where only results counted, all the kindnesses, all the good humor, all the struggles against temptation to cheat or hate or quit, all the spiritual decency of the man were simply irrelevant. Certain that he had not counted for something, he killed himself.

But on a spiritual scale, what he had tried to do mattered. Where a moral marker existed to accord respect for decency, regardless of results, there was dignity for the courage, honesty, and love, and for persevering, for prevailing in the battle for one's soul. There was a proper gauge of Willie Loman's spirit.

In a free society where no individual can be self-sufficient and able to cope with the contingencies of life alone, every person is a Willie Loman. Failure will afflict virtually everyone. Individuals fall short, fail to make it, are disappointed, flub. A mother's child disappoints, despite her care. Responsibilities impinge just when all one's energies are needed to take advantage of a once-in-a-lifetime opportunity. Sickness intervenes or some other form of misfortune strikes, and nothing comes of a vast effort. Or, as in Willie's case, a promotion goes to someone else, despite fidelity, courage, and endurance.

Moreover, in a world of limited material achievement, a pragmatic ethic implies a moral inegalitarianism. Were results the only things that mattered in the ethical realm, the world would consist of an honorable few and a mass of moral no-accounts. Denial of dignity to the latter would lead to virtually universal envy and hate, and envy and hate would make partnership and cooperation impossible and return man to a brutal state of nature.

The second effect of spiritual values was to fill an emptiness in the soul that the state would have otherwise usurped. Tocqueville warned Americans not to underestimate the size of the human soul. When filled only with little furnishings, pygmy hopes, and finite objects, it hungered to be more adequately filled. "The heart is of a larger mold," he wrote. "It was not man who implanted in himself the taste for what is infinite and the love of what is immortal; these lofty instincts are not the off-spring of his capricious will; their steadfast foundation is fixed in human nature, and they exist in spite of his efforts. He may cross and distort them; destroy them he cannot."[15]

Man's nature, asserted Tocqueville, centers on his religious impulse, on his longing for immortality: "The soul has wants which must be satisfied." If it lacks spiritual values to contemplate, it will roam the landscape, searching for a substitute to satisfy his persistent longing for the immortal. It will at length find it in the earthly institution that appears imperishable—the state. Compared with the moral individual, the state has a perpetual existence; for the godless individual, the state looms as his vehicle for immortality. The state tends to fill a spiritual vacuum. It gives the individual cause to work for lasting ends. But when the state is the sole means of preserving the individual's immortality, the individual becomes obliged to preserve it at all costs. Thus, the terrible twist. By virtue of its longevity, the state becomes superior to the individual. With its guns, its coercive instrumentalities, and its tendencies to be corrupted by worldly power, the government assumes a sovereign place over the hearts of men and women. It defines the measure of self-respect and weighs human beings on its scales. It focuses to its own ends humankind's energies to love and to hate. And there is no force left to contest its moral monopoly.

Without spiritual values, the religious instinct drives the individual to his knees, to bow down before the state. Instead of being paramount on earth, instead of being of divine worth, instead of assuming sovereignty over the government, the individual ultimately defines his worth in terms of preserving and ensuring the paramountcy of the state.

How does all this relate to pragmatism? The natural ethical competitor of religion in America was pragmatism: individualistic, materialistic, and consequentialist. In having nothing of consequence to offer the needs of the soul, it was nihilistic and left room for the elevation of the state to the level of divinity.

All this may sound far-fetched in a modern, enlightened democracy such as the United States. But consider what New York governor Mario Cuomo said to the national Democratic party convention in his keynote address in 1984. Keep in mind that his words had a galvanic effect upon the thousands of delegates gathered there:

> We Democrats still have a dream, . . . and this is our credo. . . . We believe in a government strong enough to use the words "love" and "compassion" and smart enough to convert our noblest aspirations into practical realities.
> We believe in encouraging the talented, but we believe that while survival of the fittest may be a good working description of the process of evolution, a government of humans should elevate itself to a higher order. . . .
> We believe in a single fundamental idea that describes better than most textbooks and any speech that I could write what a proper government should be. The idea of family. Mutuality. The sharing of benefits and burdens for the good of all. Feeling one another's pain. Sharing one another's blessings. Reasonably, honestly, fairly,— without respect to race or sex, or geography, or political affiliation.

We believe we must be the family of America, recognizing at the heart of the matter, we are bound one to another, that the problems of a retired school teacher in Duluth are our problems. That the future of the child in Buffalo is our future. That the struggle of a disabled man in Boston to survive, and live decently is our struggle. That the hunger of a woman in Little Rock is our hunger. That the failure to provide what reasonably we might, to avoid pain, is our failure.[16]

Of whom did "the family of America" consist? Its children were the retired school teacher in Duluth and the hungry woman in Little Rock. Its head, its mother and father, full of love and compassion and intelligence—and graced with immortality, to boot—was the government, elevated by its responsibilities to a higher order than the people themselves. That was Governor Cuomo's idea of a proper government: the mother and father of us, the people. His image so powerfully paralleled Tocqueville's democratic nightmare that we must remember what the Frenchman wrote a century and a half ago:

> I seek to trace the novel features under which despotism may appear in the world. The first thing that strikes the observation is an innumerable multitude of men, all equal and alike, incessantly endeavoring to procure the petty and paltry pleasures with which they glut their lives. . . . Above this race of men stands an immense and tutelary power, which takes upon itself alone to secure their gratifications and to watch over their fate. That power is absolute, minute, regular, provident, and mild. It would be like the authority of a parent if, like that authority, its object was to prepare men for manhood; but it seeks, on the contrary, to keep them in perpetual childhood: it is well content that the people should rejoice, provided they think of nothing but rejoicing. For their happiness such a government willingly labors, but it chooses to be the sole agent and the only arbiter of that happiness; it provides for their security, foresees and supplies their necessities, facilitates their pleasures, manages their principal concerns, directs their industry, regulates the descent of property, and subdivides their inheritances: what remains, but to spare them all the care of thinking and all the trouble of living?[17]

A government that treated the children of God as though they were idiots—that was Tocqueville's nightmare.

But how to deny primacy to the state? Ronald Reagan discussed that question in his farewell address to the United Nations on September 26, 1988. It was a time of hope, for the United States and the Soviet Union had just reached an agreement to reduce nuclear arms. The president's last words to the UN delegates were simple and personal, the more striking because the setting of the General Assembly was austere and formal. He wanted to speak of "a truth that I hope now you'll permit me to mention in these remarks of farewell":

That the case for inalienable rights, that the idea of human dignity, that the notion of conscience above compulsion can be made only in the context of higher law, only in the context of what one of the founders of this organization, Secretary General Dag Hammarskjold, has called devotion to something which is greater and higher than we are ourselves. This is the endless cycle, the final truth to which humankind seems always to return: that religion and morality, that faith in something higher, are prerequisites for freedom, and that justice and peace within ourselves is the first step toward justice and peace in the world and for the ages. . . .

I think [of my mother] and others like her in that small town in Illinois, gentle people who possessed something that those who hold positions of power sometimes forget to prize. No one of them could ever have imagined the boy from the banks of the Rock River would come to this moment and have this opportunity. But had they been told it would happen, I think they would have been a bit disappointed if I'd not spoken here for what they knew so well: that when we grow weary of the world and its troubles, when our faith in humanity falters, it is then that we must seek comfort and refreshment of spirit in a deeper source of wisdom, one greater than ourselves.

And so, if future generations do say of us that in our time peace came closer, that we did bring about new seasons of truth and justice, it will be cause for pride. But it shall be a cause of greater pride, still, if it is also said that we were wise enough to know the deliberations of great leaders and great bodies are but overture, that the truly majestic music, the music of freedom, of justice, and peace is the music made in forgetting self and seeking in silence the will of Him who made us.[18]

With his last words to the nations of the world, Reagan laid down a personal standard by which individuals should measure the worth and dignity of their lives. "The case for . . . human dignity . . . can be made only in the context of higher law, only in the context of . . . the will ✓ of Him who made us." Alexis de Tocqueville, who thought likewise, would have applauded.

8

★★★★★★★★

Mistaken Leadership: The European Parliament Speech

The central cause of the tensions of our time is the conflict between totalitarianism and democracy.

—First Draft, "Address to European Parliament,
Strasbourg, France," April 23, 1985

We live in a complex, dangerous, divided world; yet a world which can provide all of the good things we require—spiritual and material—if we but have the confidence and courage to face history's challenge.

—Final Draft, "Address to European Parliament,
Strasbourg, France," May 8, 1985

To partisans of the president, the sentiment "Let Reagan be Reagan" meant, "Let the president speak philosophically." It expressed the longing of his adherents for the president to discuss the big questions identified at the outset of this book: What is human nature? What is the measure of the good life? What is human society? The president's political instincts led him to speak to those issues, too. He knew that ideas were the stuff that kept a free society from falling apart, the center around which teams and communities were built.

His speechwriters shared his confidence in the power of ideas, as Tony Dolan explained: "The point of that wonderful book, *In Search of Excellence*, is that people who are worthwhile don't react to monetary bonuses. They react to shared values. If you state those values and build a team around them, and give them a feeling they are going somewhere, they'll respond. Ronald Reagan understands that."[1]

A president, however, also had to play several other parts in addition to that of spiritual spokesman. He was, for one thing, his party's chief legislative lobbyist and political strategist. As such, he had to speak to the elected and appointed professionals of government about the specifics of programs.[2] He was also the country's chief diplomat, and in that task he had to speak to the leaders and foreign affairs experts around the globe.

The Reagan White House was animated by the tension arising from the pull of these different roles. The chief of staff urged the president to address the concerns of the political community—what the president called the "beltway crowd"; he wanted the president to speak the language of economics and law. The State Department and the president's adviser on national security affairs pressed the president to use public forums to communicate to the leaders of foreign nations; they wanted him to speak the language of diplomacy and force.

Such internal tensions have existed in all modern presidencies. What gave the Reagan White House its special configuration was the vigor of the Speechwriting Department, which found ways to encourage the president to speak, not about policy or diplomacy, but about the intellectual and spiritual needs of the American people beyond the beltway. "Room must be given to dealing with the issues which really lurk in people's hearts," insisted Tony Dolan.

The president's own heart agreed. His head, however, told him there must be compromise. His personal style was to let the competing parties fight it out, discerning whether it was his diplomatic advisers, his chief of staff, or his speechwriters who cared most passionately about a particular speech opportunity. Always, however, his known predilection for the speechwriters' perspective tilted the likely outcome in their favor. Those in the chief of staff's office, who favored talking policy, and those in the State Department, who favored talking diplomacy, knew that the burden fell on them to dissuade the president from following his philosophical inclinations.

Despite the favorable rules of the game, the writers did not always prevail. Sometimes the president checked his instincts and allowed his domestic or diplomatic advisers their way. Every defeat caused the Speechwriting Department acute disappointment. None of its members ever liked to lose, but the knowledge that they were the true favorites of the president revived them and they would try again.

Few instances better illustrated the competition for the presidential pulpit than the European Parliament speech in May 1985. The speechwriters struggled against the State Department to shape the address. When the dust settled, the president gave the nod to the diplomatic objectives of State. Here was a case where the president himself did not let Reagan be Reagan.

The speech was a dud, barely noticed and quickly forgotten, a failure from which a lesson would be learned. In any major public address the president must be the moral teacher, and the competing imperatives to announce policy or conduct diplomacy must be reconciled with the need to maintain moral integrity and public clarity. Spiritual continuity is the basis of the enduring connection between a free people and their leaders.

But we are getting ahead of our story.

In the immediate aftermath of Reagan's reelection victory in 1984, the White House developed plans to go to Western Europe the following spring. The trip was to take ten days in May and would begin with his attendance at the economic summit. The economic summit was an annual meeting of the leaders of seven of the industrial powers of the free world—the United States, Canada, France, Italy, Japan, the United Kingdom, and West Germany. Each year the site changed, and in 1985 West Germany was the host.

The president wanted to use his visit to Germany to demonstrate that West Germany had truly renounced fascist totalitarianism and thereby had earned an honored place among the free nations of the world. Plans were made for him to go to a German cemetery at Bitburg, where German war dead lay buried, to signify forgiveness and redemption. It turned out to be ''an appalling public relations disaster,'' in the words of Donald Regan, the president's chief of staff at the time.[3] Belatedly it was discovered that the Bitburg cemetery contained not only the graves of battlefield troops, who had fought in their nation's defense, but also those of forty-eight members of the Nazi Secret Service, the interior police who carried out Nazi atrocities against innocent civilian populations.

The president held firm to his commitment to visit Bitburg, but he added a second visit, this one to the World War II concentration camp at Bergen-Belsen, where the Nazi regime four decades earlier had committed some of its worst atrocities against Jewish men, women, and children and where Anne Frank had died. Controversy vexed the entire European trip nonetheless.

But before this unexpected revelation soured the public's reception of the West German visit, chief speechwriter Bently Elliott had anticipated an important speaking event. The president was scheduled to address the 434-member European Parliament in Strasbourg, France.

The European Parliament was the congress of the Western European democracies. It was responsible for overseeing and advising the two executive institutions of European economic integration, the Commission and the Council of Ministers of the European Communities. Although the European Parliament lacked law-making power—passing legislation was the job of the Council of Ministers—it was still an important part of the consultative process on all kinds of matters, ranging from agricultural subsidies to transportation. It was a regional federation—a little United Nations—with a difference: Its members were popularly chosen. Each represented not the nation that had appointed them, but the voters who had directly elected them. The European Parliament was the first international body so constituted. It was an unprecedented democratic experiment.

The Speechwriting Department decided that the president's visit to the European Parliament was an opportunity for him to express the values of Western civilization that unify the free world. Elliott, in particular, wanted to draw attention to those precious democratic and legal procedures that made personal freedom possible. He assigned Peggy Noonan to write the speech, which she completed on April 23, two weeks before the event itself.[4]

The Noonan draft was organized around three topics—totalitarianism, democracy, and peace. The first two, concerning the dynamics of totalitarianism and the meaning of democracy, were aimed at the immediate audience, the members of the European Parliament. The third topic—peace and its connection to European unity and military strength—was aimed not at the representatives, but at the people of Western Europe.

On totalitarianism, the draft expressed the president's view that World War II had stemmed from Germany's fateful submission to "the totalitarian temptation," which had been born of a belief in the perfectibility of man.[5] The German people, according to the president, had deluded themselves into thinking that a benevolent government could lead the way to a carefree Utopia, a world free of pain and sacrifice. They had "elevate[d] [the state] to the level of God" and then had abjured all personal responsibility for how it behaved. As a consequence, "banal . . . little men" were able to bully their way into authority over the state apparatus and cloak their evil in the mantle of its divinely established purposes. Thereafter, the brutal acquisitiveness of these little men, left unchecked because Western democratic procedures had been abandoned, plunged the world into war and darkness.

> We know of the existence of evil in the human heart, and we know that in Nazi Germany that evil was institutionalized—given power and direction by the State, by a corrupt regime and the jack boots who did its bidding. And we know, we learned, that early attempts to placate the totalitarians did not save us from war. In fact, they guaranteed it. There are lessons to be learned in this and never forgotten.

The president's second point in the Noonan draft concerned Western democracy. His starting point was to be the state of current political discourse in some European circles. What troubled him, the president was going to say, was the tendency of "some of us" to "question the moral and intellectual worth of the West." Western society was weakened by doubts about its central axioms—about "what is right and what is wrong, what is a decent system and what is not, which philosophies should be resisted and which encouraged."

Adhering to his rhetorical custom, the president was to seize on particular words in contemporary discourse to demonstrate the confusion in language that made it difficult for the people to think for themselves. In the draft the president was to say:

> This terrible moral confusion is reflected even in our language. We speak of "East-West" tensions as if the West and East were equally responsible for the threat to world peace today. We speak of the "superpowers" as if they are moral equals—two huge predators composed in equal parts of virtue and vice. We speak of the "senseless spiral of the arms race" as if the West and the East are equally consumed by the ambition to dominate the world. We speak as if the world were morally neutral—when, in our hearts, most of us know it is not.

The Noonan draft attempted to restore some clarity to the discourse. It diagnosed each fuzzy phrase, explored the evidence, and drew three unequivocal conclusions.

First, the world-threatening tensions were not mutually contributed by East and West, but exclusively caused by totalitarian communism. Second, if "superpower" implied a "predator" nation that got its way by intimidation and bullying, there was only one such superpower: the Soviet Union. Third, the arms race was not a race at all, but a defense by free democracies against brute totalitarian force purposely exercised to bully and trample: "The central cause of the tensions of our time is the conflict between totalitarianism and democracy. . . . It is communism that is the destabilizing influence in the world today, and it is the acquisitive impulse of communism against which we are forced to defend ourselves." In other words, forty years after the defeat of fascism, totalitarianism still existed, was still aggressing against "the free peoples of the world" and still pursuing the totalitarian temptation. The only difference was that the new totalitarianism was communism.

The evidence for this conclusion was everywhere to be seen—the Berlin Wall, erected by the Communists to imprison their own people; refugees fleeing from Communist aggression in Indochina, Afghanistan, Eastern Europe, and Central America; the Soviet buildup of SS-20 missiles on the edge of Western Europe.

The president argued in the Noonan draft that it was not by accident that the totalitarian temptation affected Communist regimes and "not the democracies of the West." Western democracy was morally superior to communism: it made people more decent. The moral superiority of democracy was central to the case for spreading it worldwide.

The president further argued that the byproduct of democracy was peace, that of communism was war:

> All of us in this room want to preserve and protect our *own* democratic liberties—but don't we have a responsibility to foster and encourage democracy throughout the world? And not because democracy is "our" form of government, but because we have learned that democracy is, in the last analysis, the only *peaceful* form of government. It is, in fact, the greatest Conflict Resolution Mechanism ever devised by man. For only in its atmosphere can man peacefully resolve his differences through the ballot, through a free press, through free speech and free political parties, and the right to redress injustice.

Regimes were not morally equal. They were not life-styles that could be adopted or jettisoned with minor human consequence. Democracy dissipated political warfare; communism heightened it as a means of cowing the community into conformity. If "God's gifts" of diverse talents and individual outlooks were to be a source of strength and rejuvenation, then only democracy would work. The liberal procedures of free speech and assembly, universal suffrage, and effective protection of minority rights were indispensable if a plural society were to escape the extremes of chaotic license and coerced conformity. Without liberal procedures a society lacked the "conflict resolution mechanism" to resolve peacefully the inevitable political differences arising from these desirable human differences. In democratic procedures lay the secret to real peace—peace with freedom.

Then the president turned to peace, and addressed his words directly to the European people. The president sought to engage in the popular discourse in Europe. In effect, he submitted three questions for neighborhood debates.

He began by reminding the people of Western Europe how distinctive was free political debate and how much more "reasonable" and humane it made free people:

> We all want peace; we all want to protect the world. But we have a better chance of preserving the peace if we in the West see the world as it is and deal honestly with its hard realities. The peace movements of the West call for disarmament, a thoroughly laudable and understandable desire. But I cannot help note that it is the West, usually the United States, that they see as the chief aggressor in the so-called arms race. And it is the West, and only the West, to which they made their appeal. There is pathos in this, and a strange, hidden tribute.

Pathos because their decision not to confront the creator of the arms race, the chief aggressor of our time, dooms their movement to failure. And a hidden tribute because they obviously feel that at least we, the reasonable people of the West, will give them a hearing.

Much as he did when he talked directly to the American people, Reagan posed a set of questions for the people to argue among themselves. The draft had him asking the members of the peace movement in Europe:

> Does it make you feel safer to know that the peace activists of the Soviet Union are in the Gulag? Does it make you feel safer to know that the Russians who truly desire peace with the West are in psychiatric hospitals?

That was the first question: Why did the Soviet system imprison people like "you" and other sincere peace activists, who share the "laudable and reasonable desire" for disarmament? Have the members of the European peace movement faced up to the totalitarian nature of the Soviet regime?

The second question was, What should be the real objective of those who truly desire peace—was it really arms control or only the signing ceremonies?

> Arms control means *nothing* unless both sides comply. And I would ask if it is not reasonable to state the following: that anyone who talks arms control, but never about compliance is, wittingly or unwittingly, really working not for peace but for unilateral disarmament of the West. And we cannot have that, because if the West, and only the West is disarmed, then we will wind up back in 1939—and the tanks of the totalitarians will roll again.

The president then posed his final question: "History has taught a lesson we must never forget: Totalitarians do not stop—they must be stopped. And how? What is the West to do?" Reagan had some suggestions: stay strong; stay unified and remember that "our unity is the natural result of our shared love of liberty"; "foster and encourage democracy throughout the world"; and, above all, remember "that we are not powerless before history."

Here was the president at his best, taking his philosophical case to the people of Western Europe, confiding in them, separating out the troubling complex of issues, clarifying the central terms of the discussion, untangling fact and value, inviting dispute, and encouraging his supporters among "the reasonable people of the West" to wage the debate on his behalf.

The speech, as drafted, was never given. Between April 24, when the Noonan draft first began to circulate in the White House, and May 8, when the president addressed the European Parliament, the rhetorical aspirations of the Speechwriting Department were rebuffed and those who championed diplomacy and policy triumphed. The clarity of the Noonan draft was sacrificed for the sake of diplomatic overtures to the Kremlin. Great attention was paid to defining specific policies, but the public justification for them was left a confused mess. The speech was, as was said earlier, dreadful, the more disappointing because of the road not taken, the rhetorical alternative rejected.

The draft rang clear: "The central cause of the tensions of our time is the conflict between totalitarianism and democracy." The actual speech overflowed with clichés, the benumbing stuff of writers' nightmares: "We live in a complex, dangerous, divided world; yet a world which can provide all of the good things we require—spiritual and material—if we but have the confidence and courage to face history's challenge."[6] If ever there was an example of the "terrible moral confusion" against which the Noonan draft railed, that was it. Consider: Why was the world divided? What were the elements that combined to make events complex? What were "the good things we require—spiritual and material"? Not only was the speech callow, it was wrong. It misidentified the mission of the West—"to keep the peace with an ever more powerful Soviet"— and, worse, it then saddled the West with the responsibility of stabilizing the Soviet relationship.

In the final version of the address, the president said: "We in the West have much to be thankful for—peace, prosperity, and freedom. . . . Our task . . . is to keep the peace with an ever more powerful Soviet Union, to introduce greater stability in our relationship with it, and to live together in a world in which our values can prosper."[7] Note the treatment of "freedom." After a passing mention, the speech made no further reference to it. Concerning the freedoms of speech, press, assembly, and economic and political choice, the president's address fell silent. Nor was any mention made of the Western vision, that all people are entitled to personal freedom. To put it bluntly, the speech denied the great mission of the West. It advanced instead a paltry substitute: "peace," now elevated to the West's highest duty; and "prosperity," the material byproduct (and ultimate justification) of that peace.

To compound that error, the president's speech proceeded to accuse the Western democracies of doing too little to advance peace. The president's remarks could be construed as an admission that the present instability in the world was due, not to Communist acquisitiveness, but rather to the West's failure to fulfill its task to maintain peace with the Soviet Union.

At the very least, that was a possibility if the speech were interpreted in an unfriendly light. And, of course, it would be, for the speech was aimed not at the average European (as the Noonan draft was intended to be), but at the Soviet Union and its adherents within the West European peace movement. And the speech played right into their hands. There was no criticism of the Soviet Union; there was no moral defense of the democracies as guardians of personal freedom. Nor did the speech dispel the ambiguity invariably connected to the word "peace." Peace, in the final version of the president's address, could just as easily have meant surrender to superior force (the Soviet meaning) as its opposite—personal autonomy free of bullying threats (the Western meaning).

Rhetorically, the discussion of peace was unforgivably vague. And that was not the only rhetorical lapse. Consider the treatment of democracy. In the Noonan draft its features were specific: "the ballot, . . . a free press, . . . free speech and free political parties, and the right to redress injustice." It hailed democracy as "the greatest Conflict Resolution Mechanism ever devised." In contrast, what the president ended up saying at Strasbourg was abstract and meaningless:

> We will support and will encourage movement toward . . . the democratic ideals shared in Europe. . . . As we seek to encourage democracy, we must remember that each country must struggle for democracy within its own culture. Emerging democracies have special problems and require special help. These nations whose democratic institutions are newly emerged and whose confidence in the process is not yet deeply rooted need our help. They should have an established community of their peers, other democratic countries to whom they can turn for support or just advice.[8]

Virtually every word in that paragraph was diplomatically ambiguous. What democratic ideals were shared, for example, by the two German nations then existing in the very center of Europe, both of which called themselves democracies? What modifications of these democratic ideals were to be countenanced in the name of a nation's culture, and what ones resisted as destructive of the essential purposes of democracy? What were the democratic institutions that were newly emerged? And by "nations," was the president referring to the people or to a select group of political officials who were still uncertain about the advantages of the democratic process?

Such fuzzing over of reality was as purposeful as the crystalline clarity of the Noonan draft. The intention of those who wrote the final version of the European Parliament address was not to teach the people but to make diplomatic overtures to the foreign office in the Kremlin and placate it.

The diplomats from the State Department sought to remind the Soviet Union of both the power and the restraint of America and to leave U.S. intentions to use them ambiguous. Here in that flat, benumbing language of serious international diplomacy was the assertion of power:

> In the short run, we [in the United States government] have no alter-
> native but to compete with the Soviet Union in this field [of nuclear
> arms], not in the pursuit of superiority but merely of balance. It is
> thus essential that the United States maintain a modern and survivable
> nuclear capability in each leg of the strategic triad—sea, land, and air-
> based. It is similarly important that France and Britain maintain and
> modernize their independent strategic capabilities.[9]

Then, to reduce Soviet apprehensions, diplomatic protocol required the
president to make a personal pledge of restraint to the Soviet leadership.
America's goal was "fruitful cooperation with the Soviet Union . . . [and]
not . . . to undermine or change the Soviet system nor to impinge upon
the security of the Soviet Union."

In the course of the speech the president did advance a number of
specific proposals regarding military coordination. He talked of specific
things like "a permanent military-to-military communications link . . . for
exchanging notifications and other information regarding routine military
activities." Whether such steps would have been prudent or effective is
not at issue. Nor need we decide whether a diplomatic overture was best
made in a widely publicized presidential speech. What even a layman
could assess, however, was how the diplomatic and policy purposes to
which the speech was put dictated the ambiguous style, equivocal and
contradictory content, and uninspiring tone of the president's rhetoric.

As a communication between the leaders of the two so-called superpowers, it may (or may not) have been useful. As a speech by a democratic
leader to a free people, it was a travesty, and the Speechwriting Department, which had fought so hard to make it otherwise, knew it was. Its
members resolved to fight the next time with greater tenacity.

Democratic leaders invariably face a choice in how to use their
rhetorical powers: to speak to the people or to address political professionals. Speaking candidly to the people, Reagan often had to be undiplo-
matic. Making political overtures to professionals, he often had to
adulterate public understanding. His choice was unavoidable.

In the long run the repercussions from the European Parliament
speech were politically unimportant. My strong hunch is that the
most important effect of this failed speech was on the president himself. It hardened his resolve to trust his instincts as much in foreign
affairs as he did in domestic matters. The experience confirmed his
already strong belief in using his bully pulpit to address the people,
finding other means to communicate with the professionals. If sometimes no such means were at hand, if back-room deals and secret
diplomacy were now frowned upon, if it were really the case that
the president had sometimes to ascend the bully pulpit to contact the
political professional crowd, then at minimum the policy or diplomatic

message must be framed to avoid confusing the people and contradict-ing what they had been led to think.

Likewise, my hunch is that Reagan and his speechwriters became more convinced than ever of the danger of a confused citizenry. They grew convinced that a muddled public opinion eventually forced democratic government to adopt muddled policies. Therefore, to them, the first imperative of democratic leadership was candor, and the second was steadfast adherence to those axioms of Western civilization that constituted "the moral and intellectual worth of the West" and were the guarantees of the morality and stability of personal freedom.

It could be argued that to have spoken the truth of the Soviet Union would have been to insult it. But even if it were true, the point would not be decisive. The function of the presidency is to speak the truths of freedom and to make the people an enlightened citizenry. A contrary conception of the presidency is a mistake.

The president and his partners in the Speechwriting Department took steps to teach the lessons learned from the fiasco at Strasbourg. By his final year in office he was stressing repeatedly the importance of "public candor." Never did he do it more eloquently and succinctly than in his farewell review of American foreign policy, which he delivered at the University of Virginia in December 1988:

> In the years of detente we tended to forget the greatest weapon the democracies have in their struggle is public candor: the truth. We must never do that again. It's not an act of belligerence to speak to the fundamental differences between totalitarianism and democracy; it's a moral imperative. It doesn't slow down the pace of negotiations; it moves them forward. Throughout history, we see evidence that adversaries negotiate seriously with democratic nations only when they know the democracies harbor no illusions about those adversaries.[10]

The recognition and expression of that important idea—that candor strengthened democracy and weakened totalitarianism—redeemed the rhetorical error of the European Parliament speech. Or, to put it in the vernacular, "It ain't a mistake if you don't repeat it."

PART THREE

MORAL INSTITUTIONS

We have to get the word out. . . .

—Ronald Reagan (1988)

D id Reagan's public speechmaking make a difference? Did his four million words, with their notions of partnership, human imperfectibility, and spiritual values, change the personal philosophies and behavior of Americans?

Where might we look for answers to such important questions? Anecdotes? During the 1980s the media related countless stories about individual Americans. Some were upbeat, particularly during calamities (such as earthquakes) and epidemics (such as AIDS), when the newspapers and television carried tales of sacrifice and hope. Some were downers. Reporters were able to round up the usual scandalous suspects in politics and business—and even in goodly institutions like the church—proving once again (as James Madison reminded us in 1788) that we Americans were no angels. Vice remained abundantly visible.

A vice-free world, however, was not the proper standard by which to gauge the effectiveness of what the president said, if for no other reason than that was not his or his speechwriters' purpose in speaking. Effectiveness ought to be measured by the two objectives the Reagan presidency said it was trying to accomplish from the bully pulpit: to revive hope and magnify a spirit of personal generosity. Did what Reagan said achieve either of these goals?

Consider optimism. Just before Reagan entered the White House, Americans were not particularly pleased with the state of their affairs. Recall from the first chapter how President Carter used nationwide television in 1979 to announce that "a majority of our people believe that the next five years will be worse than the past five years."[1]

From such pessimism in 1979, Americans turned hopeful in the 1980s. Figure 1 depicts the state of optimism in American society, as reflected in random surveys of one thousand Americans in 1974, 1979, and 1988. Each respondent was asked the same three questions concerning the quality of their lives as represented by the rungs of a ladder, with the tenth rung symbolizing the "best possible life" and the first the "worst possible life":

1. On which step of the ladder do you personally stand *at the present time*?
2. On which step would you say you stood *five years ago*?
3. And, just as your best guess, on which step will you stand in the future, say about *five years from now*?

The three surveys revealed striking differences across time.

In 1979, the year President Carter spoke about, average Americans thought they stood below the halfway step on their "ladder of life"; those same average Americans of 1979 looked back with nostalgia to the previous five years when (they remembered) they had stood near the sixth step. As they looked ahead to the future, they saw themselves slipping still further down the ladder. That's pessimism.

In 1974 average Americans also thought that they were worse off than they had been five years earlier, having plunged a step and a half. Still, they were optimistic about rebounding in the future.

In 1988, their outlooks were radically different. Average Americans felt good about their present quality of life: they saw themselves beyond the sixth step on the ladder, a whole step higher than they had been in 1983, and they expected to rise to the eighth step in the near future. That's optimism.

Did Reagan's words have anything to do with the increase in their hopes? Or was the average person's upbeat outlook determined by economic and material factors? After all, the 1980s provided Americans ample reason to be hopeful: inflation and interest rates were down, new jobs were being created at a rate of 250,000 *per month*, the nation was enjoying the longest sustained peacetime prosperity ever, the unemployment rate was falling virtually everywhere, high school achievement scores were up, drug use and violent crime were on the decline, there was an unexpected increase in the numbers of Americans going to college, church attendance rose, technology continued to produce miracles, more minorities were participating in politics, morale in the armed services was boosted by fair pay increases, and, abroad, Americans were not engaged in any wars (the first such decade since the 1920s), democracy was spreading throughout South America and East Asia, communism seemed to be collapsing, the Soviet Union had agreed to reduce its nuclear weaponry, the Persian Gulf was secured, international trade was expanding among the nations of the noncommunist world, and America's position in the United Nations was on the ascendant.

But there was sufficient bad news to support an inclination to pessimism, too: a seeming growth in homelessness among the poor, the twin epidemics of AIDS and "crack" (a strongly addictive narcotic), a startling stock market crash in October 1987, the worrisome bankruptcy of several major financial institutions, an unexpectedly large federal

Figure 1
Perceptions of the Quality of Life
in the Past, Present, and Future, 1974–1988

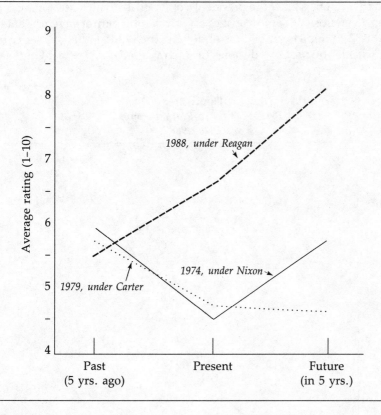

NOTE: Surveys conducted in 1974 for Nixon presidency, 1979 for Carter presidency, 1988 for Reagan presidency. Respondents ranked the current and expected quality of their lives on a scale of 1 (worst) to 10 (best).
SOURCE: Survey results presented to the Republican National Committee by the Wirthlin Group, Richard B. Wirthlin, principal investigator, 1363 Beverly Road, McLean, Virginia 22101.

budget deficit, a continuing international trade deficit, and, abroad, the intractability of war in the Middle East, worldwide terrorism, and the puzzling Iran-Contra affair, which left the Reagan presidency embarrassed by two related illegal acts: selling arms to Iran and covertly transferring financial support to the anti-Communist resistance in Nicaragua.

Given all these events, what if the Reagan presidency had said nothing, or had said something other than what it did? Would Americans have been just as optimistic? At best, any answer must be speculative. The evidence one way or another is insufficient to convince anyone with a skeptical turn of mind, but at the same time the conjunction of heightened optimism and the president's purpose in creating it gives cause to consider.

What can be said of the president's other goal—to increase Americans' personal generosity? Some statistics on private philanthropy are presented in Figure 2. It depicts, in billions of dollars, the annual gifts to charity by Americans in the past two decades (in each year about 80 percent of these

Figure 2
Private Gifts to Philanthropy,
1970–1988

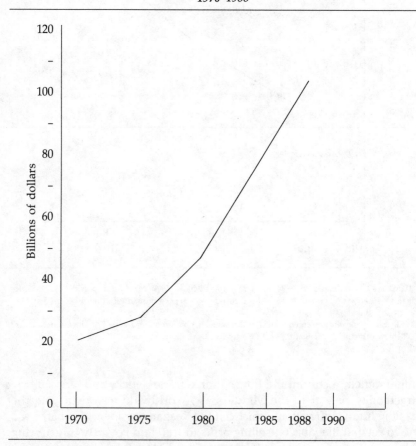

SOURCE: U.S. Bureau of the Census, *Statistical Abstract of the United States, 1990,* 110th ed. (Washington, D.C.: U.S. Government Printing Office, 1990): 72, Table 620. The original source for these estimates is the American Association of Fund-Raising Counsel (AAFRC), Trust for Philanthropy, New York, N.Y. *Giving USA,* annual.

were gifts from individual donors, and the remaining 20 percent came from charitable foundations, corporations, and bequests).

These are absolute dollars, not weighted for inflationary effects, but the raw figures are impressive. In the first eight years of the 1980s, years in which the annual inflation rate stayed close to 5 percent, charitable giving in the United States grew more than 10 percent a year, the total more than doubling from $48.7 to $104.4 billion dollars. Philanthropy ✓ flourished in the 1980s.

Was there a connection between the president's intentions to inspire personal generosity and the results? It would be hard to prove beyond a doubt; as with optimism, the conjunction of presidential purpose and result is suggestive, but that is all.

In the absence of compelling proof, is it possible to demonstrate the dynamic by which the president's ideas—his moral leadership—could have caused these significant increases in optimism and charitable giving? Yes, and what follows is an attempt to do so.

The next two chapters clarify two concepts central to the argument: that of an "idea" and a "moral institution." The remainder of the book describes the means used by the Reagan presidency to penetrate American society and root its public philosophy in the hearts and minds of the people.

President and Mrs. Reagan's private home, Rancho del Cielo, Santa Ynez, California.

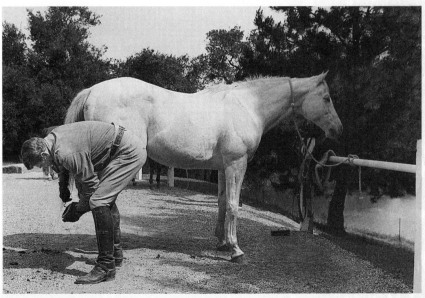

Reagan relaxing at Rancho del Cielo, Santa Ynez, April 4, 1986.

Speaking to the Japanese Diet, November 11, 1983.

In Finland, preparing for the Soviet-U.S. summit meeting, May 27, 1988.

House Speaker Thomas P. ("Tip") O'Neill, Jr., visits Reagan in the White House, January 31, 1983.

Strolling at Camp David with Prime Minister Margaret Thatcher.

At the U.S. Ranger Monument, Pointe du Hoc, France, June 6, 1984.

*President and Mrs. Reagan visit the Normandy American Cemetery in France,
June 6, 1984.*

At Andrews Air Force Base, Maryland, August 23, 1983, commemorating sixteen Americans who died in a terrorist attack on the U.S. Embassy in Beirut, Lebanon.

Memorial for crew members of the USS Stark, Mayport Naval Station, Jacksonville, Florida, May 22, 1987.

Meeting the press in the White House briefing room, April 4, 1985.

Visit to Congress Heights Elementary School, Washington, D.C., March 12, 1984.

Reagan at the NAACP Annual Convention in Denver, Colorado, June 29, 1981.

Speaking to the National Association of Evangelicals in Orlando, Florida, March 8, 1983: the "Evil Empire" speech.

In the middle of a White House press briefing, Mrs. Reagan surprised her husband with a birthday cake, February 4, 1983.

Reagan and his dog Lucky departing the White House in the presidential helicopter.

9

★★★★★★★★

The Notion of an Idea

A general idea is always a danger to the existing order.

—Alfred North Whitehead (1933)

We have frequently said that President Reagan governed with ideas. What is an idea? More particularly, what is a general idea?

In its simplest form, an idea is a pair of concepts, bonded by a relationship.[1] Picture a thick, short wire with a bead at each end. Imagine that each bead is a concept, a class of similar things. Beads come in all sizes. So do concepts: some are no bigger than a speck of dust, and others are balloon-size. Their dimensions depend on the generosity of their embrace. Freedom would be a big concept. It includes numerous activities: traveling wherever we wish, reading an uncensored newspaper, speaking critically of the government without fear of reprisal, handing in a resignation to a bad boss. These activities are similar because the individuals doing them are doing what they want to do.

Notice that the concept of freedom encompasses things that are not completely free: restraints exist on activities that we still think of as free. "Free" people, for instance, are subject to certain state regulations, the law of gravity, the need to make a living, and the influence of history. Nevertheless, they act with enough independence to fit into our concept of freedom. Freedom, like all big notions, is a matter of degree, to be defined by its user. The president, speaking at Fudan University, Shanghai, in 1984, likened his notion of a free person to a ship's navigator: "History is a river that may take us as it will. But we have the power to navigate, to choose direction, and make our passage together. The wind

113

is up, the current is swift, and opportunity for a long and fruitful journey awaits us."[2] The president's concept of freedom embraced any person having "the power to navigate, to choose direction." Freedom defined that generously was a big concept.

What does the mind do with concepts to transform them into an idea? It connects them in causal relationships. Causal connectedness between a pair of concepts: that is the essence of an idea. An idea asserts that one concept is "good for" (or "bad for") the other with which it is paired. For example, the president believed that "freedom promoted vitality." He also believed that "freedom defeated tyranny."

Freedom promoting vitality and freedom defeating tyranny: those are general ideas because the concepts of which they consist—freedom, vitality, tyranny—are vast abstract entities. As a consequence, they fit countless situations: walking a dog, raising a family, leading a business enterprise, governing a society.

Reagan often uttered general ideas during his presidency. At the two hundredth anniversary of Yorktown, the battle that ended (successfully) the American Revolutionary War, the president said: "We have come to this field to celebrate the triumph of an idea—that freedom will eventually triumph over tyranny. It is and always will be a warning to those who would usurp the rights of others: Time will find them beaten."[3] Freedom eventually defeating unfreedom: that was a big notion, a general idea.

Virtually all ideas, general or otherwise, are injected with feeling. Whenever we care about some activity that a concept represents, we end up caring about the concept, as the president demonstrated in a story he told to the 1988 Republican convention about a young boy who wrote to him shortly after he took office:

> In his letter he said, "I love America because you can join Cub Scouts if you want to. You have a right to worship as you please. If you have the ability, you can try to be anything you want to be. And I also like America because we have about 200 flavors of ice cream." Well, truth through the eyes of a child: freedom of association, freedom of worship, freedom of hope and opportunity, and the pursuit of happiness—in this case, choosing among 200 flavors of ice cream—that's America.[4]

Choosing among two hundred flavors of ice cream added a lot of love to that child's notion of freedom.

If we have strong sentiments about a concept, they color our interpretation of all things connected with it. For that reason tyrants often attempt to misrepresent their acts of tyranny as exploits of "freedom." By associating their villainy with freedom, they hope to attach to the former the favorable sentiment evoked by the latter. In Finland in 1988 the president spoke of the purposeful confusion practiced by Communist regimes, mislabeling their oppressive deeds and promising freedom, "but of a different kind than the one we celebrate." Theirs was not a vision of a society giving free scope to the common sense of individuals, but rather what the Czech writer Milan Kundera called "the freedom of imposed perfection."[5] The utopian concept of freedom was a counterfeit and brutal thing, imposed on society by a select few and was a far cry from "the democratic concept of freedom," with its infinite choices and the constitutional protections abridging those choices.

Ideas lighten the darkness of human ignorance. That darkness afflicts three realms of existence—the scientific, moral, and social. Stable ideas make it possible for us to navigate in all three areas.

First, the scientific context of ideas illuminates the cause-and-effect relationship between things and enable individuals to predict and understand events. Ideas can provide both foresight and insight. They give people hunches about what is happening and what can be done about it.

Consider the idea that "freedom promotes vitality" and vice versa. Knowing nothing about a nation except that it has just been liberated, an observer can predict with confidence that its people will become more productive and ingenious. Looking back in time to explain why the nation became free, the same observer can focus his attention on how the people acquired sufficient vitality to liberate their country in the first place.

General ideas give us a handle with which to clutch the awkward confusion of the real world and shape it to our purposes. Without general notions, we would have to wait to act until more information developed. We would constantly fall victim to what Dolan earlier called "epistemological paralysis."

Second, the passionate content of ideas provides moral meaning. If a concept is highly valued, it confers dignity—moral worth—on whatever actions we take to the concept. If freedom is a good thing, then promoting it makes us worthwhile. If a freedom-loving individual "sees" a causal connection between volunteer work and freedom (say, because voluntarism appears to reduce the need for additional "paternalistic bureaucracies"), then doing community service will bring moral fulfillment. Ideas that we care about give direction to the ways we expend our limited human energies. We become sure our lives add up to something of value when our deeds serve valued purposes. Thus, ideas dispel moral uncertainty and confer moral worth.

Third, the ideas we share with others around us give us social insight. The frightening fact of social life is that it is infinitely indeterminate; people have wills of their own and the freedom to follow them. In contrast, nonhuman phenomena are generally predictable because they lack such freedom. Human beings, being able to formulate intentions and pursue them, may, theoretically at least, change their minds and behave as they never have before.

The fact that humans try to base their actions on ideas that are consistent and stable means that their behavior will be, much more often than not, consistent and stable—and, hence, foreseeable. Such foresight makes social life less fearsome.

It is sometimes said that ideas can be easily changed. Nothing could be further from the truth. Their importance in dispelling our ignorance in the scientific, moral, and social realms means that excising them will have important consequences for ourselves and others. Untying ourselves from the support of old ideas may cause our souls and our society to collapse into intellectual confusion, moral despair, and social anarchy.

Changing ideas may result in wholesale confusion. Changing one idea disturbs the ecology of all the other notions interconnected to it. Let me illustrate.

In the Great Depression of the 1930s, a quarter of the nation's work force lost their jobs, farm products begged for buyers, businesses went bankrupt, and capital dried up. This harsh reality came as a bitter surprise to average Americans, for until the market crashed they were likely to have held the general idea that freedom promoted prosperity, and vice versa. With economic suffering spreading throughout the society, however, what were they then to think?

If this harsh reality around them led them to change their minds and think that freedom caused the depression—that is, that freedom diminished prosperity—then it would be hard to confine the implications of that change. The new idea that freedom was bad economically would affect all the other good things that revolved around freedom, too: vitality, peace, self-government. If freedom now diminished prosperity, did that mean it also worked against peace? Indeed, the alteration of one general idea jeopardized the stability of every neighboring idea. That led to confusion.

Changing ideas may lead to moral despair. If the big ideas that are changing are the moral premises on which an individual has earlier based an important decision, then that decision may appear morally mistaken. The inescapable feature of moral life is that men cannot undo history, but they can dishonor it. For instance, a laborer can work hard at his job and be proud of his progress because he assumes that his efforts will permit him to accumulate wealth for his family. If economic depression wiped out his and his family's savings after years of toil and caused him to abandon his belief that honest work and success were related, he might find that his change of mind dishonored all the past years of hard work. And, when he came to add up his life, he might find that his life did not "count" for anything, to borrow Willie Loman's term.

Changing ideas risks social chaos. As noted earlier, whenever persons share a common sense, they become understandable to one another. Their behavior, thus, becomes reliable, and they understand how to influence one another through ideas. Eliminate the center of that common sense, and things fall apart.

Shakespeare likened life to a play. Our common ideas—including our "mystic chords of memory"—constitute a script, from which we read our several parts. Let one player depart from the particular script, and the scene breaks down, much as if Juliet were suddenly to start reciting the lines of Lady Macbeth from her balcony. In the same way, the normal routines of community are disturbed when the actions of members begin to reflect nontraditional ideas. The social order—the society's center of common notions—ceases to hold, and when it disintegrates, people can no longer foresee what others are likely to do, and they must resort more and more to coercion to get their way.

Tocqueville once wrote:

> General ideas are no proof of the strength, but rather of the insufficiency of the human intellect. For there are in nature no beings exactly alike, no objects precisely identical, no rules indiscriminately and alike applicable to several objects at once. The chief merit of general ideas is that they enable the human mind to pass a rapid judgment on a great many objects at once; but, on the other hand, the notions they convey are never other than incomplete, and they always cause the mind to lose as much in accuracy as it gains in comprehensiveness.[6]

Big ideas, in other words, are too simple. "Seek simplicity, and distrust it," said the scientist and philosopher Alfred North Whitehead.[7]

But, as Tocqueville also noted, general ideas signify the insufficiency of the human intellect. They compensate for the unavoidable ignorance humans suffer about what is happening around them, what to do about it, and why. Ideas are necessary to all human action. Mortals are required to pass a rapid judgment on things they lack the time to know, on choices they suddenly find thrust at them, on persons they have never met before. Despite the possibility of error, despite the inevitable inaccuracy of the notions in our heads, individuals must take action or suffer the consequences of choosing not to act. General ideas shed light on indistinct prospects. They support us in our spiritual and worldly lives. Being so important to us, they are protected by us from tampering.

With the image of "The Silken Tent," the poet Robert Frost conveyed the importance of firm ideas to personal stability. Referring to the human personality, he wrote:

> She is as in a field a silken tent
> At midday when a sunny summer breeze

> *Has dried the dew and all its ropes relent,*
> *So that in guys it gently sways at ease,*
> *And its supporting central cedar pole,*
> *That is its pinnacle to heavenward*
> *And signifies the sureness of the soul,*
> *Seems to owe naught to any single cord,*
> *But strictly held by none, is loosely bound*
> *By countless silken ties of love and thought*
> *To everything on earth the compass round,*
> *And only by one's going slightly taut*
> *In the capriciousness of summer air*
> *Is of the slightest bondage made aware.*[8]

Undoing any of those "countless silken ties of love and thought" is delicate business and, ineptly done, may bring "the supporting central cedar pole," and the "soul" it signifies, tumbling to earth.

The resultant unwillingness of individuals to modify their ideas, however, causes a social problem. It was Edmund Burke who pointed out two centuries ago that conserving a society may depend on changing its traditional ideas.[9] Historically, cultures have had to be able to modify the content of their common sense because of changing circumstances. The problem was how to synchronize countless individual changes of ideas so that the moral center of the society would not fail and loose intellectual and moral anarchy upon the world.

Needing to change, civilizations have created moral institutions to help people undergo change. In the United States a prudent presidency, like Ronald Reagan's, wishing to alter the way Americans thought about things, was obliged to employ whatever moral institutions could be enlisted to assist in the task.

What moral institutions were available? And how did they work? To this pair of questions we now turn.

10

★★★★★★★★

The Notion of a Moral Institution

Scarcely any political question arises in the United States that is not resolved, sooner or later, into a judicial question. Hence all parties are obliged to borrow, in their daily controversies, the ideas, and even the language, peculiar to judicial proceedings. As most public men are or have been legal practitioners, they introduce the customs and the technicalities of their profession into the management of public affairs. The jury extends this habit to all classes. The language of the law thus becomes, in some measure, a vulgar tongue; the spirit of the law, which is produced in the schools and courts of justice, gradually penetrates beyond their walls into the bosom of society.

—Alexis de Tocqueville (1835)

What makes life in a free society so hard is its conditionality. Earlier we spoke of the contingent character of American life: of how it forces the individual to adjust to the private desires of others and how moral leadership is vital in dispelling the anxiety, the loneliness, and even despair that this may produce. In moments of confusion informed explanation is needed to focus energies effectively. In the midst of suspicion, leaders are indispensable in casting light on people's motives and nurturing social trust. In times of setback, philosophy is vital to comfort the afflicted and restore hope.

If the contingent character of freedom makes moral leadership imperative, however, the openness of a free society makes such leadership very difficult. For an open society is noisy, and the noise is distracting.

On one leg of his travels through America in 1979, the reporter Richard Reeves was driving to Newport, Rhode Island, listening to the car radio and finding himself "engulfed in storms of facts, of ideas, of information, of opinions, of urgings, of preachments." His account, with all its details, captures the cacophony of American society:

> There were thirty-eight different stations broadcasting on the AM band of the car radio. I had begun idly searching the little dial. . . . Then I began to actually listen.
>
> Revolution was being preached—political, social, and religious—quite openly. A convicted criminal was being interviewed—quite respectfully—about how he judged the performance of the current President of the United States. Men were speaking in a language strange to me, Portuguese, broadcast daily from WRIV in Providence, Rhode Island. From Boston, WILD was broadcasting the voices of black Americans who telephoned the station from their homes and were put on the air—live, uncensored, unedited—attacking the government, the police, white Americans. Referring to each other as "Brother" and "Sister," the callers I heard offered a consensus of opinion that the public policy of the United States was deliberately designed and executed to subjugate twenty-six million black Americans. The brothers and sisters, who obviously had little formal education, worked out, over an hour, a fairly sophisticated analysis of what they saw as a colonial policy: Ruling whites sought out the most talented and therefore the most dangerous blacks and quickly elevated them into the majority's comfortable financial structure, eliminating the leadership cadre of potential black revolution. And some of the callers were calling for that revolution—for the violent overthrow of the government. From Lexington, Massachusetts, on WROL, a Protestant evangelist named Kathryn Kuhlman, who had been dead for three years, was on tape that could play until eternity, vigorously attacking all recipients of government welfare. Work, she said, was God's welfare—and woe to the men or government that subverted Divine provisions. From New York City, WOR was broadcasting an interview with a man named John Ehrlichman, who had recently been released from jail for crimes committed while he served in the President's office, the White House. He had written a book, fiction, about Washington and was being asked to criticize the current President—the criminal's judgments being greeted with impressed murmurs of "I see." Four stations were broadcasting nothing but news. One of them, WEAN in Providence, reported with hints of shock and outrage that radio in the Soviet Union had, for twenty hours, withheld news from the Russian people that their government and the United States had completed negotiations on an arms limitation treaty. . . . Five stations were broadcasting only religious programming—Protestant services and analysis of current events—and as I began thinking about what that might mean, WCBS in New York broadcast a commentary of *Public Opinion* magazine, which had recently commented on polling data [concerning the decline in formal religious participation in the United States but the continuing acceptance of religious principles]. . . .
>
> That was one hour on the AM band of one radio—and I have recorded only a tiny fraction of the information and opinion on concerns from stock to sex that I heard in that hour.[1]

That was a lot of noise. In the years after 1979 Americans could continue to tune in a like number of radio stations; could choose among dozens of television channels; could subscribe to hundreds of magazines and newspapers; were exposed to entreaties from their labor unions, employers, and neighborhood groups; were flooded with direct-mail solicitations from countless worthy organizations; and had to put up with the constitutionally protected approaches of strangers in airports, on street corners, and even at their doorsteps. The noise of entreaty, the blare of admonition, the din of prophecy, the bombast of praise and denunciation, all constantly and indiscriminately assaulted them.

To shut out the din, Americans developed mechanisms of privacy. They learned to concentrate their senses, disregarding ideas they regarded as senseless and hearing only when they decided to listen.

In a noisy society such as ours, the president could speak; his message, however, was just one of a countless multitude. His voice was no louder or more attractive than a toiletries advertisement. He lacked the power to accost citizens in their sanctuaries without permission. In touching the heart and mind of each citizen, he enjoyed no special privileges.

In the America of the 1980s, it was difficult for citizens to discern what the president was saying; not only were they free to ignore him, but it was also probable that many people would not like what they heard if they paid any attention. The president had to expect heartfelt resistance to his ideas because he was speaking general ideas—philosophy.

The saying is that if you want to stay friends, don't talk either religion or politics. The president was talking both. The trouble with politics and religion as dinner table topics is that discussion of them often steps on the toes of people's fundamental beliefs. With his notions of the president as moral spokesman, Reagan was meddling with those self-evident truths at the heart of people's personal philosophies.

Recall that people tend to fight hard against changing the general ideas comprising their individual philosophies—ideas that are the stays of the personality and society—and loosening them tends to wreak personal disorder and social instability. In changing attitudes that touch the soul, conventional wisdom suggests that it is best and most effectively done by close and trusted acquaintances giving individualized counseling.[2] Occupants of the presidency—personally remote as they are—do not have the luxury of sitting down with the individual citizen to overcome his or her understandable resistance.

A century and a half ago Tocqueville observed much the same noisy openness in American life that Reeves did. On first disembarking in New York in 1831, he heard what he described as "a confused hum": "No sooner do you set foot upon American ground than you are stunned by a kind of tumult; a confused clamor is heard on every side, and a thousand simultaneous voices demand the satisfaction of their social wants."[3]

With time Tocqueville came to delight in the noisiness and energy of America. He also came to discern that one clear voice stood out distinctly in the uproar—the law. Americans tuned in to messages couched in the language of the law. Legal ideas pierced the clamor, while notions originating from other sources tended not to. Tocqueville took pains to explain the reasons for the power of the legal voice in the American democracy: "The language of the law thus becomes, in some measure, a vulgar tongue; the spirit of the law, which is produced in the schools and courts of justice, gradually penetrates beyond their walls into the bosom of society, where it descends to the lowest classes, so that at last the whole people contract the habits and tastes of the judicial magistrate."[4]

Lawyers impressed Tocqueville with the fact that they enjoyed a moral authority akin to that of the great landed families of Europe. Tocqueville even called them "the American aristocracy." Lawyers fashioned the ideas of the nation, teaching their language and their spirit to their fellow Americans.[5]

They were effective because they formed what Tocqueville called a "party." That is to say, lawyers were connected institutionally with a well-organized team of fellow lawyers, judges, and scholars. They were a part of an institution that lent the ideas of the judiciary a compelling authority. That's what made the law stand out amidst the "storms of facts, of ideas, of information, of opinions, of urgings, of preachments" in America.

What were the special characteristics of law that legal ideas spread widely and influentially? In Tocqueville's estimation, the explanation of the law's moral force was organizational: the profession was shaped so that it was specially fit to propagate ideas.

What caught Tocqueville's attention were six special features. First, the law was a text-centered organization. The text was a single, authoritative document, written and publicly accessible—the Constitution of the United States. Its terms were comprehensive and applicable to "the time and circumstances" of each generation. It was a text that the private citizen could invoke at any time to test the constitutionality of virtually any official action that grieved him. Tocqueville appreciated the sweeping application of the Constitution: "In truth, few laws can escape the searching analysis of the judicial power for any length of time, for there are few that are not prejudicial to some private interest or other, and none that may not be brought before a court of justice by the choice of parties or by the necessity of the case." As a result, "scarcely any political question ar[ose] in the United States that [was] not resolved, sooner or later, into a judicial question." Besides its general application, the Constitution was also virtually unchangeable, and sanctions were available to enforce it ("the Americans have acknowledged the right of judges to found their decisions on the *Constitution* rather than on the *laws*").[6]

Second, the legal system centered final interpretive authority of the text in a single body—the Supreme Court of the United States. Tocqueville was struck by the unity of the American legal system. Despite their large number, American judges recognized the dominance of the central judicial authority. Already in Tocqueville's time the Supreme Court of the United States was expected by lower-court judges, parties, and lawyers alike to have the final say on Constitutional questions. Tocqueville also noticed the justices employed their exegetic power with great prudence, habitually dignifying the interpretations of their lower-court brethren with approval. More important, they practiced moderation in the interpretation they gave to the text. "In order to uphold the traditionary fabric" of American society (in Tocqueville's words), they resisted sudden changes in interpretation of the text:

> If it is necessary to modify previous interpretations in any respect, to adapt them to the changes that time operates in society, recourse is had to the most inconceivable subtleties in order to uphold the traditionary fabric and to maintain that nothing has been done which does not square with the intentions and to complete the labors of former generations.[7]

In addition to possessing a public text and an exegetic unity, the law had a system to attract fresh recruits. These were enticed on the basis of personal interest and then taught not only the doctrines of the law, but the honor of it. In their students the American "schools . . . of justice" helped propagate a uniformity of approach to legal ideas.[8] Especially important to American legal studies was the reading of cases. Because the courts depended upon the law of precedents, the schooling of lawyers consisted of reading the past opinions of judges. Tocqueville noted with admiration that the curriculum of law students seemed to serve one dominating purpose, to perpetuate and transmit to the future the traditionary fabric of the nation.

Crucial to the moral force of the institution was a fourth feature: its mechanisms for supervising and disciplining the practitioners while they were working in the field. Lawyers were prompted by their self-interest to keep current on the latest judicial interpretations of legal texts and instruct their clients in them. They made their living that way: that was what their clients paid them to do. Said Tocqueville of American lawyers, "They are brought into contact with the people by their interests." Lawyers were driven by the dynamic of the marketplace to act as a subtle influence on their clients—to teach them the full import of the judges' interpretations of the Constitution on their private interests. Tocqueville was struck by the American lawyer's deference to the language of judges. An attorney, no matter his background and personality, happily bore "this servitude of thought which he [was] obliged to profess."[9]

Tocqueville's keen eye alighted on a fifth feature by which to explain the moral force of law in America: a system of commentary that enabled attorneys in the field to interact with and even influence the central judicial authority. Just as the marketplace obliged the lawyers to read the opinions of the judges, so every judge had to attend to the ideas of lawyers, who simply had to appear in court to get a judge to pay attention. Moreover, the judiciary was embedded in a network of legal literature common to practitioners, judges, legislators, and teachers of law. Furthermore, decisions never seemed to be made precipitously, but only after deliberate and widespread consultation. The freedom to interact so frequently and easily with the judiciary gave lawyers a feeling that they were true collaborators. When the judicial authority finally did act, the likelihood of resistance was considerably diminished by this feeling of collaboration.[10]

Sixth, lawyers had an esprit de corps, a sense of fraternity. Tocqueville noted that American practitioners wore "no badge peculiar to itself." Nonetheless, they carried in their heads a special common-law learning that enabled them to read the legal precedents by which Americans governed their private affairs. Tocqueville observed, "Nothing . . . can be more obscure and strange to the uninitiated than a legislation founded upon precedents. . . . [T]he American lawyer resembles the hierophants of Egypt, for like them he is the sole interpreter of an occult science." The visibility of the courts of justice, the common training of lawyers, the special language and methods of precedent that connected them and set them apart from nonlawyers—all these factors isolated lawyers as a distinct class, and they enjoyed a special prestige with the public as a result. To protect their respectability, they tended to hang together in a mutual assistance society.[11]

Thus, Tocqueville's curiosity about the penetrating influence of legal ideas led him to an institutional explanation. The six factors of text, authority, training, discipline, commentary, and symbols built a "common tie" among the lawyers that enabled them to propagate legal ideas and gave them a unity and a passion of unmatched moral force.[12]

If the legal system was an effective moral institution in Tocqueville's day, its institutional strength became even more formidable by the 1980s. The reasons were several. For one, there were many more lawyers in the nation in the twentieth century than there were in the nineteenth—more than 600,000 lawyers, one for every 400 persons.[13]

Numbers would mean nothing if contemporary lawyers lacked an intellectual discipline. On the contrary, however, the best evidence made it clear that the modern profession shared a consensus that could only be described as remarkable. In Herbert McClosky and Alida Brill's exhaustive study of civil liberties, American lawyers subscribed overwhelmingly to the Supreme Court's definitions of free speech, due process, and privacy—in striking contrast to the population at large. With respect to the Court's libertarian philosophy, lawyers were markedly more favorable than both the general public and community leaders—political officials, civic leaders, and representatives of the vocal classes such as writers and scholars. According to McClosky and Brill:

> Community leaders score significantly higher than the mass public on every item in the scale. The differences on most items fall between 15 percent and 20 percent and in some cases go as high as 25 percent or 30 percent. The libertarian scores of the legal elite are, as one might expect, even higher, and by a significant margin. The legal elite, for example, averages 15 percent higher on the individual items than the community leaders.

What accounted for this striking loyalty of lawyers to the central "judicial authority"? McClosky and Brill said that lawyers were required by their vocation to learn about the law of civil liberties and in applying it to their cases came to reflect on their merits and shortcomings and appreciate "the reciprocal obligations that a belief in civil liberties imposes upon individuals who claim them for themselves."[14]

McClosky and Brill's contemporary observations echo Tocqueville's description of the legal profession in the 1830s. Everyday application of the law reinforced what Tocqueville called the lawyers' servitude of thought.

Contributing to this striking consensus among lawyers was another factor—the modern law school. In each year of the Reagan administration the nation's 175 accredited law schools graduated nearly 40,000 new attorneys. Within the schools the profession perfected its use of the case study method of teaching. That meant virtually exclusive reliance on judicial appellate opinions as law school texts. Thereby each new generation of lawyers was trained in the thinking of their professional mentors.[15]

Another development was the growth in judicial apprenticeships (clerkships) as rewards to law students for high academic attainment. The unity of the judiciary thus was most indoctrinated in those most likely to be judges in the future.

To deal with the vast expansion of the number of lawyers the profession has improved the mechanisms for internal commentary.

Consider that in Tocqueville's day the kind of informal interaction between the central judicial authority and the practitioners in the field (which we have called the process of commentary) could take place in face-to-face meetings, thanks to the concentration of lawyers in a few cities. In the twentieth century the centers have multiplied geometrically, as have the numbers of lawyers and judges. But so has the means of commentary. The law schools spew out academic discussion of judicial work through countless law reviews. Modern transportation makes possible frequent meetings of bench and bar. Judicial education programs have brought judges within the clutches of law professors. A sophisticated system of indexing legal materials and scholarship makes it possible to retrieve the abundant precedents of the past.

The result is this. In a nation of 150 million adults more than half a million men and women practice law, share a common sense, and believe it is in their best interest to get the word of the judiciary out to clients. These half million men and women dominate public life; they occupy offices in state and national legislatures, city councils, school boards, private societies, and public agencies. Their training in oratory and writing gives them special advantages as spokesmen.

In President Reagan's day, as in Tocqueville's, the law was the nation's premier institution for propagating ideas. Its text remained the Constitution, the Supreme Court the chief exegete. (Since Tocqueville's time the ratification of the Fourteenth Amendment of the United States Constitution, which prohibits the states from depriving "any person of life, liberty, or property without due process of law," has vastly increased the scope of judicial review.) Its central axiom was an insistence on moral freedom: "The law," said Justice Benjamin Nathan Cardozo, "has been guided by a robust common sense which assumes the freedom of the will as a working hypothesis in the solution of its problems."[16] Its discipleship of a half million lawyers constituted a vast army trained and motivated to conduct themselves honorably in propagating the ideas of the central judicial authority. The disciplinary structures of the law—lower-court judges and bar associations—were firmly institutionalized, capable of dispensing powerful sanctions to punish the heretic and reward the adherent. The commentary apparatus ensuring informal interaction within the institution was never better organized. Finally, as in Tocqueville's day, the public singled out persons trained in law as members of a distinct fraternity.

In the 1980s the constitutional separation of powers kept the idea-transmitting apparatus of the law entirely independent of the president's direct influence. The president's appointive power, his one connection to the federal judiciary, was limited to filling vacancies due to retirement and death—and nominating candidates when Congress created new judgeships. (Even that one power was lacking over the state courts, which constituted the bulk of the American judiciary.) Since the appointments to the federal bench by a president's predecessors lasted a lifetime, his appointive power was constrained by their longevity. (In his first term President Reagan made only one appointment to the nine-justice Supreme Court; in his second term only two.)

Even when the president did make appointments, they were regarded as "junior" in rank in a system where seniority had its privileges. Moreover, time had to pass before the opinions of a new appointee could appear in law school textbooks as materials in the training stage of law students. Even at that, more years would have to elapse before those law students who learned from them would reach sufficient status to be influential within the profession. In other words, the power of judicial appointment was not likely to have much manifest effect until nearly two decades from the time a president reached the White House.

At the end of President Reagan's second term in office, his judicial appointees were just beginning to write the kind of opinions that embraced the president's ideas about human nature and limited government, about spiritual values and the social and moral consequences of economic freedom and volunteerism. At that point—but not before—it became clear to many observers that it was just a matter of time before the judiciary would reinforce the president's philosophy.[17]

Yet it was also clear that during his eight years in office Reagan had already found some way to get the word out. The ideas of the president had already penetrated the din and clamor of American society—without the assistance of the law.

How had Reagan done it? He borrowed an institution that, from a moral viewpoint, shared many of the organizational features of the law. It had a text that provided continuity, mental discipline, and comprehensive application. It had an exegetic mechanism, a way of providing some kind of final say in interpretive disputes of the text. It had a means of educating those who would teach its word and of replenishing their ranks when they tired or died. It had disciplinary mechanisms to keep their commitment to the word alive and unambiguous. It had a well-developed system of commentary, which decreased the chances of deep schism and nurtured energy and a sense of participation. And, finally, it had a set of symbols and lore that fortified a sense of identification.

In short, President Reagan found another moral institution. It was not quite the equal of the law in its effectiveness in getting the president's word out, but it was not bad. It was the religious community.[18]

11

★★★★★★★

Religion: A Fruitful
Moral Institution

*The United States political philosophy stands at the intersection of
religion and politics.*

—Peter Robinson (1984)

*America is more than just government on the one hand and helpless
individuals on the other.*

—Ronald Reagan (1984)

Without the length of tenure or the manpower to organize a nationwide
moral institution of his own, a president in the 1980s had to piggyback
his message on an established moral institution.[1] At the time the United
States was constituted of many associations that had at least some of the
characteristics of a moral institution. In addition to the law, there was
the clergy, organized labor, the business community, academia, the
literary world, the public school system, the psychoanalytic community,
the military, the entertainment business, and the news media. They were
all capable of propagating general ideas. Some had a text and a central
interpretive authority; most had extensive recruiting and post-entry
training programs; and many had commentary procedures by which the
men and women in the field could converse with authority at the center.
Religion, however, provided a pair of advantages to the president:
institutional strength and philosophical congruence.

First, the church was more widespread, more fervent, and more
intellectually disciplined than any other American institution engaged

in the propagation of ideas—except the law. The institutional power of religion lay in the number and discipline of its ministry. In the 1980s, more than 300,000 trained clergy were dispersed to virtually every locality in America.[2] A multitude of Catholic, Jewish, and Protestant seminaries was established to train recruits in the text of the Bible. Upon graduation, most clergymen and women abided by the discipline of their sectarian organizations. A rich network of commentary (pastoral letters, journals, theological presses, radio and television networks) flourished, and the symbols of the Cross and the Star of David set clergy apart from the laity and gave them a visibility and stature among their adherents, who were themselves vast in number. Forty million Americans attended church regularly, and more than 80 million Americans had received religious training as youngsters.

The weakness of religion as a moral institution was its lack of a central authority: there was no chief exegete to resolve arguments over application of the biblical text. As a result, the various sects took different approaches to such fundamental controversies as abortion, pacifism, and commerce. The unresolved discord of the clergy sharply contrasted with the organizational unity within the legal profession.

Of course, some degree of civilized debate within a moral institution can be stimulating and, in promoting excitement, can actually create cohesion. But factionalism—controversy between irreconcilable groups—blunted the force of religion as a moral institution. The competing and autonomous sects insisted on their own interpretations of the biblical text. The traditions of Protestantism, with its principle of "a priesthood of all believers," encouraged theological independence.[3] Maverick churchmen, unlike lawyers, could always continue preaching despite being defrocked; they could practice their ministry without a license—if their followers followed them.[4]

Although religion suffered from a factionalism not found in the law, its disunity was hardly of a scale that greatly enfeebled it. In terms of institutional strength, religion was second best to the law—but a powerful second best.

Philosophical congruence was the second factor that made religion a good partner of the Reagan presidency. In the president's search for moral institutions on which to piggyback, he was limited to those with compatible creeds. If he wanted to use an organization's text, exegetics, schooling, discipline, commentary, and symbolism for his own purposes, he would have to return the favor. He would have to confer prominence upon its doctrines, galvanize its disciples, and vest its commentaries with importance. He would not want to do that to an institution founded on beliefs that were fundamentally at odds with his own.[5] The church, being preoccupied with human meaning, provided a natural fit with Reagan's philosophy of human freedom.

Why were the churches willing to involve their destiny with his? In America, after all, religious organizations could choose to keep themselves apart. The president lacked the appointive power over their officers, and the principle of the separation of church and state deprived him of regulatory and fiscal authority over them.

What made them susceptible to presidential influence was their disunity. As the various religious factions competed for adherents and status, they looked for outside help. For the support of the president, they would gladly give him a platform to address their congregants.

The ingredients of a mutually profitable partnership were present. What was the nature of that partnership? What was the rhetorical consequence of it? And how effective was this collaboration of church and president in getting the president's word out?

First, the partnership of the presidency and the church was forged by a common social task. They preached the importance of not giving up. To put it another way, both defined the moral worth of trying and of instilling hope by emphasizing the unique dignity of human life.

Recall a remark by Peter Robinson mentioned in Chapter Four: "the United States political philosophy stands at the intersection of religion and politics."[6] By "the United States political philosophy" Robinson meant the moral revolution the president was seeking to bring about, but what did he mean when he said that it stands at the intersection of religion and politics?

He was suggesting that the president and the clergy occupied common ground—their intersection—because they both supplied the public with an answer to Hamlet's famous question, why undertake "enterprises of great pitch and moment" when, after all, we eventually die? President Reagan expected churchmen to speak to that question, and they expected him to do the same. No matter their denomination, clergy were in the business of speaking to their congregants about the meaning of mortality.

And so was the president. He held an office that had, from the earliest days of the nation, taken the responsibility for providing solace and hope to a people troubled by death. For example, as commander-in-chief of the nation's armed forces and chief diplomat, Reagan was notified of every death in the ranks. He personally called the kin of all military and diplomatic personnel killed in attacks by terrorists, major accidents, and police actions. He honored the dead and consoled the survivors of public calamity. He met with the kin of Vietnam veterans still missing in action. His presence was often requested when survivors of the Holocaust held commemorative ceremonies in Washington. He represented the nation at the Tomb of the Unknown Soldier and the Vietnam War Memorial.

All speechwriters understood the importance of this presidential function. Peggy Noonan discussed Reagan's recurrent appearances at commemorations and the appropriateness of his speaking philosophically on those occasions: "These speeches speak to the drama of man. They look at life with a broader point of view. They provide a context for life."[7]

Dolan, too, emphasized the importance of the president's presence at times of great national sorrow, to redeem the loss by reminding men of the brevity of existence on earth and the preciousness of their living well: "There are just some important things you must know about human existence. And probably the most important of them is, we come into the world to die."[8]

The commemoration of countrymen—the funeral oration—offered constant opportunity to the president to speak of death's inevitability and put that fact into "a context for life." What was life? And was there life after death? Did the effects of personal honesty and love and decency abide beyond a man's lifetime? In contrast, did barbarity and greed, the evil of men, fall into dishonor as soon as their perpetrators died? Was there any such thing as immortality, and if so, what difference might it make in the ways a person chose to conduct his life?

When the president addressed these existential questions, the religious community sat up and took notice. Clergymen had a professional stake in paying attention to him if he could help them do their jobs better. Engaged in a profession where they spoke to the very same issues as he, they were willing to learn from their fellow professional.

In short, they were prepared to hear, if Reagan was willing to make the effort to speak. And Reagan was plenty willing to exert himself to speak. In his eight years as president nearly one speech in ten was devoted to what might be called religious discourse: orations at funerals, lectures to clerical audiences, and speeches on themes of professional interest to the clergy (Table 1).

In 1984, for example, a year in which one speech in eight was religious in nature, the president gave eighteen funeral orations, commemorating (among others) Princess Grace of Monaco, President Harry Truman, Senator Henry Jackson, Vice President Hubert Humphrey, Terence Cardinal Cooke, along with American servicemen who had died over the previous four decades in Normandy (1944), Vietnam (1963–1976), and Grenada (1983). In addition, he addressed nine different religious audiences, including the National Religious Broadcasters, the Baptist Fundamentalists, the National Association of Evangelicals, the New York State Federation of Catholic School Parents, and B'nai B'rith. On fifteen more occasions he devoted his remarks primarily to religious issues of importance to the clergy, the most significant of which was a speech at an ecumenical prayer breakfast at the Republican national convention in Dallas.

Table 1
Religious Discourse of President Reagan, 1981–1989

Year	Total prepared remarks[a]	Total religious discourse (no.)	(%)	Speeches to religious audiences	Funeral orations	Speeches with religious themes
1981	160	13	8.1	1	7	5
1982	245	24	9.8	9	6	9
1983	282	24	8.5	4	12	8
1984	334	42	12.6	9	18	15
1985	210	20	9.5	4	10	6
1986	257	20	7.8	2	9	9
1987	262	21	8.0	3	7	11
1988	298	27	9.1	4	12	11
Total	2,048	191	9.3 (ave.)	36	81	74

a. Does not include remarks prepared for visits by foreign leaders and for press conferences and interviews with journalists.

To put in perspective the sheer quantity of Reagan's religious discourse, let us compare his schedule with that of a previous president who was thought to be a devout man. Take the third year of Reagan's presidency (1983), and contrast it with the third year of the presidency of his immediate predecessor, Jimmy Carter (1979). Even though Carter was a self-described born-again Christian, he gave eleven religious discourses (and only if you stretch that term to the absolute limit), whereas Reagan gave twenty-four. More interesting, Carter scheduled himself to speak to no clergy: he addressed not a single audience of clericals. The only religious audience he spoke to was a group of laymen, the National Conference of Catholic Charities (a speech in which he did not discuss religion).[9] Moreover, Carter gave only one funeral oration that commemorated an individual.

An even more important difference was in the quality of the discourses of the two presidents. Where Reagan's discussions of religion were always serious and usually elaborated, Carter's religious allusions could best be described as perfunctory. Not one demonstrated even the most elementary development. Even at the National Prayer Breakfast, Carter devoted virtually every word to questions of government policy.[10]

What was the rhetorical consequence of the president's collaboration with the church "at the intersection of religion and politics"? His general political philosophy became more coherent and restrained as a result of his religious discourse. In harmonizing moral notions of personal responsibility with religious beliefs of brotherhood and charity, the speechwriters orchestrated the president's political convictions and pruned out earlier partisan excesses. The president's philosophy was reset in principles sufficiently universal and abiding that the clergy was pleased to amplify it.

What enabled the Reagan presidency to recompose its ideas so fittingly that the religious community found it attractive? Repetition. The president kept showing up—repeatedly.

Repetition is a big part of any president's rhetorical life, but it was especially instrumental in Reagan's penetration of the nation's religious institutions. He reappeared before the same audiences. He repeated the same ceremonial functions. He returned to the same philosophical subjects.

This repetition had three effects on the president's speechwriting team. First, it provided second chances; the president could speak once, learn from his mistakes, and have the speechwriters take another go at the same subject. Second, reappearing before the same audiences kept him consistent; audiences had memories, which forced him to adhere to the same themes. Third, in rehashing old topics he was forced to deepen their development and advance new applications.

Just as professors refine the statement of their ideas through repeated presentations of them, so it was with the president and the speechwriters. And presidential reappearances before the same audience, besides their obvious political utility, offered valuable opportunities to expand upon old notions.

In the dozen funeral orations President Reagan gave each year, he could not avoid facing the question, what was life's meaning? A funeral was about a man or woman who was born and lived among us and died. No mortal was free from that fate. Think of the questions an audience thought about at a funeral: What might I do with the remainder of my brief life? Was anything important, important enough to die for, if death was final? Why try, why sacrifice, why do something that would only benefit the long run? What motivated this dead man or woman to have lived a good life, and what could I learn from it to apply to my conduct? If the person being commemorated was the victim of someone else's brutality, what caused people to do such harm? What were the effects of good and bad acts? Was there hope of immortality?

Now, no individual elected to the presidency was likely to have had more than minimal experience commemorating the dead. The typical public-spirited citizen—even a governor of a populous state like

California—was comparatively inexperienced in honoring the dead and consoling the living.

Therefore, comparing the president's commemorative remarks at the beginning and end of his first term provides a chance to see the effects of repetition in "improving" his philosophical discourse. In Reagan's case, let us look for the things not done at first, but done with experience.

In this light consider the president's commemoration of Senator Robert Kennedy in 1981, and contrast it with what the president said in 1984 in praise of the late senator Henry Jackson and the late vice president Hubert Humphrey.

Thirteen years after his assassination in 1968, Robert Kennedy was honored with a Congressional Medal in his memory. At a White House ceremony President Reagan's remarks to his widow and friends were gracious:

> Robert Kennedy's service to his country, his commitment to his great ideals, and his devotion to those less fortunate than himself are matters now for history and need little explanation from me. The facts of Robert Kennedy's public career stand alone. He roused the comfortable. He exposed the corrupt, remembered the forgotten, inspired his countrymen, and renewed and enriched the American conscience.[11]

Although the president suggested that Kennedy's works were so well known that they required little explanation, a listener might have said that an explanation was exactly what was needed—an explanation, for example, of why Kennedy chose life and to serve, while others—for example, his assassin—chose death and to slay? What was it in the make-up of Robert Kennedy that led him to expend his days on earth doing useful work? What difference did it make that he chose to do so? And, finally, was he different from the rest of mankind, or was he typical? To none of those questions did the president's eulogy speak.

Three years later the president conferred posthumously the Presidential Medal of Freedom on another Democratic senator, Henry ("Scoop") Jackson. Like Kennedy, Jackson had run for the presidency and lost his party's nomination. Like Kennedy, he was a brave and committed public servant.

The president, however, made an explanation of Jackson's deeds the centerpiece of his remarks.[12] He avoided portraying the late senator as a man heroically fashioned by providence. Rather, Reagan depicted him as the son of immigrant parents, whose Norwegian homeland was invaded by the Nazis in World War II. In that national tragedy Jackson saw how bullies brutalized a population too undefended to protect themselves. "And from then until the day he died," the president explained, "he rejected isolationism as an acceptable way for a great democracy to comport itself in the world." Then the president exposed a deeper level of the man. He spoke of Jackson's first glimpse of the Nazi death camp at Buchenwald and how it had moved him. Jackson's commitment to protect Israel and other free countries, according to the president, was crystallized by Buchenwald: "It wasn't some grand geopolitical abstraction that made him back the creation of Israel; it was seeing the concentration camps first hand at the end of the war. At Buchenwald he saw the evil, as he said, 'written in the sky,' and he never forgot." Buchenwald was why "Scoop was always at the side of the weak and the forgotten."

From Buchenwald's effect on Jackson, Reagan turned to demonstrating Jackson's effects on others:

> A few years ago [Senator Jackson] was invited to visit the Soviet Union. The invitation was withdrawn when he said he could not go without calling on Andrei Sakharov. If Scoop were here today, I know he would speak out on behalf of Sakharov, just as Sakharov, a man of immense courage and humanity, stood up in Moscow and hailed the Jackson amendment as a triumph of "the freedom-loving tradition of the American people."

Goodness inspired goodness in others and ignited human energies in ways that could never be completely anticipated. The principled goodness of Jackson and Sakharov mutually inspired immense courage. In a second tale the president demonstrated how the good that men did in their lifetimes survived their deaths.

> The principles which guided [Senator Jackson's] public life guided his private life. By the time he died, dozens of young men and women had been helped through school by a scholarship fund that he established and sustained. No one knew the money came from Scoop, until a change in the financial disclosure laws many years later forced him to 'fess up. He had never told the voters; he'd never even told his staff.
> Other people were embarrassed when the disclosure law revealed their vanities. Scoop was embarrassed when it revealed his virtues.

The particularity of the events depicted in the president's eulogy of Senator Jackson helped teach general lessons about human character—its causes and its consequences—in a way missing from the earlier, more abstract praise of Robert Kennedy.

Several months later, the president conferred the Congressional Gold Medal on a third Democratic senator, the late Hubert Humphrey of Minnesota.[13] The commemorative remarks contained the same loving detail as the ones for Jackson. The stories about Humphrey not only captured his zest and love, but provided, in the president's words, "a surer sense of [Humphrey's] real dimensions . . . his nature, his character, his personality."

> In the last few weeks of [Senator Humphrey's] life, as he lay dying, an amazing healing process began. He got a WATS line, and he called his old friends and his old adversaries, and one after one he told them, "I wish you well." And the calls came in, too, from all across the country. Old opponents called in, and young people just entering politics. Powerful political figures called, and obscure farmers. It was as if all of them were trying to reconnect with a part of an unchanging political past, trying to touch for the last time a special spirit and a special style that would go with Hubert Humphrey's passing. It's said that a lot of love passed along the lines those last few days. There was a lot of forgiving and a lot of encouraging and a lot of sharing of wisdom.

The president spoke fondly of Senator Humphrey's faults ("and then there were others that said he was downright garrulous") and virtues ("he'd laugh when someone said he'd never had an unuttered thought") lovingly intermixed.

Out of the loving description of the particulars of Humphrey's and Jackson's lives, the president sought to draw general lessons about the human impulse to benevolence, the importance of memory, the pervasiveness of evil in the world and the moral choice to resist it, and above all the personal strength derived from commitment to causes larger than the self. Jackson's and Humphrey's lives gave the lie to any illusions about human nature, either its perfectibility or its impotence. In repeating the commemorative ceremony, the president and the Speechwriting Department learned to teach about the human heart.

An audience's expectations often dictated what the president could talk about. The reactions he anticipated would encourage (or discourage) him and his speechwriters to take up a particular topic. Of course, the president had considerable freedom to choose his audiences, but once that choice was made, the range of topics he could discuss narrowed considerably. An audience that expected to hear about the economy, for example, would resist a speech on some other topic, and the president had to respect their expectations. If a particular audience dictated a particular topic, the president's choice to reappear before that audience signified his desire to continue to keep talking about that topic.

Each year from 1982 to 1988, the president talked to the National Association of Religious Broadcasters, which held its annual convention in Washington, D.C. The number who came was staggering: 3,500 or more clergy (Protestant, Catholic, and Jewish), who regularly discussed matters of religion on radio and television. Some broadcasters were well-known Protestant evangelists, like Ben Armstrong, Jerry Falwell, and Jim Bakker; the bulk of them, however, spoke to local audiences only.

Over the years the president's speeches to the National Association of Religious Broadcasters covered many topics, but he always returned to one, What was the church in a free society? In 1982 in his first appearance as president, he spoke to them of the origins of American churches. He recalled America's starting point: The United States was "a country [that] was created by men and women who came not for gold but mainly in search of God."[14] "Faith in their maker" caused Americans to form local, voluntary churches on the basis of their shared values.

American churches, said the president, were institutions of the people. They were places where friends came together. Churches tapped "a deep spirit of love—of caring and willingness to work together." Churches focused their members' energies on the accomplishment of significant and visible objectives. Churches made it possible for people to accomplish important and worthwhile deeds. As a result each church community discovered the secret of collective power. They found they were not impotent and isolated individuals, and by learning the arts of cooperation, they could help each other surmount sizable problems beyond the power of any single individual. Having learned how to be effective, they applied their skills to benevolent purposes. Said the president:

> But too many people have been told that what they do is not as important or worthwhile as what government does. I don't buy that. Last week at the Annual Prayer Breakfast, I spoke of the parable of the good Samaritan. And I've always believed that the meaning and the importance of that parable is not so much the good that was done to the beaten Pilgrim [as] it was to the Samaritan who crossed the road, who knelt down and bound up the wounds of the beaten traveler, and then carried him into the nearest town. He didn't take a look and hurry on by into the town and then find a caseworker and say, "There's somebody out there on the road I think needs help."

What churches did was to give outlet to the soul's need to be an effective Samaritan. They gave men the confidence to be good. By joining "friends" with common aspirations, the church focused their love into a powerful social force. Churches functioned to enhance the chances of successful benevolence: "We'll never find every answer, solve every problem, heal every wound, or live all our dreams. But we can do a lot if we work together down that one path that all know provides real hope."

Churches taught the morality and the skills of working together: they reinforced the reciprocal rule of freedom, "what we give will be given back many times over." Not only did American churches teach the art of cooperation, but they played the broker's role by connecting volunteers with those in need.

A year later the president again appeared before the religious broadcasters. Again his speech covered a great many political topics (like school prayer, tax credits for parochial school tuition, and abortion), but at the end he returned to the topic of the church in a free society, this time turning to the economic consequences of the good works done by an effective congregation.[15]

He repeated much that he had said the year before: The church was a voluntary association, within which "we gather together" to keep alive and give outlet to our spiritual instinct to build a better community—to help "needy families," "to provide food, clothing, furniture, and job bank centers at no cost," "to exercise the 'good' in America's heart."

Having summarized the previous year's speech, he touched on the difference churches could make if they organized a community's instinct for benevolence. The more active the church became, the less active the government would have to be: "Each year, government bureaucracies spend billions for problems related to drugs and alcoholism and disease. Has anyone stopped to consider that we might come closer to balancing the budget if all of us simply tried to live up to the Ten Commandments and the Golden Rule?"

In 1984 he made his third appearance before the religious broadcasters.[16] He did not return to the possible budgetary implications of church volunteerism. Rather, this time he spoke of the church's importance in political and moral terms. He put the church in its larger social context, as mediator between the powerful state and the individual.

> Look at projects like CBN's [Christian Broadcasting Network] "Operation Blessing," Moody Bible Institute's "Open Line" radio program, "Inner City" of Chicago, and the work of Dr. E. V. Hill of Mount Zion Baptist Church in Los Angeles. They show us that America is more than just government on the one hand and helpless individuals on the other. They show us that lives are saved, people are reborn and, yes, dreams come true when we heed the voice of the spirit, minister to the needy, and glorify God. That is the stuff of which miracles are made.

"That America is more than just government on the one hand and helpless individuals on the other"—with that phrase the president and his speechwriters defined for the church a social role strikingly akin to Tocqueville's notion of "intermediate powers." The church provided ordinary citizens the chance to associate and learn about problems beyond their own private lives. They listened—through broadcasts such as "Open Line"—to the needs of others and enlarged their horizons as a result.

Through their direct involvement in benevolent enterprises, they developed confidence in themselves and found the courage to stand up for what they believed. Church membership enabled willing individuals to escape isolation and selfishness.

That was the theme the president developed in his repeat performances before the religious broadcasters. At first, his notions were inchoate and particular ("But too many people have been told that what they do is not as important or worthwhile as what government does. I don't buy that."). In subsequent iterations his theme expanded. The church became the archetypal intermediate power, bringing individuals together in common concern, bolstering self-confidence in collective enterprise, and encouraging them to act independently of government.[17]

The president, by returning to the same audience year after year, returned to the same questions. The expectations of the audience almost compelled him to do so. In the case of the religious broadcasters, once the president began discussing the topic of the church's role in a free society, their favorable reactions encouraged him to stick to the subject.

There was a third kind of repetition, the repetition of a story, and with each occurrence the point got more and more finely expressed and the implications more fully evoked. The president and his speechwriters would return again and again to a particular text, sensing increasing significance with every repetition. (Such might happen because more than one speechwriter would work with the same story.)

Whittaker Chambers's description of his conversion from communism to freedom is a case in point. Chambers (1901–1961), an American journalist, had joined the Communist party in the 1930s and performed espionage in Washington, D.C., for the Soviet Union. After a decade's experience with the party, he renounced communism. In 1948 he told the Federal Bureau of Investigation about the spy ring he had joined, and when one of its alleged members, Alger Hiss, denied Chambers's allegations, the lawsuit between the two men became one of the great dramas of our time. Chambers subsequently wrote his memoirs, *Witness*, in which he spoke of the reasons for his renunciation of communism and embrace of Christianity. We have already encountered one of the speeches in which the president mentioned Chambers, the so-called evil empire speech to the Evangelicals in Orlando in 1983. Chambers's description of his disenchantment with communism appeared often in the president's remarks.

His first reference to Chambers was in 1981 before the Conservative Political Action Conference (C-PAC). C-PAC was an umbrella organization embracing the American Conservative Union, the Young Americans for Freedom, the *National Review* (William Buckley's magazine), and

Human Events (another conservative periodical). The president met with C-PAC in every year of his administration. It was always his friendliest audience, and he used the affection of his adherents to speak of his conservative principles. The members of C-PAC wanted Reagan to be Reagan, and he was every bit of that.

At the first of his eight C-PAC dinners, Reagan expressed his political creed much as he had formulated it throughout the campaign of 1980: "robust individualism," "regard for the social consensus that gives stability to our public and private institutions," the removal of "government's smothering hand from where it does harm," revitalizing "those social and economic institutions which serve as a buffer and a bridge between the individual and the state," renewal of "our spiritual strength," and so on.[18] In defining the difference between the Western heritage and the Marxist vision, the president turned to Whittaker Chambers for a description of his disillusionment with communism:

> That's why the Marxist version of man without God must eventually be seen as an empty and a false faith—the second oldest in the world—first proclaimed in the Garden of Eden with whispered words of temptation: "Ye shall be as gods." The crisis of the Western world, Whittaker Chambers reminded us, exists to the degree in which it is indifferent to God. "The Western world does not know it," he said about our struggle, "but it already possesses the answer to this problem—but only provided that its faith in God and the freedom He enjoins is as great as communism's faith in man."

What did that passage mean in the president's speech in 1981? Religious faith made men humble. Men must resist the temptation of putting their faith in other men. The illusion of the perfected society, on the one hand, was false and tempted those who believed otherwise to use "barbed wire and terror"—totalitarian powers—to pursue human perfection and reap the wind. Religion, on the other hand, gave courage to the individual to admit his original and inescapable sin and to construct a free society according to that human truth.

In suggesting that religious faith was necessary to be a decent human being, Whittaker Chambers posed an intellectual challenge to explain why that should be so. No less than four times during 1982 the president was drawn back to the Chambers text.

In his second appearance at the C-PAC dinner the president talked of the importance of economic recovery as a means for individuals "to better their own lives and those of millions of others around the world."[19] That betterment occurred only where there existed "the great civilized ideas of individual liberty, representative government, and the rule of law under God." The president again referred to Chambers, "who sought idealism in communism and found only disillusionment." His awakening occurred one morning at breakfast as he was looking at the delicate ear of his baby daughter: "He knew that couldn't just be an accident of nature. He said, while he didn't realize it at the time, he knows now that in that moment God had touched his forehead with his finger."

Religion not only required political humility, but also justified freedom and the political institutions that made it possible to live free—the rule of law, democracy, and personal rights. The president quoted Chambers directly:

> For in this century, within the next decades, will be decided for genera-
> tions whether all mankind is to become Communist, whether the
> whole world is to become free, or whether in the struggle civilization
> as we know it is to be completely destroyed or completely changed.
> It is our fate to live upon that turning point in history.

But Chambers's insight compelled the president to deepen the inquiry. Why was it that if an individual did not "awaken" to God, he would not even attempt to preserve the institutions that made a free society possible? Why was religion essential to the preservation of freedom? He addressed that question a year later in Orlando, Florida, in the so-called evil empire speech (see Chapter Six).

His argument was as follows.[20] Personal morality was invariably subordinate to a higher purpose. Individuals, in interpreting the letter of their personal moral codes, looked to the spirit that they saw lying behind their principles of right and wrong. Otherwise, there was no way to bridge the gap between abstract principle and concrete situation. The formulation of higher purpose grew out of the individual's instinctive hankering for immortality. Man's instinct was to resist mortality by connecting with something permanent. That instinct was man's religious sense, and since man had entered the world, he had been thrown back upon one or the other of two ideas about this immortal connection. One was a spiritual god, and if persons embraced a loving version of that god—that is, one who demanded "concern for others"—then each interpretation of their personal morality would be biased to serve that higher purpose, regard for "the sacredness of human life." Between one's obligations to a loving god and respecting individuals, there would be no conflict.

If, however, one rejected a spiritual notion of god, man's religious nature still had to be satisfied. He had to have a star to attach his moral sense to. He had to connect himself to something immortal on earth, and the state invariably was the sole candidate. If he made the state the object of his religious sense, then the state's preservation became the higher purpose within which one's personal morality was recurrently interpreted. It became "the final cause," elevated to the position of god, with a higher dignity than the mortal instruments of its preservation. The state had its privileges when it was elevated to the level of god. The president quoted William Penn: "If we will not be governed by God, we must be governed by tyrants."

The president turned to the insight of Whittaker Chambers to make his point: "The crisis of the Western World exists to the degree in which the West is indifferent to God, the degree to which it collaborates in communism's attempt to make man stand alone without God." While quoting the same words of Chambers as he had in 1981, he construed them to emphasize that the essence of human nature was the religious sense. Men were critically enfeebled when they denied its centrality.

A year later, on March 6, 1984, the president met again with the Evangelicals, this time in Columbus, Ohio. The topic was "religious values in public life." He repeated the story of Whittaker Chambers, adding, "When men try to live in a world without God, it's only too easy for them to forget the rights that God bestows—too easy to suppress freedom of speech, to build walls to keep their countrymen in, to jail dissidents, and to put great thinkers in mental wards."[21]

Without the countervailing power of religion, said Reagan, those who seized the mantle of the state indulged their envy and their hatreds, exercising the state's monopoly of organized coercion and cruelty. Where there was religion with a loving god, there was a widespread moral consensus that made it difficult, not easy, for bullies to consolidate their control of the state's terrible weapons. The dilemma of modern politics—how to make government strong enough to be effective, yet weak enough to keep it safe—rested on a fundamentally medieval answer: the cross-purposes of Caesar and God.

In exploring why religion was necessary to make humanity decent, the president spoke before friendly audiences, out of sight of the general public. But once he had tried the argument out and it felt satisfactory, the president gave it the broadest public exposure, at a time when the press and citizenry were paying maximum attention. The site he chose to set out his mature thinking was the 1984 Republican convention in Dallas, Texas. The occasion was the ecumenical prayer breakfast, with thousands in attendance and the whole event nationally televised. It was an eloquent testimony to the importance of religion in a free nation.[22]

As he often did, he sketched the importance the Founding Fathers placed on religion as "the bedrock of moral order" and decried the attacks upon religion over the past two decades by "those who care only for the interests of the state." But as he came to his conclusion, he expressed the relationship between religion and the individual.

The truth is, politics and morality are inseparable. And as morality's foundation is religion, religion and politics are necessarily related. We need religion as a guide. We need it because we are imperfect, and our government needs the church, because only those humble enough to admit they're sinners can bring to democracy the tolerance it requires in order to survive.

A state is nothing more than a reflection of its citizens; the more decent the citizens, the more decent the state. If you practice a religion, whether you're Catholic, Protestant, Jewish, or guided by some other faith, then your private life will be influenced by a sense of moral obligation, and so too, will your public life. One affects the other. The churches of America do not exist by the grace of the state; the churches of America are not mere citizens of the state. The churches of America exist apart; they have their own vantage point; their own authority. Religion is its own realm; it makes its own claims.

We establish no religion in this country, nor will we ever. We command no worship. We mandate no belief. But we poison our society when we remove its theological underpinnings. We court corruption when we leave it bereft of belief. All are free to believe or not believe; all are free to practice a faith or not. But those who believe must be free to speak of and act on their belief, to apply moral teaching to public questions. . . .

Without God, there is no virtue, because there's no prompting of the conscience. Without God, we're mired in the material, that flat world that tells us only what the senses perceive. Without God, there is a coarsening of the society. And without God, democracy will not and cannot long endure. If we ever forget that we're one nation under God, then we will be a nation gone under.

Whittaker Chambers was not mentioned in the speech, but it was his testimony on which the president drew, the "witness" of one who discovered that "without God" he had suppressed the prompting of his conscience. Without religion Chambers found himself "coarsening" and, worse, subservient to a belief in a corrupt and increasingly purposeless state.

With each religious occasion the speechwriters developed the president's argument further. They played with subtle distinctions, and they fleshed out the connections between ideas.

Many factors contributed to this development. First was the president himself. He had religious convictions, and the speechwriters knew it. They knew he cared about the problems being puzzled over, and he conveyed how much he cared to the Speechwriting Department by the care with which he spoke to religious audiences, by his suggestions for topics (such as Chaplain Resnicoff's letter about the Marine barracks in Beirut; see Chapter Seven), and by his editing of religious talks. His reactions permitted the speechwriters to be open to their own religious faith and intuition. He never showed fatigue or rancor about repeating over and over again some of the same words.

Second was the license the president and the speechwriters had in developing their own thinking independently of the rest of the executive. Unlike other topics, religion and spiritual themes were of no interest to executive agencies, which left such speeches alone. As Peter Robinson pointed out in sincere surprise, when speaking of the president's 1984 address to the National Association of Evangelicals, "On this speech no agency was involved at all."[23]

And there was a third factor: the reaction of the religious audiences. They were galvanized by the president's words and thrust themselves into the debates raging within the religious community. They took his ideas into the discourse of the ministry. They confronted fellow professionals with his words, and if there was disagreement, they confidently put their opponents on the defensive. They egged the president on to think through his ideas more deeply. Professional journals on the subject of religion and politics were begun or revived in the spirit of his ideas.[24] They were debated in the corridors of theological seminaries and religious universities, written about in newspaper columns, and talked about from pulpits and public lecterns.[25] The president's words entered into an ongoing commentary within the religious community.[26]

Did the words spoken by the president and spread by the religious community make a difference? The evidence is hard to gather: How many sermons were given more confidently? How many counseling sessions advanced differently because the clergyman felt inspired?

But think about those two thousand evangelical Methodist and Baptist ministers in convention in Florida in 1983. They appreciated the president making a coherent and eloquent connection between the theological axiom of original sin and the political realities of the day. Or think of those four thousand religious broadcasters, who year after year cheered his efforts to define the place of the church in a free society. When the clergy went home to their congregations and the broadcasters returned to their studios, their memory of the president, dealing with the theological and social problems at the center of their ministry, must have reinvigorated them. And with that extra vigor these communicators, these counselors to others, these *verbal* men and women, spread the president's words.

12

★★★★★★★

Business: A Shallow Moral Institution

President Coolidge, a man I greatly admire, said, "In all our economic discussions we must remember that we cannot stop with the mere acquisition of wealth. The ultimate result is not the making of money, but the making of people. Industry, thrift, and self-control are not sought because they create wealth, but because they create character."

—Ronald Reagan (1982)

To spread his word further the president enlisted the assistance of a second institution, business. Or rather he tried to. As he did with America's religious institutions, he sought to formulate a fundamental notion, repeat it, and have the converted go forth to propagate it in the commercial world.

The idea that Reagan advanced was that commerce supplied personal freedom with manners: those who participated in the marketplace were made kind and trustworthy. But the business community proved to be a poor transmitter. Unlike the clergy, it lacked the sustained ardor necessary to spread the president's word effectively. The kind of intense discourse that led to a society's changing its mind never occurred within the business community.

Why? I believe the answer has to do with what I have called the process of commentary. The business community lacked a forum where philosophical questions were debated in depth among its members and up and down political hierarchies. That missing feature mortally weakened business as a moral institution for the president's purposes. But we are jumping ahead to the conclusion. We need some background.

Karl Marx, one of capitalism's most perceptive observers, insisted on two truths about economic freedom: it made men energetic, and it produced unparalleled prosperity. At the same time, the marketplace produced one vice—it corrupted human nature, driving out love and stimulating greed and mean-spiritedness. Although freedom of competition was personally invigorating and a bonanza economically, it was a disaster morally. Capitalism deserved two cheers, not three.

The president dissented. Could it be that capitalism ennobled, that it supported generous instincts and created habits of public-spiritedness? Was it not apparent under closer scrutiny that the moral byproduct of the competitive marketplace was to "unlock what is best in human nature"?[1] Was not Calvin Coolidge right when he said, "The ultimate result [of capitalism] is not the making of money, but the making of people [with character]"?[2] To the president it seemed plausible that the foremost value of economic freedom was not that it made good products, but that it made producers good. Three cheers for capitalism!

The notion that commerce civilized, that business turned its practitioners into benefactors, was a strangely unconventional idea in the public discourse of the United States during much of the twentieth century. Since the Great Depression, in fact, many who had occupied the presidency had frequently maintained the opposite. In his inaugural address in 1933, to recall one example, Franklin Roosevelt denounced the morality of commerce, scorned the pettiness of profit-seeking, and accused business leaders of knowing only the rules of "a generation of self-seekers. . . . The money changers have fled from their high seats in the temple of civilization. We may now restore that temple to the ancient truths. The measure of the restoration lies in the extent to which we apply social values more noble than mere monetary profit."[3]

The morals of money changers and business leaders were ignoble, predatory, and self-seeking.

It was true that once in a while Roosevelt might turn a conciliatory glance on the private sector. The president said to the Chicago Chamber of Commerce during his 1936 presidential campaign that he had always believed in private enterprise as "the backbone of economic well-being in the United States." But Roosevelt never said that private entrepreneurs were good people, nor that they were the moral backbone of American society. Quite the contrary. Even as some of his words denied that all businessmen were greedy and unscrupulous, his rhetorical flourishes actually focused hatred against the business leadership:

> Let me make one simple statement. When I refer to [the immorality of] high finance, I am not talking about all great bankers, or all great corporation executives, or all multimillionaires—any more than

> Theodore Roosevelt, in using the term "malefactors of great wealth,"
> implied that all men of great wealth were "malefactors." I do not even
> imply that the majority of them are bad citizens. The opposite is true.[4]

"Malefactors of great wealth," "bad citizens"—if those were phrases repeated in a spirit of conciliation, think of what he said in a more agitated spirit or before an audience more ready to credit direct denunciation. Then he would talk of "war" against the profit seekers. In speaking to a partisan Jackson Day Dinner crowd in 1936, he said: "The Government of the United States seeks to give [the people] a square deal, and a better deal—seeks to protect them, yes, to save them from being plowed under by the small minority of businessmen and financiers against whom you and I will continue to wage war."[5]

In these more gentle times the imagery of civil war, pitting American against American, might surprise, but the violence with which Roosevelt denounced businessmen and financiers was unmistakable.

He repeated his attack on commerce on numerous occasions. In his 1936 annual message to Congress, for example, he denounced the private sector as "a resplendent economic autocracy," in which the "rulers" of the marketplace, financed by "unscrupulous money-changers," played by rules in which "the advantages . . . went to the ruthless and the strong."[6] The achievement of the New Deal, he said, had been to overthrow the capitalist regime of yesteryears and to establish the government as the "trustee of the public interest." "Our aim was to build upon essential democratic institutions, seeking all the while the adjustment of burdens, the help of the needy, the protection of the weak, the liberation of the exploited and the genuine protection of the people's property." But this meant waging a battle against "entrenched greed."[7]

Roosevelt's public philosophy that commerce corrupted would later echo in the history books, legal briefs, and rhetoric of Roosevelt's heirs, and thus it became a part of America's collective memory.[8] The cry to rise up against the rapacity of commerce was to animate political leaders for a long time to come. Five decades later, in the middle of the Reagan presidency, politicians who came of age in the New Deal, like House Speaker Thomas ("Tip") O'Neill (who was born in 1912), were still decrying anyone who saw things otherwise as "a cheerleader of selfishness."[9] Thus, a president's ideas can have enduring consequences.

One important feature of Roosevelt's public philosophy was that it consisted not of one theme, but of two. There was the obvious point that commerce corrupted. But there was a second point, as well: government was honorable, filled with warriors whose hearts and minds were untainted by the seamy business of profit seeking. Because of their purity, officials of the national government had vision and were the ideal trustees of the public interest, the perfect priests in the temple of civilization. Politics ennobled.

The Reagan presidency tried to contest this intellectual heritage and recruited the assistance of business institutions to rebut it. What was the nature of that rebuttal? How did it prod business to spread the word? And to what effect?

Reagan employed his inauguration as president in January 1981 to challenge Roosevelt's New Deal notions. Like many initial rhetorical efforts, however, Reagan's first inaugural address was far from a complete success. Under examination, its flaws were very evident.

Reagan began well by observing that the businessmen and women he knew were much more than mere self-seekers:

> Those who say that we're in a time when there are not heroes, they just don't know where to look. You can see heroes every day going in and out of factory gates. Others, a handful in number, produce enough food to feed all of us and then the world beyond. You meet heroes across a counter, and they're on both sides of that counter. There are entrepreneurs with faith in themselves and faith in an idea who create new jobs, new wealth and opportunity. They're individuals and families whose taxes support the government and whose voluntary gifts support church, charity, culture, art, and education. Their patriotism is quiet, but deep. Their values sustain our national life.[10]

The depiction of manufacturers, farmers, merchants, and entrepreneurs as heroes was an attempt to challenge the first of Roosevelt's two ideas, that business bred greed.

But Reagan did not contest the allied theme about the nobility of government. If anything, he reinforced it. In speaking to "the citizens of this blessed land," the president said:

> Your dreams, your hopes, your goals are going to be the dreams, the hopes, and the goals of this administration, so help me God.
> We shall reflect the compassion that is so much a part of your makeup. How can we love our country and not love our countrymen; and loving them, reach out a hand when they fall, heal them when they're sick, and provide opportunity to make them self-sufficient so they will be equal in fact and not just in theory.[11]

In other words, people in government ("we") were filled with compassion and committed to accomplishing the people's goals—just as the New Deal had been. The apparent intellectual continuity between Roosevelt and Reagan left some things unclear. For example, did the Reagan administration, with its commitment to compassion, intend to continue to do battle against "an entrenched economic autocracy," as Roosevelt and his heirs had said a compassionate government must do?

The speech became even more puzzling when it turned about and accused government of being a pain-in-the-neck: "In this present crisis, government is not the solution to our problem; government is the problem."[12] The message seemed incoherent. How could government be compassionate, yet harmful?

The way out of this rhetorical muddle lay in locating the origin of the American people's goodness. What were the causes of their decency? Was a well-intentioned government a hazard to those moral forces that made people caring and courageous?

The answer had been foreshadowed in the inaugural, where the president hinted that the marketplace was "the core of our system," where "idealism and fair play" were learned and practiced every day.[13] The marketplace disciplined men by rewarding those who made themselves useful to others and denying prosperity to those who did not.

It followed that individuals working in nonmarket institutions were not exposed to the benign discipline of economic reciprocity. Those in the business of managing the state, especially, escaped its civilizing ties. What made it worse was that they were exposed to the great temptation of statecraft, the power to tax—the power to take without giving.

In a nationwide address on February 5, 1981, Reagan spoke eloquently of the dangers of government:

> Some say shift the tax burden to business and industry, but business doesn't pay taxes. Oh, don't get the wrong idea. Business is being taxed, so much so that we're being priced out of the world market. But business must pass its costs of operations—and that includes taxes—on to the customer in the price of the product. Only people pay taxes, all the taxes. Government just uses business in a kind of sneaky way to help collect the taxes. They're hidden in the price; we aren't aware of how much tax we actually pay.[14]

The state, far from being worthy of being entrusted with the public interest, as Roosevelt would have it, was more like a trickster, using "sneaky" techniques to support itself. It forced the people to pay inflated prices on the useful goods and services produced in the private sector and fobbed off on the public. its own shoddy work.[15]

This effort to warn the public of the moral defects of government (and to praise the elevating moral effects of market freedom) was broadcast nationally on television. Thereafter, the president turned to business audiences to elaborate on the themes.

Table 2 summarizes the business discourse of President Reagan during the years 1981 through 1989. Notice that the president spoke

Table 2
Business Discourse of President Reagan, 1981–1988

Year	Total prepared remarks[a]	Total business discourse (no.)	(%)	Number of speeches: to large-business audiences	to small-business audiences[b]	with a business theme	on voluntarism (PSI)[c]
1981	160	12	7.5	2	1	6	3
1982	245	14	5.6	4	4	1	5
1983	282	19	6.8	7	10	1	1
1984	334	20	6.0	3	9	7	1
1985	210	26	12.4	15	1	9	1
1986	257	19	7.4	12	3	1	3
1987	262	36	13.7	26	2	7	1
1988	298	26	8.8	17	2	6	1
Total	2,048	172	8.4 (ave.)	86	32	38	16

a. Does not include remarks prepared for visits by foreign leaders and for press conferences and interviews with journalists.
b. Typically, companies, associations, and industries with fewer than 500 employees.
c. PSI stands for "private sector initiative" speeches to big business on the subject of voluntarism.

to the business community with much the same frequency as he did to the religious institutions (8.4 percent for business as against 9.3 percent for religion). The president, however, changed the time allotted to the business community in his second term. He met much more frequently with large-business audiences: seventy times in 1985–1988, compared with only sixteen in 1981–1984. But he met much less often with small-business audiences. As a matter of fact, he virtually fell silent, presidential appearances declining from twenty-four in 1981–1984 to a mere eight in 1985–1988.

This redirection of energy from one segment of the business community to another affected the substance of the rhetoric. What Table 2 does not reveal is that the content of Reagan's speeches depended on the audience he was addressing. In the eighty-six times that he addressed officials of large corporations employing more than five hundred individuals, he rarely spoke philosophically. Instead, he advocated specific policies—policies for which he needed popular support in the Congress— tax reforms, MX missile site placements, and the like. (The exceptions were the sixteen additional occasions when he gathered officials of large corporations to talk about voluntarism, the subject discussed in

Chapter Five.) When he talked to small-business people, that is, companies with fewer than five hundred employees, however, he virtually always touched on matters of the public philosophy.

Since Reagan's early philosophical efforts with the business community were directed at small business, it behooves us to examine what the small-business community was like. In 1981 there were twelve million small firms doing business in the United States. Most were involved in construction, retail trade, and services. Proprietors of small businesses were busy people, often jacks-of-all-trades. For that reason the small-business community did not look too promising as a moral institution. Individuals in small enterprises were too busy and lacked organization, discipline, and the luxury of time to deal with ideas. Unlike those in the clergy and the law, the lot of small-business persons was action and results. They had little practice in the arts of reflection, debate, and philosophy. They were practical men, not scribblers.[16]

They had no text to unify them (notwithstanding the availability of Adam Smith's *The Wealth of Nations*). There was no single authority to which they might look for an interpretation of events. And although business schools existed, none of them nurtured those homiletical and rhetorical skills in which preachers and lawyers received so much training. Virtually every element of what we have identified as a necessary characteristic of a moral institution seemed to be missing.

A second glance, however, revealed that small businesses were largely local in nature. Their owners had countless intimate ties to the nation's neighborhoods. Local business organizations flourished in nearly every community—Rotary, Kiwanis, Lions, Women Business Owners. On a bigger scale, an association of small businesses, the National Federation of Independent Business (NFIB), had developed an institutional device to give its membership a sense of participation: it regularly polled its membership on issues of government regulation, taxation, and spending and fairly reported the results, conditioning its members to comment on matters of public policy and philosophy.

In these several respects the small-business community was a more promising moral institution than first appeared. The White House had some reason to hope that it might be able to turn its potential strength to moral advantage. What could it do?

For one thing, it could galvanize the Small Business Administration (SBA) into an active office in the national government. It could change the dominant character of the SBA from that of a lending agency to that of a political advocacy group, coordinating small-business lobbying efforts in the legislatures of the states and localities. Having to lobby public lawmaking bodies would prod small business to take their case to the public. They would need reasons and ideas to support their legislative positions; the president would be in a position to fill their need.

The White House did just that, appointing Frank Swain to the SBA Office of Chief Counsel for Advocacy. It also gave him an additional responsibility—to maintain the momentum of the first White House Conference on Small Business (held in 1980 and organized by the Carter administration) and initiate a second one. From a moral standpoint, the climactic event of these conferences—the convening in Washington, D.C.—was far less important than the countless local meetings of small-business delegates preceding it. Nominally, these local gatherings were to select delegates for meetings one level up, but interwoven with the delegate-selection process was considerable discussion of the appropriate relationship between government and small business. The White House conference thus induced busy people to take the time to collaborate and think abstractly about the large questions, Was government good or bad? Was commerce good or bad? This mechanism thus served as a temporary process of commentary, enabling small businesspersons to converse with each other and with the president's speechwriters.[17]

The SBA had one more task. It prepared an annual report on the state of small business for submission to Congress. Its rhetorical significance was that the president always marked its publication by gathering representatives of small business in Washington and talking to them about the import of economic freedom. In 1982, for example, Reagan used the occasion to challenge the New Deal antibusiness philosophy: "We [in the Reagan administration] are not members of that Washington fraternity that believes that profits for business are dirty, but profits for government should be guaranteed."[18] In saying that profits for business are not dirty, Reagan directly confronted Roosevelt's notion that profits flowed to entrenched greed.

The president also used these annual friendly occasions to try out new formulations of the moral case for economic freedom. In 1982 he advanced the idea that both government and private business had to accrue profits. (The government's profits were called taxes.) By assimilating private profits and public taxes—as the share of the gross national product the private and public sector took to accomplish their work—the president could compare which did the greater good with its profits. In the president's assessment small business did more, materially and morally: "You know, it's small business . . . not the Federal Government, which creates four out of every five new jobs, employs more than half the work force, provides the livelihood for some 100 million Americans, and gives us new technology and real hope for our future—and that's not bad."[19]

Private profits enabled those with the will to solve other people's problems build the teams to do it. Profit earners had vision and were the true idealists of the nation:

> When you're talking about the strength and character of America, you're talking about the small business community, about the owners of that store down the street, the faithful who support their churches, and defend their freedom, and all the brave men and women who are not afraid to take risks and invest in the future to build America.

To show up, to please, to care about the community, to take risks—these were the habits the free market reinforced. As the president would say, quoting former president Calvin Coolidge, "The ultimate result [of private enterprise] is not the making of money, but the making of people."

Over the course of his first term, Reagan and the speechwriters developed a more articulate analysis of the mechanisms by which the marketplace shaped the character of persons in business.[20] The import of reciprocity was the central theme: the marketplace rewarded people who could find some way to help others. In a radio talk in May 1983, the president said:

> That word "invest" helps explain why entrepreneurs are a special breed. When small business people invest their money, they have no guarantee of profit. They're motivated by self-interest. But that alone won't do the trick. Success comes when they can anticipate and deliver what you, the customer, wants, and do it in a way that satisfies you.[21]

"Motivated by self-interest"—that key piece of conventional wisdom attracted the president's attention. In his opinion, self-interest was an inadequately analyzed concept, for it made no distinction between the self-centered, predatory practices of the greedy and those of the customer-centered, caring relationship required in the world of commerce. There was a vital difference between self-centeredness and customer-centeredness, and attention had to be paid it. The difference was between taking and giving.

In that connection the president quoted the anthropologist-economist George Gilder:

> Entrepreneurs intuitively understand one of the world's best kept secrets: Capitalism begins with giving. And capitalism works best and creates the greatest wealth and human progress for all when it follows the teachings of Scripture: Give and you will be given unto. . . . [S]earch and you will find. . . . [C]ast your bread upon the waters and it will return to you manyfold.[22]

The glue of a free society was the giving and getting of countless reciprocal relationships. The habits of reciprocity made it possible for society to develop a reliable division of labor. The norms of reciprocity forbade taking from someone else without consent. The practice of reciprocity exercised personal talents so that they could be put to use for the benefit of others. The incentives of reciprocity induced the widespread sharing of productive ideas. Reciprocity cultivated man's potential for cooperation in many ways.

Reagan and his speechwriters constructed their argument carefully. They presented the idea—economic freedom nurtured personal generosity—eloquently. The small-business community seemed both highly motivated and well equipped to carry the notion into the larger American society.

Somehow, however, the process never worked effectively: The idea that human goodness was the byproduct of economic freedom never penetrated society as deeply as did the notion of man's moral freedom. The religious community was a more effective propagator of the president's public philosophy than the business community. Although it is hard to document that such was the case, it certainly is noteworthy that the president himself stopped beating the philosophical drum in the business community in the second term and started talking about policy and other less abstract matters, as pointed out earlier. Had he felt that his philosophical efforts were succeeding in the business community, he would more likely have stayed with them.

There were three reasons to explain his rhetorical ineffectiveness within the business community. One was historical. The business community had never learned to be a strong moral institution. In the United States it had rarely carried its own philosophical water. Throughout the nineteenth and the early twentieth centuries, the U.S. Supreme Court had been the moral spokesperson for business, the cheerleader capitalism had relied on. Typical of the Court's rhetoric was Justice George Sutherland's opinion striking down a minimum-wage law for women and children because it violated their freedom of contract: "To sustain the individual freedom of action contemplated by the Constitution [that is, to nullify labor-standards regulations] is not to strike down the common good but to exalt it."[23]

The unfortunate thing, of course, was that the Supreme Court intermingled its exalting of the marketplace with a laissez-faire political agenda—an insistence, as Franklin Roosevelt depicted it, "that Government has no right, in any way, to interfere with those who were using the system of private profit to the damage of the rest of the American citizens."[24] In 1937, with the appointment of the so-called Roosevelt Court, the Supreme Court changed its collective mind and refused to entertain any further constitutional challenges to business regulation. Coincidentally, however, it also stopped acting as capitalism's advocate. The Roosevelt Court took its lead from former justice Oliver Wendell Holmes's dissent in *Lochner* v. *New York* (1905), which had urged the Court to withdraw its sponsorship of laissez-faire and cease being the apologist for American business:[25]

> This case [*Lochner* v. *New York*] is decided upon an economic theory which a large part of the country does not entertain. If it were a question whether I agree with that theory, I should desire to study it further and long before making up my mind. But I do not conceive that to be my duty, because I strongly believe that my agreement or disagreement has nothing to do with the right of a majority to embody their opinions in law. . . . The 14th amendment does not enact Mr. Herbert Spencer's *Social Statics*. . . . But a Constitution is not intended to embody a particular economic theory, whether of paternalism and the organic relation of the citizen to the state or of laissez faire. It is made for people of fundamentally differing views.

The consequence of the Court's new passivity in economic matters was that after 1937 it fell silent about the meaning of economic freedom. The business community seemed ignorant of how to fill the vacuum. So one-sided did the debate become, so powerful and uncontested was the voice of capitalism's detractors, that the economist-philosopher Joseph Schumpeter asked himself, "Can capitalism survive?" and sorrowed, "No, I do not think it can." . . . "The bourgeois order no longer makes any sense to the bourgeoisie itself and . . . when all is said and nothing is done, it does not really care."[26]

Schumpeter's remark reflected the fact that the Supreme Court had fallen silent in articulating the moral meaning of economic freedom and the business community did not seem to care about filling the moral gap left by the Court's withdrawal.[27] Thus, one explanation of Reagan's ineffectiveness in rallying the business community to spread his philosophy was the intellectual inexperience of businesspeople.

A second explanation was the weakness of the message. That economic freedom produced benign moral consequences was a highly disputable proposition, as everyday events often proved. Humankind not being angels, there was always a scoundrel and a scandal to point to in the business community. Sometimes the president's rhetoric fell victim to events. Soon after Reagan honored John Mariotta, the head of WedTech, as an entrepreneurial hero, for example, Mariotta was indicted for bribing members of Congress to pressure the Defense Department to purchase his firm's products.[28]

I was struck, however, by a third factor, the institutional weakness of the business community. It lacked a means of sustaining a process of commentary. Yes, there were places where philosophical discourse went on—the national daily newspaper, the *Wall Street Journal*, for one. Yes, there was a text to expound if anyone wanted to read it—Adam Smith's *Wealth of Nations* was a rich source of moral insight. Yes, there were temporary devices to stimulate commentary, such as the White House Conference on Small Business. And yes, big corporations like IBM and the phone company appeared, in their size and organizational discipline, to be model moral institutions.[29]

Nevertheless, the business community was a shallow moral institution. Discussions of the ideas of Adam Smith were not the fare of executive suites, and in contrast to the religious community, business provided few places where the president's words resonated in active debate. Even such gifted thinkers and publicists as Milton Friedman of the University of Chicago and Irving Kristol of *Public Interest*, for all their stress on capitalist productivity, said little about its value for the virtues of the workman. Kristol's famous title, "Two Cheers for Capitalism," signified the lack of support for a debate on the moral issue.

Therefore, the assumption that the marketplace exacerbated greed, avarice, and the desire to exploit others was left regnant. What debate there was in the academies, the economic and business journals, the business conferences, and the business institutions themselves assumed that the system produced greed. The only lively questions were, how much, and how bad must it get before the government should enter the fray to regulate it? The premise—that capitalism worsened men—was always granted. Marx's critique, that the bourgeoisie were greedheads because they were bourgeois, was the frame of reference, not the issue, of the debate.

The puzzle was, why? After all, over the past fifty years business had professionalized. Graduate business schools had been developed and legitimated. Business scholars abounded, and so did degree candidates.

But within business schools, the matter was seldom debated. The philosophy of capitalism was basically left untaught. At least, that was the case as late as 1987, if we are to believe a convincing description of the Harvard Business School by a young Harvard Law School student. Fareed Zakaria compared Harvard's business school with its law and medical schools.

> Law and medical schools create an atmosphere in which students see their fields as noble and themselves as socially useful. . . . If business schools stood for the proposition that business is an honorable endeavor, and that businessmen are socially useful, students could learn to take pride in their profession and, conversely, feel ashamed to let it down. . . .

This does imply a moral defense [of] capitalism, obviously a controversial position for business schools to take. But, as the Critical Legal Studies Group has pointed out, the argument that our legal system is a beneficial one is equally tendentious, and yet it may well help to make better-behaved lawyers. Ironically, professional "ethicists" sometimes object to taking any such definitive moral stance at all. . . . But by staying away from an advocacy of the free market, business schools are refusing to defend themselves. If capitalism is morally neutral, the schools are at best self-interested corporations that identify a need for a product (MBAs) and make a morally neutral decision to produce it. If capitalism is unambiguously good, they are educating an integral part of a prosperous and just society.[30]

His point was that the halls of business schools were silent in defining (and asserting) the moral nature of economic freedom, in contrast to the "tendentious" position taken by law and medical schools that their professions were honorable both in principle and consequence. Business schools lacked people who gave full time to propagating the honor of business and using that code to make sense of the marketplace.[31] They lacked a starting point of view, and hence there was no debate on fundamental questions.

As a consequence, the moral nihilism of Marx flourished uncontested in the graduate education of the business community. Without a point of entry in the business community, the president's rhetoric never penetrated it. Graduates of the school were left without the language or the frame of reference even to comprehend the philosophical discourse to which the president's words spoke. And so they lacked a shield against the charges of self-seeking, dishonesty, greed, and ruthlessness that stemmed from an antithetical philosophy. The fundamental moral concept underlying economics, reciprocity, went unexplored and unnoted and unknown. Without an echo chamber to amplify his message, without an ongoing debate that his disciples were able to join, the president found himself silenced. The lesson was that no moral leader, even one as skillful as Reagan and his speechwriters, could be effective without a moral institution in good condition.[32]

13
★★★★★★★

The Media: A Thorny Moral Institution

The press was an inferior pulpit. . . .
—*Henry Adams,* The Education of Henry Adams *(1918)*

Toward the end of March in 1984, Steven Weisman of the *New York Times* interviewed the president for a feature article. The president began with a gentle dig. "Before we get under way," he smiled, "I just have one question of my own—on the other side of the political fence and all. I found this, that my popularity had improved, but I had to turn to the second section on the sixth page to find it."

"Well, it's no longer news," Weisman responded.

"I've heard that before," the president laughed.

Weisman answered, "Well, it's a good answer."[1]

Why was it "a good answer"? Why was the president's improved popularity—his approval rating had risen from 32 to 65 percent in less than fifteen months—no longer news? My suspicion is that the editors of the *New York Times* believed readers would not be surprised that the president was popular. After all, the public's general idea was that in a democracy nice guys were popular: since President Reagan was a nice guy, and he was now popular, what else was new? "News" was defined as something counterintuitive: front-page prominence was reserved for events that ran counter to the general ideas the editors thought were in the average reader's mind, like reports that a nice guy was not popular, or a ruthless one was. The anomaly was always newsworthy.

The brief exchange revealed an important constraint on American presidents with moral objectives. The purpose of Reagan the leader was to certify certain general ideas, that of Weisman the journalist to question them. "That [incompatibility of purpose] makes for friction," as the president told the White House correspondents in his last annual dinner with them.[2]

Once in a rare while, however, this natural friction between press and presidency has been overcome, and they have collaborated in common cause. One of those occasions when the media, rather than challenging a president's ideas, propagated them, occurred a half century ago. It is instructive to ask why it happened then.

The unusual collaboration occurred in the first administration of Franklin Roosevelt. Times were hard. Economic emergency pervaded every corner of the world. The Great Depression paralyzed American economic life. Unemployment soared above 25 percent. Banks were without the cash to redeem the demands of their depositors. Farmers were going bankrupt because they were producing food few customers had the money to buy.

Beneath the despair of the people lay paralyzing confusion about what was to be done. The source of the confusion was the common sense of the day, laissez-faire. Laissez-faire was an economic and social philosophy in which five ideas about what constituted a good society interconnected: first, that individual effort was justly rewarded; second, that personal poverty was due to an able-bodied individual's irresponsibility; third, that an active national government was incompetent and oppressive; fourth, that local government, because of its limitations, was best suited to preserving personal liberty; and, fifth, that personal liberty exercised in the unregulated marketplace produced prosperity.

Roosevelt believed that the worldwide depression of the time was so beyond the power of the individual or local government that the national government had to undertake unprecedented economic initiatives. If he were to take such measures in the perspective of widely held beliefs in laissez-faire, he would worsen the present confusion, his programs would be misunderstood and resisted, and eventually he would lose public support. He therefore had no choice but to tamper with the public philosophy, excise the extant notions of a good society and replace them with an image that would make sense of the political and economic programs he felt were necessary to meet the emergency. In other words, President Roosevelt set out to propagate anomalous philosophy.

In his first words as president, Roosevelt spelled out his intention to change the people's understanding of the importance of government and their relation to it. That is, he intended to replace an outworn tradition of laissez-faire with a new and better idea.

What was that new idea, that appropriate "image" of the good society? It was an army at war:

> If we are to go forward, we must move as a trained and loyal army willing to sacrifice for the good of a common discipline, because without such discipline no progress is made, no leadership becomes effective. We are, I know, ready and willing to submit our lives and property to such discipline, because it makes possible a leadership which aims at a larger good. This I propose to offer, pledging that the larger purposes will bind upon us all as a sacred obligation with a unity of duty hitherto evoked only in time of armed strife.[3]

Roosevelt's metaphor called on citizens to be obedient and disciplined soldiers and to wage "war against the emergency" and the miscreants who caused it—"the resplendent economic autocracy" we met in Chapter Twelve.

The intellectual distance between the old and the new visions was vast. The concentrated authority of Roosevelt's popular army was nearly the total reversal of the dispersed independence of the self-regulating, laissez-faire society. It was the measure of Franklin Roosevelt that he was not daunted by the size and danger of his moral undertaking.

Roosevelt needed messengers to spread this revolutionary word and fit it into the hearts and minds of Americans, to whom it was initially uncomfortable. Where was President Roosevelt to find such a cadre to penetrate the public mind?

His prospects were hardly promising. The legal profession, led by the Republican-appointed Supreme Court, had created and propagated the very outworn tradition he decried. The justices *were* the enemy.

What of the churches? At first glance, the clergy seemed ideally situated for the president. After all, ministers were in a profession providing spiritual and material succor to the Great Depression's victims. Moreover, Christianity contained ideas fully in consonance with the president's New Deal. Religion's compassion for the suffering poor and its tolerant attitude toward "Caesar and the things that are Caesar's" were principles that looked as if they would fit comfortably into Roosevelt's philosophy of the benevolent state.[4]

The usual constitutional barriers to the collaboration existed, but as Reagan's experience in the 1980s would attest, those were not insuperable. The fact of economic emergency provided the president some leeway to reach out to any set of Americans who wanted to help.

Roosevelt apparently gave much thought to enlisting the church in his philosophical crusade. Following the first year of his presidency, for example, Roosevelt addressed the Federal Council of Churches, which consisted of representatives from twenty-five Christian denominations.

He invited the religious leaders there to join him in his war against laissez-faire philosophy:

> During a quarter of a century more greatly controlled by the spirit of conquest and greed than any similar period since the American and French Revolutions you have survived and grown. You have come through to the threshold of a new era in which your churches and the other churches—gentile and Jewish—recognize and stand ready to lead in a new war of peace—the war for social justice.[5]

In this "war for social justice" Roosevelt envisioned himself and the federal government as fellow foot soldiers side by side with the church, making "a collective effort which is wholly in accord with the social teachings of Christianity": "That human agency which we call government is seeking through political and economic means the same goal which the churches are seeking through social and spiritual means." That common goal was "a more abundant life" for all Americans. Of course, Roosevelt warned the clergymen, in order to spread the prosperity wide, the economy would have to be "socially controlled for the common good." Effecting such social controls was going to be unpopular in some corners and would be made difficult because democratic government was vulnerable to popular resistance. To survive periodic elections, Roosevelt needed the church to help "crystallize a public opinion so clear that Government of all kinds will be compelled to practice a more certain justice." The urgent need was for the church to spread the general idea that government was benign in character, dedicated to defending the people against the predatory character of business (enterprises "controlled by the spirit of conquest and greed"). He urged the churches to make common cause with him and teach the people the benevolence of the welfare state, to teach them that "they have the right to demand of the Government of their own choosing" a better life.

The government was God's "human agency": Just as the church served God by bringing about social and spiritual fulfillment, so the Government served God by bringing about political and economic fulfillment.

Unlike President Reagan fifty years later, Roosevelt did not energetically follow up his overture to the church, although in 1935 he did write individually addressed letters to thousands of clergymen, enlisting each of them in his army of social justice. In those letters he repeated the suggestion that church and government work together to improve the spiritual and material lives of the American people. The church's end of this partnership would consist of expressing its impartial views about the lofty goals of the welfare and public works programs which the government enacted to serve the people and find solutions to their problems. He noted that the clergy, with their regular personal contact with parishioners, were ideally positioned to help them overcome their objections to an activist government.[6]

That was about as far as Roosevelt went in inviting the ministry at large to propagate New Deal ideas. Instead, he concentrated his efforts on cultivating an alternative moral institution, the White House press corps, and through them the national media.

Even in the 1930s the correspondents covering the presidency numbered several hundred, the White House press corps having grown steadily since President Grover Cleveland's time in the late nineteenth century. The bustle and activity of the New Deal government, however, required reporters to understand more economics and law than they had ever had to master before. Roosevelt, understanding this need for knowledge, saw his opportunity to cultivate them.

Twice a week he would call them into his Oval Office, two hundred strong, and speak off the record of newsworthy accomplishments of the national government. In 1937 Roosevelt opened the first press conference of his second term as president by expressing to the reporters his appreciation of their sympathetic rendering of New Deal philosophy in their columns, despite the widespread editorial criticism of his policies and administration, especially by the larger newspapers: "I consider it an interesting fact that . . . the great majority of newspaper correspondents who cover the White House are personally friendly to the Administration, and in general approve its objectives, most of its methods, and legislation adopted to accomplish its goal."[7]

Roosevelt confided to the correspondents that he enjoyed being connected to their team as they spread their friendly words. And what made their collaboration the more zesty was that their bosses were often on the opposing side. The spirit of common accord between president and correspondents was noted by President Herbert Hoover's former personal secretary, who wrote that Roosevelt "has been and is ace high with most of the corps." He even characterized the atmosphere of Roosevelt's press conferences as comradery since he had come nearer than any president "to meeting the expectations of the four hundred men and women who, in these times of stress, write half a million words a day to bring to our firesides news of developments at the seat of the Government," while they "functioned quite satisfactorily to the president."[8]

What satisfied Roosevelt was that they carried out their duty to bring a favorable view of government into American homes. They were the good soldiers of the New Deal.

In turn, what satisfied the White House reporters was the inside dope Roosevelt gave them. Former president Hoover's personal secretary noted a further perquisite the correspondents enjoyed—a heightened professional status resulting from covering an activist president, one who generated a lot of far-reaching governmental programs:

> The White House today is more the center of news than it ever has been in history.
> With a regularity that is almost monotonous the Executive Offices have provided the setting for events that make the headlines streaming across the pages of the newspapers. Because it is the one best source for news, more writers, serious-minded journalists, and the garden variety of reporters alike gather there than at any time since the Fourth Estate became an adjunct of Government.[9]

The White House beat became the spot where the dominating news story was made each day. Covering it was a feather in any journalist's cap. It made a somebody out of even the garden variety of reporter. Heightening reporters' self-importance added to the comradery between an activist White House and the press.

It is revealing to read the transcripts of these press conferences—all off the record, for neither attribution nor quotation. (Like a general talking to his lieutenants, Roosevelt clearly spelled out the rules regarding background information and off-the-record information at his first press conference.)[10] Each conference was recorded verbatim by a White House stenographer, but only with White House permission was a word, phrase, or remark made public.

Roosevelt's conduct of the conferences—in the Oval Office, the front row of reporters crushed against his desk by late-arriving reporters squeezing through the door into the room—was witty, dominating, and brilliant. He spiced each meeting with an air of emergency and complicity between himself and his media comrades.

A typical example of the friendly character of the presidential press conference of the time can be found in the spring of 1935, two days after the U.S. Supreme Court had decided the *Schecter* (or "Sick Chicken") case, voiding the National Industrial Recovery Act (NIRA) of 1933.[11] The NIRA was one of the first pieces of New Deal legislation—and doubtless one of its most far-reaching and revolutionary. It repealed the application of the antitrust laws to America's industries and delegated to cartels of private employers virtually absolute authority to fix wages and prices. Their collective decisions on hours and working conditions, as well as wages and prices, if approved by the president as "fair," were enforced by the police and taxing powers of the U.S. government, without any further action by Congress. The NIRA was public policy of such unprecedented intrusiveness and constituted so expansive a delegation of public authority to private power that two years after its passage the Supreme

Court unanimously struck it down as unconstitutional. In fact, the universally esteemed Justice Benjamin Nathan Cardozo, a so-called liberal on the Court who voted to uphold virtually every other piece of New Deal legislation, termed the NIRA "delegation running riot."[12]

The day after the Court announced its judgment in *Schecter*, Roosevelt called a press conference, which lasted nearly two hours and dealt only with the Court's opinion in the case.[13] The meeting with the correspondents began like this:

> THE PRESIDENT: What is the news?
> Q: That's what we want.
> THE PRESIDENT: Have you any questions to ask?
> Q: What did you do yesterday?
> THE PRESIDENT: I saw lots of people. I telephoned to a lot more, and I am continuing to do it.
> Q: Do you care to comment on the NIRA?
> THE PRESIDENT: Well, Steve [Early, the president's own press secretary: note that the president's man asked the question], if you insist. That's an awful thing to put up to a fellow at this hour of the morning just out of bed. Suppose we make this background and take some time because it is an awfully big subject to cover, and it is just possible that one or two of you may not have read the whole twenty-eight or twenty-nine pages of the Supreme Court decision.
>
> I have been a good deal impressed by—what shall I call it?— the rather pathetic appeals that I have had from all around the country to do something. They are very sincere as showing faith in the Government. They are so sincere that you feel in reading them—and so far there have been somewhere between two and three thousand by letter and telegram and I haven't seen this morning's mail yet—so sincere that you feel the country is beginning to realize that something in the long run has to be done.

Roosevelt then read fifteen of these letters and telegrams and next turned to the Supreme Court opinion itself. Minutely, paragraph by paragraph, he described, analyzed, and condemned the decision, whose implications were, in FDR's words, "much more important than almost certainly any decision of my lifetime or yours, more important than any decision probably since the Dred Scott case, because they bring the country as a whole up against a very practical question."

For the next hour, without interruption, he focused on the constitutional authorization that Congress shall have the power "to regulate commerce among the several states'' and deplored the Court's narrow interpretation of what constituted interstate commerce. Carefully he demonstrated to the press corps' unquestioning satisfaction that the Court was denying to Congress its power to regulate virtually all construction, mining, manufacturing, and farming activity because of their intrastate aspects. With telling effect Roosevelt claimed that the Court was about to declare that ''the United States Government has no control over any national economic problem.''

Here, by way of illustration, was what Roosevelt taught the press about the NIRA and the destructive effect of the Supreme Court's opinion:

> The other example is that of a department store which puts in a book department and sells all the latest detective stories that retail ordinarily at $1.50—I ought to know because I read them—for ninety cents. Up to the time that their code went through, bankruptcies of small book stores throughout the country where those practices were engaged in were increasing. They were being put out of business because they could not afford to do it, because people who went into that department store to save sixty cents on a detective story undoubtedly bought a good many other things in that department store, and the store was able to make up the loss.
>
> Now, all that seems to be ''out of the window.'' We made a very sincere effort to eliminate things that were called unfair trade practices not only because they were giving advantage to people with lots of capital or with nationwide systems—advantages over smaller men or local men.

With color and drama he depicted the bitter sectional competition that would arise if the national government had ''no right . . . to better national social conditions'' and had to leave matters up to the forty-eight states to take separate action to solve economic and social problems that were national in scope.

FDR went on to demonstrate that the major implication of the *Schecter* opinion was that the Court would declare unconstitutional the bulk of New Deal legislation—the Securities and Exchange Acts, the Agricultural Adjustment Act, and so on—because the commercial activities the president and the Congress were attempting to regulate were not in ''commerce among the several states''; not being so, they were outside the constitutional powers of Congress to regulate.

> You see the implications of the decision. That is why I say it is one of the most important decisions ever rendered in this country. And the issue is not going to be a partisan issue for a minute. The issue is going to be whether we go one way or the other. Don't call it right or left; that is just first-year high school language, just about. It is not right or left—it is a question for national decision on a very

important problem of government. We are the only Nation in the world that has not solved that problem. We thought we were solving it, and now it has been thrown right straight in our faces. We have been relegated to the horse-and-buggy definition of interstate commerce.

During the entire ninety minutes of virtually uninterrupted and brilliant political advocacy, the atmosphere was informal and friendly. The press raised not a single hostile question—in fact, hardly an inquiry worthy of being defined as a question. There was not a single skeptical word said about Roosevelt's assertion of the good intentions and competency of the government. There was not a single inquiry into such controversial matters as, Why should both the presidency and Congress have surrendered authority to employers to set maximum wages and minimum prices (including even the price of a mystery paperback book)? What did the NIRA mean by "fair competition"; had not the NIRA permitted established businesses to eliminate *all* their competition? How would he answer Justice Cardozo's charge that the NIRA was "delegation running riot?" How could he explain the unanimity of the Court's opinion, including the votes of liberal justices like Louis Brandeis, Harlan Stone, and the revered Cardozo? Present-day journalists would have hung their heads in shame at their predecessors' subordination to the man in the White House.

With the entire press conference conducted on background, the president enlisted the White House press corps to bring the issue of the Supreme Court's "horse-and-buggy definition of interstate commerce" to the people. The correspondents agreed to warn the people that democracy was being rendered powerless to solve its problems by the "perfectly ridiculous and impossible situation" created by the Court.

Such obedience of correspondents would be inconceivable to us today. Little wonder that Roosevelt thought the press functioned quite satisfactorily, showering the country with half a million friendly words every day.

Why did President Reagan, in contrast, fail to turn the media into agents of his ideas? There were several explanations, some of which might be obvious but need mention.

The first answer was historical. During the presidencies of Lyndon Johnson (1963–1969) and Richard Nixon (1969–1974), the professional norms of White House journalism were radically altered. The Vietnam War and the cover-up of the Watergate burglary of Democratic party headquarters emboldened correspondents to become aggressive, even prosecutorial, and above all suspicious of a possible cover-up. The job of the Washington journalist was redefined in the presidencies of Johnson and Nixon.

A second explanation was the prosperity of the Reagan years. With no emergency, there was no requirement to hang together. With no war or depression, there was no need to bring assurance to the people "at their firesides." Instead, a journalist's patriotic duty was to expose the governmental muck—the role of the "wealthy and selfish advisers" around the president and the "macho," "reckless," and "dangerous" actions that "personify your foreign policy."[14]

Third, the press corps felt a natural resentment of Reagan's particular message. His humble vision of national government as a minor partner of the people humbled the correspondents who made the national government their beat. In the president's eye, the places—the spots—where important events were occurring were private—the family, the churches, the neighborhoods, the voluntary associations, and the private work place. If the president's views were right about where the real action was, then veteran Washington journalists were writing stories of less moment than the ones written by local reporters back home.[15]

A fourth explanation of Reagan's inability to coopt the correspondents was their genuine political disagreement with him. At least, most of his advisers believed that the reporters' presuppositions about politics were contrary to his.[16]

A fifth reason—and perhaps the most important of all—was the journalists' conception of what was news. The simple fact was that Reagan's notion of presidential leadership—as moral spokesman—required continual repetition of the word. Repeated messages, however, words and paragraphs that the reporter had heard before, were not new, hence not news. Charlotte Saikowski, White House correspondent for the *Christian Science Monitor*, once told me how she reported the president's speeches: "I look at the speech he's giving and lay it side-by-side the previous speech he made on the same topic. And I go right down the speech to find the paragraph, or even the sentence, which is new, which he had not said before. That's what I pay attention to."[17] The "poetry" of the Reagan presidency, the president's moral premises, repeated in speech after speech, was no longer news, and did not warrant publication or exposure on television's nightly news.

Thus, the change in professional standards, the lack of a compelling national emergency, the professional threat of diminished White House importance, philosophical differences, and the definition of newsworthiness all combined to make it impossible for Reagan to enlist the media in his revival of the American spirit.

Yet he tried. At least in 1983 and 1984 he devoted much time to wooing the Washington press corps. Admittedly, his effort did not measure up to Roosevelt's. (The reader may judge Reagan's effort by taking as a benchmark Roosevelt's 337 press conferences during his first administration.) In Reagan's two terms there were 235 press conferences, 87 of them (roughly 36 percent) occurring in 1983 and 1984.

By "press conference" I mean (1) a meeting with one or more reporters (2) in a formal setting (which meant the reporters were seated, not standing) (3) where the reporters were invited (either explicitly or by circumstance) to ask a number of questions and (4) where they had an opportunity to prepare questions. I exclude any meeting with reporters where fewer than five questions of substance were asked and any encounters in the White House Rose Garden (the site of countless public ceremonies) or on the South Portico or South Lawn of the White House (where television lurked to catch the president's movements in, or departures from, the White House). I also exclude those occasions when the president gave formal talks to media groups but took few or no questions after his remarks.

Press conferences nonetheless took in many kinds of meetings between members of the press and the president, including but not limited to the forty-six "Presidential News Conferences" where the White House press corps would assemble for television. They included all wide-ranging press conferences, those off-television meetings where correspondents were invited to discuss any matter of domestic or foreign importance. Also included would be single-issue briefings, where the president would expect the correspondents to confine their questions to exploring a single topic, and those sustained interviews that offered to a handful of prominent reporters the chance to discuss matters with the president for a significant period of time. (Also included were meetings with correspondents who were not a part of the White House press corps: reporters from foreign nations and U.S. journalists from outside Washington, D.C.)

Table 3 reveals Reagan's efforts to meet the press. Note that in the last three years of his administration, Reagan cut virtually all connections with the White House press corps. No wonder the correspondents laughed when he opened his farewell presidential news conference with the quip, "We've got to stop meeting like this."[18] Even in 1983 and 1984 Reagan met the press only three times a month, whereas Roosevelt would have met with them eight times.

The reader should keep in mind, of course, the ways that Reagan's and Roosevelt's press conferences differed. Virtually nothing of what Roosevelt said was on the record. Whatever he said to a reporter was unquotable, unattributable, and eminently deniable. All of what Reagan said—even his efforts at facetiousness before the press conference formally began—was in the public domain. Roosevelt had no problems in answering difficult or untimely questions; because there could be no adverse publicity, he would simply refuse to answer them. With everything on the record, Reagan had no such leeway.

Table 3
President Reagan's Press Conferences (1981–1989)

Kind of conference	Total	1981	1982	1983	1984	1985	1986	1987	1988–1989
Presidential news conferences	46[a]	6	8	7	5	6	7	3	4
Wide-ranging press conferences	38	3	6	16	4	4	1	3	1
Single-issue briefings	34	8	5	6	3	6	4	2	0
Sustained interviews	33	2	3	4	10	6	6	1	1
Total meetings with White House press corps	151	19	22	33	22	22	18	9	6
With foreign journalists	31	0	2	4	6	5	4	3	7
Regional press conferences	53	3	10	14	8	7	3	4	4
Total	235	22	34	51	36	34	25	16	17

a. Includes two presidential news conferences at the economic and Moscow summit meetings in 1988.

But having said that, I think it plain why Reagan met the press so infrequently. The press was not in league with him the way it had been with Roosevelt, and so he devoted his precious time to more productive purposes.

One of the epigraphs beginning this book tells the parable of the sower. It is a tale symbolizing a teacher spreading his word in the world. Some seeds of thought never lodge themselves in the soil, but are borne away by birds. Some take root where they fall, but are quickly strangled by thorns. Some grow fast, but the soil in which they fall is shallow and their roots are too close to the earth's surface to survive the heat of the midday sun. Finally, some seeds drop onto deep soil and flourish. As with the notions of religious prophets, so with the ideas of the bully pulpit. President Reagan spoke constantly, but his ideas did not always take root. The Constitution, like a flock of birds, intercepted any presidential effort to influence the law directly. The media grew thorny and hostile. The business community, though initially responsive, lacked the depth of commentary to sustain the hard work necessary to propagate the president's public philosophy. Only in the inviting soil of the religious ✓ community did Reagan's words take firm root and spread.

14

★★★★★★★★

The Cabinet: The President's Personal Moral Institution

Mr. President, in your Inaugural Address you said that no arsenal, no weapon in the world "is so formidable as the will and moral courage of free men and women." I think, as you often do, you put succinctly the essence of the matter, and I say to you that I will take these words of yours as my touchstone and foundation as I approach the conduct of this great office.

—George Shultz (1982)

The president depended primarily on religion to penetrate American society with his ideas. But a president who took his moral agenda seriously, out of prudence, did not want to be solely dependent on a moral institution he could not dominate. The White House undertook to build a secondary pulpit, one over which Reagan could exercise direct supervision of the instruction of his followers, in case events deprived him of the collaboration of the church.[1] A personal institution had a second advantage: it could be used to influence not public opinion, but the thinking of administration officials; it could serve as a pulpit to speak to the executive branch of government.[2]

A moral institution, even a secondary one, is grounded in a text. The text of Reagan's intragovernmental institution was "A Time for Choosing," referred to by his speechwriters simply as "The Speech."[3] It was the repository of Reagan's prepresidential views.

Delivered to a nationwide television audience on October 27, 1964, and repeated in whole or in part countless times since, the speech consisted of a single, abstract idea, universal in application. The idea was that a centrally administered government tended to weaken a free people's

175

character. By overregulation and fiscal overindulgence, a distant government demoralized and enervated its citizenry. The president argued that the runaway bureaucracy of the federal government stripped people of their will to be self-reliant and their capacity for self-government. By spreading "bounties, donations, and benefits," a centralized administration first lightened, and then assumed, the "responsibility for our own destinies." Moreover, its unreasonably nitpicking restraints weakened the people's sense of responsible self-restraint. As a result individuals lost any feeling of pride in their own accomplishment and even a desire for accomplishment.

The speech elaborated the idea comprehensively to explain why craftsmen lost pleasure in their work, business managers countenanced inefficiencies, farmers planted unwanted crops, and parents separated and left their children. It accounted equally well for engineers who built unnecessary projects, city officials who laid waste decent neighborhoods, bureaucrats who expanded their dominions excessively, courts that turned a blind eye to the erosion of civil liberties, and citizens who grew frightened to speak up against runaway government. In short, the central state, by acting "outside its legitimate function," transformed a hardy people into a crowd of dispirited and unscrupulous individuals, lacking self-respect.

The speech was eloquent, humorous, lucid, brilliantly partisan, and at the same time argued from a set of fundamental principles about free and democratic government. Consider a paragraph on the limits of majority rule:

> Somewhere a perversion has taken place. Our natural unalienable rights are now presumed to be a dispensation of government, divisible by a vote of the majority. The greatest good for the greatest number is a high-sounding phrase but contrary to the very basis of our Nation, unless it is accompanied by recognition that we have certain rights which cannot be infringed upon, even if the individual stands outvoted by all of his fellow citizens. Without this recognition, majority rule is nothing more than mob rule.[4]

The White House Speechwriting Department was the chief interpreter of the text. Some of the speechwriters said they almost knew passages of the speech by heart. It was the focus of their art.

They saw their job as one of elaborating its core idea—the suffocating moral effects of an overgrown central government—and applying it to give direction to the agencies in the executive branch. Al Meyer, for example, described how he felt about the continuous repetition of the president's point of view to those who worked in the federal government:

For any administration to be effective in its relations with the executive branch, there must be a clear understanding throughout the Executive Office of the President and in the upper echelons of the executive branch—the political appointees—or, if you will, what I like to call the "conscience of the Presidency." I mean by that that both in foreign and domestic policy matters the President has not been elected as a mere caretaker, but as an activist for a point of view and with an expectation to improve on the present state of things. That means action, and action requires direction. And those who are charged by position within the executive branch and the Executive Office of the President to give direction must keep their fingers clearly pointing in that direction.

If the political appointees were the "conscience of the presidency," the six writers in the Speechwriting Department had the special responsibility of interpreting the principles of that conscience coherently and justifying their particular applications. That was what made the speechwriting team crucial to the president.

This compound [the White House and the Old Executive Office Building] consists of the crucial people who keep and maintain a handle on that direction, and if they don't do it, no one else will. Can you imagine? Who in the Department of Education would submit a budget of zero dollars for the next year? The place is full of career government officials, good ones, people who believe in what they're doing, and they're not going to eliminate themselves. . . . [T]he direction to do that has to be in this compound. The conscience of the presidency is in this compound and in the political levels of the Executive Branch. This president makes the federal government get smaller, and it's in the interest of the Department of Education and all the rest to make it bigger. And if you do not have a conscience, it will get bigger.[5]

The documents embracing "the principles of the conscience of the presidency" were the president's speeches. They were treated as the ongoing interpretation and application of the president's philosophy, and like interpretations of any sacred text, they were collected, published, and carefully indexed for easy retrieval. The publication in which they were contained was the *Weekly Compilation of Presidential Documents*, a government periodical first established in 1965. Each issue, typically about fifty pages long, contained everything the president had written or said publicly in the preceding seven days. Like the advance sheets that inform judges and lawyers of the latest judicial precedents, the *Weekly Compilation* made available to every federal department—and particularly every political appointee in it—the latest presidential word.

But a printing press alone would not have been a sufficient condition for starting a moral institution. To establish a presidential network for getting the word out, Reagan and his speechwriting team had to cultivate an inner circle of followers. They needed a small, closely knit group of sympathetic, yet persuasive evangelists to magnify the president's presence. Building an inner circle required Reagan to be in sufficiently close contact with its members to be able to instruct and converse and to share experiences with them all. All successful moral institution building depends on this process of discipleship, and presidential efforts were no exception.

Who did the president know well enough to recruit as his principal "disciples"? And how could he instruct them so that they could pass the word effectively? The president turned to his cabinet, consisting of the heads of the principal agencies of the executive branch. Their classrooms of instruction were the cabinet councils.[6]

The cabinet has long been a problematic institution, perpetually engaged in the task of finding a function. Typically, all department heads, except at State, Defense, Treasury, and Justice, have been invisible and isolated from the president.[7] Surrounded by career employees, often housed in buildings miles from the White House itself, beset by ardent clienteles and importunate congressional committees, frequently ill-informed about the inner workings of their own bureaucracies, the heads of these secondary departments historically have eventually resigned or filled their time by undertaking a few pet projects of their own. Moreover, in those cases where they did stick around, they usually began to identify with the agency they headed. As political scientist James Q. Wilson summed up the Washington wisdom, the agency secretary is more a representative *of* the agency to the president than *his* representative to the agency and "probably wants the president to do things that are very different from what the [president] would like him to do."[8]

Reagan and his speechwriting team reversed that pattern. He transformed the fifteen members of his cabinet into his representatives to carry his word out to their specialized bureaucracies and their clienteles.

To maintain their loyalty and discipline their thinking, President Reagan and his counselor, Edwin Meese, created seven cabinet councils, each dealing with a broad subject area.[9] Each council consisted of half a dozen cabinet members, along with the president, Chief of Staff Jim Baker, Vice President George Bush, and Meese himself. The task of each council was to identify problems and design acceptable solutions to them.

The sheer number of the councils made excessive demands on their members' time, and in the president's second term he and Meese decided to reduce them to three.[10] But for the purposes of building a moral institution within the presidency, the cabinet councils were key to the discipleship process in three ways.

First, the cabinet councils effectively involved the secretaries in important matters. For example, Secretary of Agriculture John Block regularly left his office once a week—sometimes more often—to go to the White House, where he was able to put aside the day-to-day complications of administering agricultural policy. There he would join with colleagues on the Cabinet Council on Commerce and Trade, and together they would be instructed in and would deliberate upon the nation's foreign trade relations. The sense of being involved, as much as any single factor, kept the secretaries from resigning. Their commitment to stay on gave them the opportunity to master the Reagan philosophy.[11]

Second, with time the cabinet council structure also helped school and discipline them in the practical application of the president's principles. The cabinet councils often met with the president, confronted urgent and complicated problems, and had to make responsible judgments. As happens at such times, they found abstract principles useful in cutting through the confusion of dazzling, disorganized fact. In applying repeatedly a few central ideas on which they could agree—and that inevitably meant the president's general ideas—they found it easier to make difficult decisions. The cumulative exercises of applying principle to practice emboldened them, built their confidence in the president's philosophy, and acquainted them with the implications of this increasingly familiar "touchstone."[12]

Third, their regular exercise in principled thinking built solidarity among the cabinet members. As a result, when they returned to their separate and specialized domains of agency and clientele, they not only were able to speak consistently with the president's philosophy, but, knowing they were part of a team, they felt reinforced in their courage and will to speak out.[13]

The secretaries, to justify new decisions that proved troubling to conscientious employees, found themselves explaining the president's philosophy. Moreover, in responding to the endless questions of reporters and members of Congress, they repeated his principles in explanation. Finally, in speaking to the public clientele of their agencies, they invoked the president's general ideas.[14]

In short, the cabinet councils fortified them to go into the world, not to be taught what was wrong, but to teach the president's definition of what was wrong.[15]

As the cabinet was turned into the White House's own moral institution, the speechwriters of the cabinet secretaries observed the development. I spoke with ten of them about their bosses' role in spreading the president's public philosophy.

The cabinet speechwriters were a varied lot: some were young and some were old; a couple were heirs of affluent Ivy League traditions and a few were brought up in labor families; some were political novices just getting their feet wet; several were individuals of considerable independent accomplishment. Among them were former journalists and former clergy; career agency employees and temporary hangers-on; isolated wordsmiths and close personal confidants to the secretaries.

Their bosses were no less diverse. They included long-time presidential intimates, such as Interior Secretary William Clark and Attorney General Edwin Meese (after he ceased to be counselor to the president); former members of Congress, such as Budget Director David Stockman and Trade Representative William Brock (later to be secretary of labor); clientele specialists, such as Agriculture Secretary John Block, Transportation Secretary Elizabeth Dole, and Housing and Urban Development (HUD) Secretary Samuel Pierce; and men and women of national repute, such as Secretary of State George Shultz, United Nations Ambassador Jeane Kirkpatrick, Treasury Secretary Donald Regan, and Secretary of Commerce Malcolm Baldrige. Their departments varied, too, from the intimate International Trade Representative's Office to the sprawling clientele agencies like Agriculture, HUD, Interior, and Labor. Yet in the speechwriters' accounts of what they and their bosses did, they repeatedly made the same four points.

First, all the cabinet members made a lot of speeches. They spoke to their specialized clientele. A list of their audiences was endless: the American Mining Conference, the American Water Resources Association, the cattle ranchers, the mortgage bankers, the Western States Dairy Conference, the Dairy Farmers Association, the National Corngrowers Association, the American Meat Institute, export groups and economic groups, the NAACP, the AFL-CIO, the Trilateral Commission, and so on. They spoke three and four times a week. "It's incredible," said Don Smyth, the Labor Department speechwriter. "I have never seen a schedule like Bill Brock's nowadays." Ed Dale, speechwriter for Budget Director Stockman and a former economics reporter for the *New York Times* and the *New York Herald Tribune*, explained why such "incredible" schedules were necessary: If the president was going to change how Americans thought, his message had to be repeated countless times. Moreover, he said, since the ideas would lose their news value unless they were attached to some current problem they had to be presented to specific audiences in person. In a pluralist America, there were so many different audiences that Reagan needed his inner circle to speak repeatedly for him on his behalf.

On top of addressing these countless private groups, the secretaries also had to appear before congressional committees, where—often in quite adversarial circumstances—they would have to rebut critics and fortify political allies. Finally, they spoke to their agencies, conveying to the career employees the unfamiliar ideas of a new president. As Jayne Gallagher, the principal speechwriter at HUD, put it, "The Secretary talks philosophy [in order] to theme the agency."

Second, the cabinet members and their speechwriters were very clear about what Reagan's principles were. Justice Department speechwriter Terry Eastland summed up his understanding, "In a nutshell, he is seeking a rebirth of the idea of liberty in this country." The president's purposes seemed no less clear to his speechwriting colleagues in other departments: "to shrink back the role of the federal government"; to bring America back ("four years ago the most depressing statistic was that we thought our kids would be worse off than we are. And the Government was taking us down"); to be aware of "the nation's sense of morale"; to stand for the conservative philosophy ("the country runs the government, not vice versa. It's the country's own intrinsic vitality which is this nation's strength, not the government's vitality"); to demonstrate "that we are not guilty as a nation for the wrongs of the world. . . . Our values are right, and it's right to defend those values when attacked."

The president's words were frequently read by the cabinet speechwriters. "I look at the Reagan speeches. I try to let them influence me," said one. Another recalled, "Reagan's State of the Union speech [in 1985] really did move me very strongly, and at a number of levels. It had a tremendous impact on my wife and me, very moving, and it hit a lot of points. It talked to us about the meaning of ourselves as Americans and our American place in the world." "You know," said Gene Hemphill, speechwriter in the Department of Agriculture, "Reagan came to Joliet, [Illinois], years ago, maybe it was 1976, and I still have a copy of his speech, and it is not much different from the things he said in 1980 and even today. What he intends to do . . . is to leave America a little more in charge of its own destiny, instead of letting government be in charge of its destiny." Reagan's ideas, repeatedly stated, became a part of the way cabinet speechwriters tended to think.

Third, by virtue of the cabinet members' familiarity with Reagan's philosophy, their speeches were framed in terms of those principles. They could express his ideas as easily as he could. They conceived their role as one of conveying the administration's outlook. The cabinet speechwriters drew confidence from the president's speeches. "I have the most fun," said one of the more youthful of them, "when there is a philosophical slant to a speech that I can write out of my own head. I use a 'slant' which I feel certain the president would agree with. . . . When I get the chance with a speech, I like to include material which I know is aligned with the President's tilt of thought. I put his philosophy into any speech I get a chance at."

Speechwriter Bob Walker showed me a speech Interior Secretary Clark was going to give to the Ranchers Association. With its emphasis on partnership, it sounded like a paraphrase of Edmund Burke's *Reflections on the Revolution in France* ("Society . . . becomes a partnership . . . between those who are living, those who are dead, and those who are to be born"). It read: "We have a partnership—you who live on, and care for and use the land to raise livestock, and those of us in government charged with managing these federally owned resources. Together we preserve the remaining remnants of pioneer America." Walker commented: "Government has a partnership with business and provides that framework of life. We're beating on that approach of partnership because the secretary likes it, and I like it. It's gotten so I don't put a draft on the secretary's desk without mentioning partnership."

Fourth, the cabinet enjoyed talking in philosophical terms and thought it important to do so. The cabinet speechwriters would say things like, "Secretary Pierce is beginning to enjoy the bully pulpit since he's starting to talk big ideas" and "the beauty of working with Cabinet-level officials is that you're talking about ideals and principles, not facts."

Joe Dugan, who served as speechwriter for both U.N. Ambassador Kirkpatrick and Transportation Secretary Dole, summed up the satisfaction of being a part of the president's philosophical team:

> The president is unique among all high officials in the government because of his role as a teacher, as a communicator, as a preacher of the public philosophy. We look to him to do that. There is one school of political theory that gives a lot of emphasis to that role. I don't think I agreed with that school so much, until Ronald Reagan came along. I had a teacher who stressed the role of the president as Chief Magistrate, as Magister, a teacher. "Let's not forget the meaning of that word," he would say. . . .
>
> Now communication is not all there is to it. That's asserting too much, that's assuming too much interest among the people in abstraction and philosophy. But philosophy is part of the people, and the people experience Reagan, and they resonate with the fit between his philosophy and theirs.

The secretaries were only the most conspicuous propagators of the president's ideas. There were adherents to his principles throughout the vocal classes and the government itself. They, too, did their missionary work whenever they could. They maintained contact among themselves and with the president (and his speechwriters) through an important process of commentary. Commentary permitted ever-widening circles of adherents to discuss the president's text and argue its interpretation among themselves and with the president (and his speechwriters). The means of commentary consisted in part of a network of conservative journals.[16] Of greatest importance was the "administration's newspaper," the *Washington Times*.[17] Established in the second year of the Reagan administration and financed by South Korean businessmen (all were members of the Reverend Sun Myung Moon's Unification Church), the *Washington Times* opened its columns to dozens of eloquent and experienced conservatives. It had a small circulation (about 100,000) that masked its importance. Virtually all the spokesmen of the Reagan administration read it, especially its three-page "Commentary" section. In the *Washington Times* scores of philosophers and columnists (for example, Michael Novak and Pat Buchanan), economists and political scientists (Warren Brookes and Ben Wattenberg), military officers and White House staff (Elmo Zumwalt and former Nixon speechwriter Raymond Price), scholars and lawyers (Thomas Sowell and Alan Dershowitz), and even a former president (Richard Nixon) routinely debated the appropriate ways to apply the president's philosophy. Here, in the liveliest intellectual forum in town, the president's words were quoted, discussed, controverted, and reinforced. Ideas from one column would be discussed in someone else's column the next week and sooner or later would appear in some official's speech. The daily appearance of the *Washington Times* stirred an abundance of controversy within the presidency. The dialogue built a philosophical solidarity that produced fealty and courage among the president's adherents.

Alexis de Tocqueville once wrote that newspapers had an important part to play in a free society. They united like-minded individuals not otherwise aware of each other into communities. Tocqueville could have been describing exactly the relation between the *Washington Times* and the substantial army of Reaganauts that inhabited Washington:

> In democratic countries . . . it frequently happens that a great number of men who wish or who want to combine cannot accomplish it because as they are very insignificant and lost amid the crowd, they cannot see and do not know where to find one another. A newspaper then takes up the notion or the feeling that had occurred simultaneously, but singly, to each of them. All are then immediately guided towards this beacon; and these wandering minds, which had long sought each other in darkness, at length meet and unite. The newspaper brought them together, and the newspaper is still necessary to keep them united.[18]

The newspaper as a beacon in the night, guiding wandering minds to a common meeting point—as florid as the image might sound, it was an apt depiction of the *Washington Times*.

Thus, within the government there had come into being a process of propagation possessing all the features of a mature moral institution—a text, an exegetic organ, a school of instruction and instrument of discipline, and a commentary network. Even the word "Reaganaut" was useful in identifying the committed carrier of the president's public philosophy.

Was it effective? I asked Peter Rodman that question. He was chief of the Office of Policy and Planning in the State Department and sometime speechwriter for Secretary George Shultz. He had been a part of several presidencies in his relatively young life, having been brought to Washington by his former professor, Henry Kissinger. He thought carefully before he spoke about the Reagan method of governing, and then he said: "The striking thing about this president . . . is that he has placed his stamp on this government by virtue of a coherent philosophy everyone understands. . . . I doubt if any president has so permanently and so widely left his mark on government as Reagan."

Reagan taught from both his primary and his secondary pulpits. He spoke to the people from the former and to his administration from the latter. One key to his success was the harmony between the ideas transmitted at the two levels. The administration theme, that centralized government weakened the hearts and nerve of the citizenry, was premised on the very ideas that constituted the popular sermon: that human nature was a divided nature, evil impulse struggling with good; that the ethical measure of individual human worth was spiritual, signifying the victory within of good over evil; that a society organized around private exchange fortified the individual in his spiritual battle; that reciprocity provided countless tiny compulsions to please others; and that a welfare society robbed individuals of the demands to reciprocate that fortified them in their inner battles with their worse side.

The White House's rhetorical strategy left the president's mark so pervasively on the country precisely because the president spoke at these two levels of discourse. The message from the primary pulpit reduced people's expectations of government, and from the secondary pulpit the president justified to the nation's bureaucracies their reduced, but honorable role:

> Economic growth does not spring from the numbers and graphs in government bureaus but from the hope and aspirations of ordinary people. . . . [T]he key to the future is in a simple human face. It's not the face of someone famous, someone whose name is likely to appear in the history books, but of someone, a man or a woman, who carries in his or her heart a dream, an excitement, a drive. And despite others calling that person impractical, he or she goes out and builds a dream into a business. Sometimes the dream is technologically sophisticated. Sometimes it's as simple as the store on the corner. Either way, this person, this dreamer, this entrepreneur, whether on

his or her own or as a determined leader in a firm, is the driving
force behind all growth. And because he or she can come from any
part of society with ideas that will often seem eccentric, at least until
they are tested, we in government cannot help this individual. We
can't effectively target money or other assistance. We can only keep
out of his or her way. We can . . . reduce taxes and regulations and
open markets. We can give freedom.[19]

"We can give freedom"—that was a coherent and intelligible philosophy
to imprint on the hearts and minds of those who inhabited the great
federal bureaucracies.

15

★★★★★★★

Presidential Power and Presidential Leadership

Ideas are the stuff of politics.

—Anthony Dolan (1985)

In his classic study of the American presidency, political scientist Richard Neustadt observed, "Presidential *power* is the power to persuade."[1] As any dictionary buff knows, the verb "persuade" has two quite distinct meanings: to convince and to coax. Neustadt used the term in its latter sense, to coax by offering material inducements. A president got his way, not by spreading the word convincingly, but by distributing favors enticingly.

Neustadt's *Presidential Power* thus was not about presidential leadership, not about "the sharpening of spirit and of values and of purposes." His study did not concern itself with how presidents shaped the public philosophy, or prompted private activity, or moved the people to be generous, hard-working, and brave. Rather, *Presidential Power* was about how presidents made members of the political class do what was unpleasant to do. It dwelt exclusively on how presidents got Congress to legislate, regulators to regulate, and bureaucrats to carry out orders. To Neustadt, the principal responsibility of the president was to move the machinery of the national government into action.[2]

That was a formidable task. According to Neustadt, a president found it virtually impossible to persuade other officials to see the world as he did. Instead, to get their cooperation he had to offer them favors.

187

Exchange, not attitude change, was the name of the presidential game. A good president depended exclusively on bargaining, for he got "no help he did not pay for."[3]

A president's store of incentives derived from his control over government appointments, his influence in the budget process, and his willingness to act on behalf of (or in opposition to) projects that others wanted. He also could pay for help with such intangible inducements as charm, status, and publicity. A president was always negotiating with others, first figuring out what they believed they needed and then striking deals.[4]

In Neustadt's drama of power in Washington, the public stayed largely out of sight. They made a minor appearance as the audience of presidential events, and their applause for him could augment the value of the resources with which he made his bargains. The people could confer on him a popularity that made his charms more irresistible and his recognition more desirable to Washington insiders. If the public liked the man in the White House, if his popular approval ratings were high, then his bargaining power appreciated, and the price that politicians had to pay to deal with him soared. On the other hand, if his popularity declined, then being associated with him became less attractive, and his status inside Washington was whittled down to insignificant proportions.[5] The role of the people was about as simple as that.

Of all the president's resources, the one of greatest potential value was his ability to offer his support to governmental initiatives that others wanted. The greater the president's reputation for getting things done in Washington, the higher the price he could demand for presidential support. According to Neustadt, one way the president demonstrated his political acumen to the Washington community was in speaking publicly to the nation as a whole. Washingtonians were always scrutinizing the president's capacity to arouse intense public reaction. A president with demagogic skills made a favorable impression on Washingtonians.[6]

Neustadt ended *Presidential Power* by emphasizing the importance of governmental action. "We are confronted," he said, "by an evident necessity for government more energetic, policies more viable, than we have been enjoying in the Fifties."[7]

If it appeared obvious to Neustadt that the decades following the 1950s would need an infusion of more government to cure the nation of its practical problems, events turned out otherwise. The actuality was that the 1960s and 1970s were dominated by spiritual problems—urban riots, skyrocketing crime rates, a segment of the younger generation opting out, the sexual revolution, an acute sensitivity to inequalities of every kind, hopelessness, a lack of support for governmental actions in the Vietnam

War, mendacity in the presidency, panic in the face of enlarged Soviet nuclear capability, and a loss of confidence in the rightness of democracy and the values of a free society. As Joan Didion pointed out (quoting Yeats), the rough beast of hate slouched toward (and into) an alienated and uncomprehending America in the 1960s and 1970s. Things really did fall apart, the center failed to hold, and a larger governmental presence of the kind urged in *Presidential Power* did little to keep hope from shattering. What might presidents do to lead a free people in times of spiritual crisis? Being about presidential power and government action, Neustadt's book was virtually silent on values and purposes. Neustadt never intended to write a book about presidential leadership of the American society and of its 235 million citizens.[8]

If we define presidential power as the capacity to stir government to action, it is reasonable to claim that Ronald Reagan exercised a great deal of presidential power in his eight years in the White House. Admittedly, he was far from perfectly effective. Many problems exceeded his capacity or will to cure: drugs, mental illness, barbaric violence in the ghettos of our central cities, a big central government deficit. Still, he did obtain the favorable action of Congress on all his major initiatives: control of runaway inflation, tax rate reductions, the termination of new federal domestic welfare spending, legislation requiring a balanced federal budget and providing a tolerable transition to this end, tax reform on a comprehensive scale, reduction of federal regulation in the private sector, a strengthened national defense, elimination of Soviet missiles from Europe, and mutually verifiable nuclear arms reductions by the Soviet Union and United States. Even by the assessment of his most severe critics, Ronald Reagan stirred up a lot of governmental action. In respect of exercising presidential power within the Washington community, he doubtless often behaved in the best Neustadtian style, wheedling and bargaining to get the necessary cooperation of Washington insiders.

But the successful employment of presidential power was only half of his achievement. He also provided presidential leadership to the people. From his bully pulpit he shaped the public philosophy. To the American public he restored a common sense of human nature, human goodness, and human society. He renewed public confidence in America's private and public institutions, not least the American presidency. Furthermore, virtually everywhere on earth he inspired popular appreciation of the free market and liberal democracy.

There were six principal factors contributing to his success as a presidential leader. He was fortunate, he cared, he appreciated that general ideas had social consequences, he was careful about his rhetoric, he enlisted the aid of moral collaborators, and he was wise (that is, he developed the right ideas).

Let us touch on the first of those six secrets of effective presidential leadership: good fortune. Events beyond control can strip a president of his respectability, and without respectability rhetoric is empty. *Fortuna*, as Machiavelli warned five hundred years ago, can be fickle. During the Reagan years, 1981 to 1989, she was not fickle, although she nearly was.

Consider the effect of the Iran-Contra scandal, when the president's integrity and competence were put in question. On November 3, 1986, disclosures broke that led the nation to question Reagan's integrity and competence. It was alleged that he authorized the trading of military weapons to Iran as ransom for innocent hostages seized at the behest of that outlaw state. He was further charged with diverting public funds to support one side in a civil war in the Central American nation of Nicaragua, willfully disobeying a law forbidding him to do so. With respect to both offenses, he was accused of lying to the American public to cover up his stupidity or his deceit, or both.

In the twelve months following these charges, Reagan's public approval rating plummeted from 67 percent to a "weak" 49 percent.[9] He and his speechwriters were preoccupied in self-defense. Four times between November 1986 and October 1987 the president had to preempt nationwide television to protest his innocence.

The necessity for self-defense distracted his energies from speaking about the public philosophy.[10] Three months into the ordeal, at the annual Conservative Political Action Conference (always his friendliest audience), he spoke of the strain of justifying questionable deeds. As usual, he spoke with humor.

> You know these last several weeks, I've felt a little bit like that farmer that was driving his horse and wagon to town for some grain and had a head-on collision with a truck. And later was the litigation involving claims for his injuries, some of them permanent. And he was on the stand and a lawyer said to him, "Isn't it true that while you were lying there at the scene of the accident someone came over to you and asked you how you were feeling, and you said you never felt better in your life?" And he said, "Yes, I remember that." Well, later he's on the stand and the witnesses were there—the lawyer for [his] side is questioning—and he said, "When you gave that answer about how you felt, what were the circumstances?" "Well," he said, "I was lying there and a car came up and a deputy sheriff got out." He said, "My horse was screaming with pain—had broken two legs." The deputy took out his gun, put it in the horse's ear, and finished him off. "And," he said, "my dog was whining with pain—had a broken back. And," he said, "he went over to him and put the gun in his ear. And then," he says, "he turned to me and says now, how are you feeling?"[11]

Although it turned out that the humiliation and threat of permanent injury to his presidency eventually subsided, much of his second term was spent with a gun in his ear.

It must be repeated that all presidents will encounter tragedy and setback. With their reactions to failure and their reflections on it, they may maintain (and even enhance) their respectability. Nevertheless, presidents beset by the appearance of unacceptable behavior become fair game for their political detractors. Under suspicion is not the best presidential posture for managing a moral revolution.

For the most part, however, *fortuna* permitted Reagan a reasonable opportunity to concentrate his energies. The economy turned up, and foreign aggression affecting America's vital interests turned down.

The five remaining conditions that make presidential leadership possible were within Reagan's control, and he fulfilled them. First, he caused good speechwriters to be initially selected, and they learned quickly from the speeches he personally composed in his prepresidential days. By his skill in delivering what his speechwriting team wrote, he conveyed to them its personal importance to him and that he cared very much how well his speeches were crafted. He always was the complete professional, prepared, elevating his public performance despite distractions and personal fatigue.

Second, Reagan personally seemed to appreciate the importance of the human spirit. He communicated to Americans that he cared about their feelings by expressing encouragement, cheering them, consoling them, and speaking of their daily deeds. He repeatedly expressed publicly to his administration that his most important objective was the renewal of hope in America.

Third, he seemed to sense that ideas were "the great moving forces of history" (as Tony Dolan put it). With "A Time for Choosing," he set an example for his speechwriting team in how to express general notions carefully. He paid attention to the fact that humans were philosophical animals, and he targeted his rhetoric to strengthen (or change) their personal philosophies, thereby influencing the actions that were based on them. In speaking to the people, he and the Speechwriting Department took pains to speak publicly in a way completely consistent with what he said privately to legislators, governmental agencies, and the international diplomatic community. His arguments were not only consistent, but they had order, and he worked to demonstrate how the policies of his administration derived from explicit and fundamental principles.[12] No matter that the philosophy departments of our nation's colleges would likely reject his application for a job, Reagan appreciated the importance of identifying (and challenging) the general ideas of those whose conclusions differed from his. He also had the physical endurance to carry out the exhausting repetition of his argument. He acted as if he knew that perseverance was fundamental to changing a nation's public philosophy.

Fourth, by intuition, luck, or otherwise, Reagan sensed the usefulness of moral institutions in penetrating the robust American society with his ideas. The president responded positively to Meese's suggestion of cabinet councils—a critical step in turning the cabinet into an effective moral institution. In reaching the people themselves, he felt comfortable piggybacking on an established and comforting institution, the church, to affect (and ratify) the citizenry's profoundest moral beliefs. He drew upon the common spring of American religious thought, with its notions of imperfect human nature, spiritual dignity, and social partnership. His numerous appearances before sympathetic religious organizations disciplined him and his speechwriters to speak about the spiritual questions inherent in America's religious traditions. In turn, his solicitude for the concerns of the clergy and religious laymen galvanized them to advocate the ideas they held in common. He also seemed to understand that no peacetime president was going to have the time and resources to create a nationwide network de novo. "You can't make brick without straw," the saying goes, and the point had special application to a moral leader like Ronald Reagan. His White House understood that he could not go it alone, and he made the commitment to collaborate with an established moral institution.

Last, Reagan and his speechwriting team had the right ideas, ideas that gave hope to the souls of many of his people. Some ideas oppress and deaden the human spirit. Others, like Shakespeare's, enliven it—universally. These beliefs we call wisdom because they speak to the needs of the human spirit. Reagan, together with his speechwriters and other collaborators, spread a philosophy that helped in healing the three great afflictions of living free—ignorance, despair, and loneliness. They understood that these spiritual needs were enduring ones. Thus, they were confident that they could become morally effective today by emulating those who had been moral leaders yesterday. They turned to history to learn from it. The past revealed the ways to govern well—with philosophy. "I suppose," Reagan once said to the National Governors' Association, "it's the destiny of every second generation or so to think for a while that maybe they're wiser than our Founding Fathers. And it's the destiny of the generation that follows to realize that this almost certainly is not true and to try to bring the nation back to its first principles."[13]

PART FOUR

EPILOGUE

★★★★★★★

I've always said that in our democracy, the people tell you, the politician, what is needed, not the other way around.

—Ronald Reagan (1989)

A t the end of this inquiry into presidential leadership, we need to ask one more question, a personal one. How did Ronald Reagan, a motion-picture and television actor until his mid-fifties, learn to be an effective moral leader? Whence came his understanding of the profound philosophical questions embedded in the souls of free people?

To me, an admirer of Reagan the president, that question was mystifying enough because Reagan the man did not appear to be the typical philosopher. He was too gregarious, too unabashed in his enthusiasms, too simplistic in his thinking, too full of corny (and attractive) stories to fit the image of the profound thinker. For readers with more skeptical (or even hostile) attitudes toward the man, the puzzle must have been intensely baffling.

One summer morning in Los Angeles in 1989, I raised this question in an interview with Reagan, now a former president. It had been some seven months since he had turned the White House over to his elected successor, George Bush, the former vice president.

Typically, Reagan never offered a direct answer. Rather he spoke in anecdotes, but his chain of stories disclosed a seeming paradox. By speaking to democratic audiences, he heard their ideas; by listening to him, his audiences disclosed the contents of their hearts to him. This was what he said.[1]

He began with his after-dinner speaking experiences in Hollywood, where he had tried to correct the "false image" of "rampant immorality" in the movie business:

> And then I got interested in the next question: What difference did it make? What was this false image doing to us? What was the result of it? And the answer was that the rest of the country was becoming indifferent to what was being done to Hollywood. What did they care about people who misbehaved all the time and made so much money, and so fast? Because of this false image about the movie business, no one would go to bat for it when it was in trouble.

And it was in trouble, for the government was putting it to the entertainment business. There was discrimination taxwise. Some actors and artists may become big wage earners—but people in the entertainment business have only a short time in which they are going to be successful, if they ever are. And so forth.

Once that theme was added—about the political consequences of the false image people had about things—others would come up to me after my talk, and they'd tell me stories about what was happening to them because of the ideas people had about their business and not caring about what was happening. And pretty soon I was including more and more about government's ever greater interference in our lives. I talked about what seemed to me the adversarial nature of government toward the business sector. And as time went on, the material on Hollywood became less and less a part of the speech, and I expanded the ideas and the subjects I covered.

Reagan next discussed his work at General Electric as a corporate spokesman:

Well, there's always a demand for public speakers. And General Electric heard of me, and hired me, and put me on the road for twelve weeks a year.[2] And I'd visit all the plants. There were 139 of them. And it's interesting: never once was I told what to say.[3]

Well, one day, being a Democrat at the time, I went home to Nancy [Reagan, his wife] and said, "I go out making these speeches, calling attention to government's faults. Then, every four years, I campaign for the people responsible for those faults. Back when I was first voting, the Democrats were the party for low tariffs and free trade. Today the Democrats have become the party for protectionism."

What happened was that I was bothered by the way the Democratic party was changing. I never had any ambition to run for any office. I loved the entertainment world, and if I could have stayed in it, I would have been very content. But as I talked publicly, I realized how much certain views of politics had changed, and I put together all my ideas in a speech, which I called "A Time for Choosing."[4]

"A Time for Choosing" brought Reagan into the Republican party:

I was asked to give ["A Time for Choosing"] in behalf of Barry Goldwater in 1964. Later, a group of leading Republicans asked me whether, if they bought the air time on national television, would I give the speech? "Yes," I said, "I would." And I did. Later, I was told that it had raised eight million dollars for the campaign.

Well, the next thing I knew, this same group of leading Republicans came to me and said I'd have to run for governor of California, against [the incumbent governor] Pat Brown. What with the split in the Republican party—between [Nelson] Rockefeller and Goldwater and so forth—we didn't have a chance to win other than if I was the candidate.

I thought they were out of their minds, and I told them so. But they kept after me. With them it was simply a matter of winning or losing: Never mind whether I'd be a good governor or not. Well, I finally said, "You make it possible for me to go out on the road and provide me some speaking engagements, places where I can make some speeches, and we'll see."[5]

Reagan then detailed his campaign experiences, which included speaking throughout California.

So for the next six months, I did that. They hired a firm—Spencer Roberts—to develop a schedule, and there I was, out on the road, driving myself all over the state. And the more I talked, and the more the people reacted, the greater impression it had on me. I went back to Nancy. "You know, I think they're right," I said. "I think the people want a change in government. It's a funny thing, because they're making up their minds all based on a speech." Then Nancy and I talked over the big question: If they're right, and if I didn't make a race for governor, could I live with myself?

With all that speaking, I found that at the end of six months, by that time I had a program. I suppose it was the entertainer in me that made me want to please the people. I wanted to hear their questions, and I wanted to give them answers that would satisfy those questions.

Well, once we got in the campaign, Pat Brown began saying to everybody that I'm an actor. "He's just reading words written by others. Who writes those speeches?"

Well, the answer was, I did. And the question was, How to counter the question and the implied criticism? And I made a suggestion which scared the heck out of the people who were advising me. I would shorten my speech and leave more time for questions and answers. That way, with my answers having to be extemporaneous, they could not say that someone else was writing the answers.[6]

So, whenever I'd speak—it didn't make a difference if it was three or three thousand—I'd first start the meeting with a few remarks, and then I'd open the meeting to question-and-answer. They [Reagan's advisers] were scared, but that's what I did, and I learned from the people's questions what the issues were that were bothering them. And I kept hearing the same questions from them—it didn't make any difference whether it was Northern California or Southern California or whatever: they were the same questions from all over the state. And it assured me that I knew what was on the people's mind.

And I began doing some research on the things they asked me about, and then I learned I had not been wrong on things. Yes, the government was mismanaging things. Yes, they were playing bookkeeping tricks to cover up the costs of what they were doing. You know, the Constitution of California prohibits deficit spending, but they were spending a million more dollars a day than they were taking in, and they had to deny it. When I went into office, I tried to turn things around.

Finally, he told of his countless speeches after stepping down from the office of governor. Reagan had set his eye on getting elected president, and he had to go back to being an after-dinner speaker.

> By the time I'd had eight years of experience as governor of the state of California (a state which, if it were a nation would be the seventh ranking economic power in the world), I had a very definite sense of what the people wanted. In the years after that—between stepping down in Sacramento [in 1974] and running for the presidency [for a second time, in 1980]—I went back to the mashed-potato circuit as a public speaker.
>
> I've always said that in our democracy, the people tell you, the politician, what is needed, not the other way around. And after a couple of years, I found I had listened and developed answers to their questions, and then I found I had in mind a program. It was quite simple. I came to the presidency with that program, and I intended to get that program in place. I knew what I wanted by that time.[7]

By paying attention to the reactions and comments of his audience, Reagan learned profound things. An attentive leader, he listened to people by talking to them; "they began telling me stories about what was happening to them." With their individual reactions to his words and ideas ("I kept hearing the same questions from them"), they told him about their values, their histories, and the foundations of their hopes. Their reactions caused him to reshape what he would say to them next time ("I suppose it was the entertainer in me that made me want to please the people"), and trying his answers out on the next audience permitted him to verify his hunches about what made the people tick ("It assured me that I knew what was on the people's mind").

In order to connect with his audiences, he sought to articulate what he believed were their aspirations. In order to honor them, he tried to reflect back to them the significance of their lives. In order to inspire their whole-hearted response, he attempted to anticipate their questions and give them coherent answers.

In short, Reagan spoke to countless audiences, and they shared with him their own experiences. In exchange, he instructed them in a public philosophy that enlarged their insight, hope, and sense of teamwork. A capacity like Reagan's, for learning from and teaching the people, is the indispensable virtue of a good presidential leader.

APPENDIX

"A Time for Choosing"

(Address on behalf of Barry Goldwater's presidential candidacy at the Republican National Convention, San Francisco, California, 1964)

I am going to talk of controversial things. I make no apology for this. I have been talking on this subject for ten years, obviously under the administration of both parties. I mention this only because it seems impossible to legitimately debate the issues of the day without being subjected to name-calling and the application of labels. Those who deplore use of the terms "pink" and "leftist" are themselves guilty of branding all who oppose their liberalism as right wing extremists.

How long can we afford the luxury of this family fight when we are at war with the most dangerous enemy ever known to man? If we lose that war, and in so doing lose our freedom, it has been said history will record with the greatest astonishment that those who had the most to lose did the least to prevent its happening. The guns are silent in this war but frontiers fall while those who should be warriors prefer neutrality. Not too long ago two friends of mine were talking to a Cuban refugee. He was a business man who had escaped from Castro. In the midst of his tale of horrible experiences, one of my friends turned to the other and said, "We don't know how lucky we are." The Cuban stopped and said, "How lucky you are? I had some place to escape to." And in that sentence he told the entire story. If freedom is lost here, there is no place to escape to.

It's time we asked ourselves if we still know the freedoms intended for us by the Founding Fathers. James Madison said, "We base all our experiments on the capacity of mankind for self-government." This idea that government was beholden to the people, that it had no other source of power except the sovereign people, is still the newest, most unique idea in all the long history of man's relation to man. For almost two centuries we have proved man's capacity for self-government, but today we are told we must choose between a left and right or, as others suggest, a third alternative, a kind of safe middle ground. I suggest to you there is no left or right, only an up or down. Up to the maximum of individual freedom consistent with law and order, or down to the ant heap of totalitarianism, and regardless of their humanitarian purpose those who would sacrifice freedom for security have, whether they know it or not, chosen this downward path.

Plutarch warned, "The real destroyer of the liberties of the people is he who spreads among them bounties, donations and benefits." Today there is an increasing number who can't see a fat man standing beside a thin one without automatically coming to the conclusion the fat man got that way by taking advantage of the thin one. So they would seek the answer to all the problems of human need through government. Howard K. Smith of television fame has written, "The profit motive is outmoded. It must be replaced by the incentives of the welfare state." He said, "The distribution of goods must be effected by a planned economy."

Another articulate spokesman for the welfare state defines liberalism as meeting the material needs of the masses through the full power of centralized government. I for one find it disturbing when a representative refers to the free men and women of this country as the masses, but beyond this the full power of centralized government was the very thing the Founding Fathers sought to minimize. They knew you don't control things, you can't control the economy without controlling *people.*

So we have come to a time for choosing. Either we accept the responsibility for our own destiny, or we abandon the American Revolution and confess that an intellectual belief in a far-distant capital can plan our lives for us better than we can plan them ourselves.

Already the hour is late. Government has laid its hand on health, housing, farming, industry, commerce, education, and to an ever increasing degree interferes with the people's right to know. Government tends to grow; government programs take on weight and momentum, as public servants say, always with the best of intentions, "What greater service we could render if only we had a little more money and a little more power." But the truth is that outside of its legitimate function, government does nothing as well or as economically as the private sector of the economy.

What better example do we have of this than government's involvement in the farm economy over the last thirty years? One-fourth of farming has seen a steady decline in the per capita consumption of everything it produces. That one-fourth is regulated and subsidized by government. In contrast, the three-fourths of farming unregulated and unsubsidized has seen a 21 percent increase in the per capita consumption of all its produce. Since 1955 the cost of the farm program has nearly doubled. Direct payment to farmers is eight times as great as it was nine years ago, but farm income remains unchanged while farm surplus is bigger. In that same period we have seen a decline of five million in the farm population, but an increase in the number of Department of Agriculture employees.

There is now one such employee for every thirty farms in the United States, and still they can't figure how sixty-six shiploads of grain headed for Austria could disappear without a trace, and Billy Sol Estes never left shore. Three years ago the government put into effect a program to curb the overproduction of feed grain. Now, two and a half billion dollars later, the corn crop is 100 million bushels bigger than before the program started. And the cost of the program prorates out to $43 for every dollar of the price we pay for government meddling.

Some government programs with the passage of time take on a sacrosanct quality. One such considered above criticism, sacred as motherhood, is TVA. This program started as a flood control project; the Tennessee Valley was periodically ravaged by destructive floods. The Army Engineers set out to solve this problem. They said that it was possible that once in 500 years there could be a total capacity flood that would inundate some 600,000 acres. Well, the engineers fixed that. They made a permanent lake which inundated a million acres. This solved the problem of the floods, but the annual interest on the TVA debt is five times as great as the annual flood damage they sought to correct.

Of course, you will point out that TVA gets electric power from the impounded waters, and this is true, but today 85 percent of TVA's electricity is generated in coal-burning steam plants. Now, perhaps you'll charge that I'm overlooking the navigable waterway that was created, providing cheap barge traffic, but the bulk of the freight barged on that waterway is coal being shipped to the TVA steam plants, and the cost of maintaining that channel each year would pay for shipping all of the coal by rail, and there would be money left over.

One last argument remains: The prosperity produced by such large programs of government spending. Certainly there are few areas where more spending has taken place. The Labor Department lists 50 percent of the 100 counties in the Tennessee Valley as permanent areas of poverty, distress, and unemployment.

Meanwhile, back in the city, under Urban Renewal, the assault on freedom carries on. Private property rights have become so diluted that public interest is anything a few planners decide it should be. In Cleveland, Ohio, to get a project underway, city officials reclassified eighty-four buildings as substandard in spite of the fact their own inspectors had previously pronounced these buildings sound. The owners stood by and watched $26 million worth of property destroyed by the headache ball. Senate Bill 628 says, "Any property, be it home or commercial structure, can be declared slum or blighted and the owner has no recourse at law." The Law Division of the Library of Congress and the General Accounting Office have said that the Courts will have to rule against the owner.

In one key Eastern city a man owning a blighted area sold his property to Urban Renewal for several million dollars. At the same time, he submitted his own plan for the rebuilding of this area and the government sold him back his own property for 22 percent of what they paid. Now the government announces, "We are going to build subsidized housing in the thousands where we have been building in the hundreds." At the same time, FHA and the Veterans Administration reveal they are holding 120,000 housing units reclaimed from mortgage foreclosure, mostly because the low down payments and the easy terms brought the owners to a point where they realized the unpaid balance on the homes amounted to a sum greater than the homes were worth, so they just walked out the front door, possibly to take up residence in newer subsidized housing, again with little or no down payment and easy terms. Some of the foreclosed homes have already been bulldozed into the earth; others, it has been announced, will be refurbished and put on sale for down payments as low as $100 and 35 years to pay. This will give the bulldozers a second crack.

It is in the area of social welfare that government has found its most fertile growing bed. So many of us accept our responsibility for those less fortunate. We are susceptible to humanitarian appeals.

Federal welfare spending is today ten times greater than it was in the dark depths of the Depression. Federal, state, and local welfare combined spend $45 billion a year. Now the government has announced that 20 percent, some 9.3 million families, are poverty stricken on the basis that they have less than a $3,000 a year income. If this present welfare spending was prorated equally among these poverty stricken families, we could give each family more than $4,500 a year. Actually, direct aid to the poor averages less than $600 per family. There must be some administrative overhead somewhere. Now, are we to believe that another billion dollar program added to the half a hundred programs and the $45 billion will, through some magic, end poverty?

For three decades we have tried to solve unemployment by government planning, without success. The more the plans fail, the more the planners plan. The latest is the Area Redevelopment Agency, and in two years less than one-half of one per cent of the unemployed could attribute new jobs to this agency, and the cost to the taxpayer for each job found was $5,000. But beyond the great bureaucratic waste, what are we doing to the people we seek to help?

Recently a judge told me of an incident in his court. A fairly young woman with six children, pregnant with her seventh, came to him for a divorce. Under his questioning it became apparent her husband did not share this desire. Then the whole story came out. Her husband was a laborer earning $250 a month. By divorcing him she could get an $80 raise. She was eligible for $330 a month from the Aid to Dependent Children Program. She had been talked into divorce by two friends who had already done this very thing.

But any time we question the schemes of the do-gooders, we are denounced as being opposed to their humanitarian goal. It seems impossible to legitimately debate their solutions with the assumption that all of us share the desire to help those less fortunate. Well, it isn't so much that Liberals are ignorant. It's just that they know so much that isn't so.

We are for a provision that destitution should not follow unemployment by reason of old age. For that reason we have accepted Social Security as a step toward meeting that problem. However, we are against the irresponsibility of those who charge that any criticism or suggested improvement of the program means we want to end payment to those who depend on Social Security for a livelihood.

We have been told in millions of pieces of literature and press releases that Social Security is an insurance program, but the executives of Social Security appeared before the Supreme Court in the case of *Nestor* v. *Fleming* and proved to the Court's satisfaction that it is not insurance but is a welfare program, and Social Security dues are a tax for the general use of the government. Well, it can't be both, insurance and welfare.

Later, appearing before a Congressional Committee, they admitted that Social Security is today $298 billion in the red. This fiscal irresponsibility has already caught up with us. Faced with a bankruptcy, we find that today a young man in his early twenties, going to work at less than an average salary, will with his employer pay into Social Security an amount which could provide the young man with a retirement insurance policy guaranteeing $230 a month at age 65, and the government promises him $127.

Now, are we so lacking in business sense that we cannot put this program on a sound actuarial basis, so that those who do depend on it won't come to the cupboard and find it bare, and at the same time can't we introduce voluntary features, so that those who can make better provision for themselves are allowed to do so? Incidentally, we might also allow participants in Social Security to name their own beneficiaries, which they cannot do in the present program. These are not insurmountable problems. We have today thirty million workers protected by industrial and union pension funds that are soundly financed by some $70 billion invested in corporate securities and income-earning real estate.

I think we are for telling our senior citizens that no one in this country should be denied medical care for lack of funds, but we are against forcing all citizens into a compulsory government program regardless of need. Now the government has turned its attention to our young people, and suggests that it can solve the problem of school dropouts and juvenile delinquency through some kind of revival of the old C.C.C. camps. The suggested plan prorates out to a cost of $4,700 a year for each young person we want to help. We can send them to Harvard for $2,700 a year. Of course, don't get me wrong—I'm not suggesting Harvard as the answer to juvenile delinquency.

We are for an international organization where the nations of the world can legitimately seek peace. We are against subordinating American interests to an organization so structurally unsound that a two-thirds majority can be mustered in the U.N. General Assembly among nations representing less than 10 percent of the world population.

Is there not something of hypocrisy in assailing our allies for so-called vestiges of colonialism while we engage in a conspiracy of silence about the peoples enslaved by the Soviet in the satellite nations?

We are for aiding our allies by sharing our material blessings with those nations which share our fundamental beliefs. We are against doling out money, government to government, which ends up financing socialism all over the world. We set out to help 19 war-ravaged countries at the end of World War II. We are now helping 107. We have spent $146 billion. Some of that money bought a $2 million yacht for Haile Selassie. We bought dress suits for Greek undertakers. We bought 1,000 TV sets, with 23-inch screens, for a country where there is no electricity, and some of our foreign aid funds provided extra wives for Kenya government officials. When Congress moved to cut foreign aid they were told that if they cut it one dollar they endangered national security, and then Senator Harry Byrd revealed that since its inception foreign aid has rarely spent its allotted budget. It has today $21 billion in unexpended funds.

Some time ago Dr. Howard Kershner was speaking to the prime minister of Lebanon. The prime minister told him proudly that his little country balanced its budget each year. It had no public debt, no inflation, a modest tax rate, and had increased its gold holdings from $70 to $120 million. When he finished, Dr. Kershner said, "Mr. Prime Minister, my country hasn't balanced its budget twenty-eight out of the last forty years. My country's debt is greater than the combined debt of all the nations of the world. We have inflation, we have a tax rate that takes from the private sector a percentage of income greater than any civilized nation has ever taken and survived. We have lost gold at such a rate that the solvency of our currency is in danger. Do you think that my country should continue to give your country millions of dollars each year?'' The prime minister smiled and said, ''No, but if you are foolish enough to do it, we are going to keep on taking the money.'' And so we built a model stock farm in Lebanon, and we built nine stalls for each bull. I find something peculiarly appropriate in that.

We have in our vaults $15 billion in gold. We don't own an ounce. Foreign dollar claims against that gold total $276 billion. In the last six years, fifty-two nations have bought $7 billion worth of our gold and all fifty-two are receiving foreign aid.

Because no government ever voluntarily reduces itself in size, government programs once launched never go out of existence. A government agency is the nearest thing to eternal life we'll ever see on this earth. The United States Manual takes twenty-five pages to list by name every congressman and senator, and all the agencies controlled by Congress. It then lists the agencies coming under the executive branch, and this requires 520 pages.

Since the beginning of the century our gross national product has increased 33 times. In the same period the cost of federal government has increased 234 times, and while the work force is only 1½ times greater, federal employees number nine times as many. There are now 2½ million federal employees. No one knows what they all do. One Congressman found out what one of them does. This man sits at a desk in Washington. Documents come to him each morning. He reads them, initials them, and passes them on to the proper agency. One day a document arrived he wasn't supposed to read, but he read it, initialed it, and passed it on. Twenty-four hours later it arrived back at his desk with a memo attached that said, ''You weren't supposed to read this. Erase your initials, and initial the erasure.''

While the federal government is the great offender, the idea filters down. During a period in California when our population has increased 90 percent, the cost of state government has gone up 862 percent and the number of employees 500 percent. Governments, state and local, now employ one out of six of the nation's work force.

If the rate of increase of the last three years continues, by 1970 one-fourth of the total work force will be employed by government. Already we have a permanent structure so big and complex it is virtually beyond the control of Congress and the comprehension of the people, and tyranny inevitably follows when this permanent structure usurps the policy-making function that belongs to elected officials.

One example of this occurred when Congress was debating whether to lend the United Nations $100 million. While they debated the State Department gave the United Nations $217 million and the United Nations used part of that money to pay the delinquent dues of Castro's Cuba.

Under bureaucratic regulations adopted with no regard to the wish of the people, we have lost much of our Constitutional freedom. For example, federal agents can invade a man's property without a warrant, can impose a fine without a formal hearing, let alone a trial by jury, and can seize and sell his property at auction to enforce payment of that fine. An Ohio deputy fire marshal sentenced a man to prison after a secret proceeding in which the accused was not allowed to have a lawyer present. The Supreme Court upheld that sentence, ruling that it was an administrative investigation of incidents damaging to the economy.

Somewhere a perversion has taken place. Our natural unalienable rights are now presumed to be a dispensation of government, divisible by a vote of the majority. The greatest good for the greatest number is a high-sounding phrase but contrary to the very basis of our Nation, unless it is accompanied by recognition that we have certain rights which cannot be infringed upon, even if the individual stands outvoted by all of his fellow citizens. Without this recognition, majority rule is nothing more than mob rule.

It is time we realized that socialism can come without overt seizure of property or nationalization of private business. It matters little that you hold the title to your property or business if government can dictate policy and procedure and holds life and death power over your business. The machinery of this power already exists. Lowell Mason, former antitrust law enforcer for the Federal Trade Commission, has written, "American business is being harassed, bled and even black-jacked under a preposterous crazy quilt system of laws." There are so many that the government literally can find some charge to bring against any concern it chooses to prosecute.

Are we safe in our books and records? The natural gas producers have just been handed a 428-page questionnaire by the Federal Power Commission. It weighs ten pounds. One firm has estimated it will take 70,000 accountant man hours to fill out this questionnaire, and it must be done in quadruplicate. The Power Commission says it must have it to determine whether a proper price is being charged for gas. The National Labor Relations Board ruled that a business firm could not discontinue its shipping department even though it was more efficient and economical to subcontract this work out. The Supreme Court has ruled the government has the right to tell a citizen what he can grow on his own land for his own use. The Secretary of Agriculture has asked for the right to imprison farmers who violate their planning quotas. One business firm has been informed by the Internal Revenue Service that it cannot take a tax deduction for its institutional advertising because this advertising espoused views not in the public interest.

A child's prayer in a school cafeteria endangers religious freedom, but the people of the Amish religion in the State of Ohio, who cannot participate in Social Security because of their religious beliefs, have had their livestock seized and sold at auction to enforce payment of Social Security dues.

We approach a point of no return when government becomes so huge and entrenched that we fear the consequences of upheaval and just go along with it. The federal government accounts for one-fifth of the industrial capacity of the nation, one-fourth of all construction, holds or guarantees one-third of all mortgages, owns one-third of the land, and engages in some nineteen thousand businesses covering half a hundred different lines. The Defense Department runs 269 supermarkets. They do a gross business of $730 million a year, and lose $150 million.

The government spends $11 million an hour every hour of the 24, and pretends we had a tax cut while it pursues a policy of planned inflation that will more than wipe out any benefit with depreciation of our purchasing power. We need true tax reform that will at least make a start toward restoring for our children the American dream that wealth is denied to no one, that each individual has the right to fly as high as his strength and ability will take him. The economist Sumner Schlicter has said, "If a visitor from Mars looked at our tax policy, he would conclude it had been designed by a Communist spy to make free enterprise unworkable."

But we cannot have such reform while our tax policy is engineered by people who view the tax as a means of achieving changes in our social structure. Senator Clark (D-Pa) says the tax issue is a class issue, and the government must use the tax to redistribute the wealth and earnings downward. On January 15th in the White House, the President told a group of citizens they were going to take all the money they thought was being unnecessarily spent, "take it from the haves and give it to the have-nots who need it so much." When Karl Marx said this he put it: "from each according to his ability, to each according to his need."

Have we the courage and the will to face up to the immorality and discrimination of the progressive surtax, and demand a return to traditional proportionate taxation? Many decades ago the Scottish economist, John Ramsey McCulloch, said, "The moment you abandon the cardinal principle of exacting from all individuals the same proportion of their income or their property, you are at sea without a rudder or compass and there is no amount of injustice or folly you may not commit." No nation has survived the tax burden that reached one-third of its national income. Today in our country the tax collector's share is thirty-seven cents of every dollar earned.

Freedom has never been so fragile, so close to slipping from our grasp. I wish I could give some magic formula, but each of us must find his own role. One man in Virginia found what he could do, and dozens of business firms have followed his lead. Concerned because his 200 employees seemed unworried about government extravagance he conceived the idea of taking all of their withholding out of only the fourth paycheck each month. For three paydays his employees received their full salary. On the fourth payday all withholding was taken. He has one employee who owes him $4.70 each fourth payday. It took only one month to produce 200 conservatives.

Are you willing to spend time studying the issues, making yourself aware, and then conveying that information to family and friends? Will you resist the temptation to get a government handout for your community? Realize that the doctor's fight against socialized medicine is your fight. We can't socialize the doctors without socializing the patients. Recognize that government invasion of public power is eventually an assault upon your own business. . . . If some among you fear taking a stand because you are afraid of reprisals from customers, clients, or even government, recognize that you are just feeding the crocodile hoping he'll eat you last. If all of this seems like a great deal of trouble, think what's at stake. We are faced with the most evil enemy mankind has known in his long climb from the swamp to the stars. There can be no security anywhere in the free world if there is not fiscal and economic stability within the United States.

Those who ask us to trade our freedom for the soup kitchen of the welfare state are architects of a policy of accommodation. They tell us that by avoiding a direct confrontation with the enemy, he will learn to love us and give up his evil ways. All who oppose this idea are blanket indicted as war-mongers. Well, let us set one thing straight, there is no argument with regard to peace and war. It is cheap demagoguery to suggest that anyone would want to send other people's sons to war. The only argument is with regard to the best way to avoid war. There is only one sure way—surrender.

The specter our well-meaning liberal friends refuse to face is that their policy of accommodation is appeasement, and appeasement does not give you a choice between peace and war, only between fight or surrender. We are told that the problem is too complex for a simple answer. They are wrong. There is no easy answer, but there is a simple answer. We must have the courage to do what we know is morally right, and this policy of accommodation asks us to accept the greatest possible immorality. We are being asked to buy safety from the threat of the Bomb by selling into permanent slavery our fellow human beings enslaved behind the Iron Curtain, to tell them to give up their hope of freedom because we are ready to make a deal with their slave masters.

Alexander Hamilton warned us that a nation which can prefer disgrace to danger is prepared for a master and deserves one. Admittedly there is a risk in any course we follow. Choosing the high road cannot eliminate that risk. Already some of the architects of accommodation have hinted what their decision will be if their plan fails and we are faced with the final ultimatum. The English commentator Tynan has put it that he would rather live on his knees than die on his feet. Some of our own have said "Better Red than dead." If we are to believe that nothing is worth the dying, when did this begin? Should Moses have told the children of Israel to live in slavery rather than dare the wilderness? Should Christ have refused the Cross? Should the patriots at Concord Bridge have refused to fire the shot heard round the world? Are we to believe that all the martyrs of history died in vain?

You and I have a rendezvous with destiny. We can preserve for our children this the last best hope of man on earth, or we can sentence them to take the first step into a thousand years of darkness. If we fail, at least let our children and our children's children say of us we justified our brief moment here. We did all that could be done.

Draft of Presidential Address to the European Parliament, Strasbourg, France, Wednesday, May 8, 1985

(All italicized language was substantially cut from the final version.)

(Noonan/BE)
April 23, 1985
6:00 P.M.

Thank you, ladies and gentlemen. It is an honor to be with you on this day.

We mark today the anniversary of the liberation of Europe from tyrants who had seized this continent and plunged it into a terrible war. Forty years ago today, the guns were stilled and peace began—a peace that has endured to become the longest of this century.

On this day forty years ago, they swarmed onto the boulevards of Paris, rallied under the Arche de Triomphe and sang the "Marseillaise" in the free and open air. In Rome, the sound of church bells filled St. Peter's Square and echoed through the city. On this day forty years ago, Winston Churchill walked out onto a balcony in Whitehall and said to the people of Britain, "This is your victory"—and, the crowd yelled back, "No, it is yours," in an unforgettable moment of love and gratitude. Londoners tore the blackout curtains from their windows, and put floodlights on the great symbols of English history. And for the first time in 6 years Big Ben, Buckingham Palace, and St. Paul's Cathedral were illuminated against the sky.

Across the ocean, a half million New Yorkers flooded Times Square and, being Americans, laughed and posed for the cameras. In

Washington, our new President, Harry Truman, called reporters into his office and said, "The flags of freedom fly all over Europe."

On this day forty years ago, I was at my post in an Army Air Corps installation in Culver City, California, and as I passed a radio I heard the words, "Ladies and gentlemen, the war in Europe is over," and like so many people that day I felt a chill, as if a gust of cold wind had just swept past, and I realized: I will never forget this moment.

This day can't help but be emotional, for in it we feel the long tug of memory; we are reminded of shared joy and shared pain and the terrible poignance of life. A few weeks ago in California an old soldier touched on this. With tears in his eyes he said, "It was such a different world then. It's almost impossible to describe it to someone who wasn't there, but when they finally turned the lights on in the cities again it was like being reborn."

If it is hard to communicate the happiness of those days, it is even harder to remember Europe's agony.

So much of it lay in ruins. Whole cities had been destroyed. Children played in the rubble and begged for food. The concentration camps had been opened, and had yielded their terrible secrets, secrets that gave us a symbol of Europe: a hollow-eyed woman, dazed with pain and disoriented from loss, staring out from an empty doorway.

By this day forty years ago, forty million lay dead, and the survivors composed a continent of victims. And to this day, we wonder: How did this happen? How did civilization take such a terrible turn? After all the books and the documentaries, after all the histories, and studies, we still wonder: How?

Hannah Arendt spoke of "the banality of evil"—the banality of the little men who did the terrible deeds. We know what they were: totalitarians who used the State, which they had elevated to the level of "God," to inflict war on peaceful peoples and genocide on an innocent race.

We know of the existence of evil in the human heart, and we know that in Nazi Germany that evil was institutionalized—given power and direction by the State, by a corrupt regime and the jack boots who did its bidding. And we know, we learned, that early attempts to placate the totalitarians did not save us from war. In fact, they guaranteed it. There are lessons to be learned in this and never forgotten.

But there is a lesson too in another thing we saw in those days: perhaps we can call it "the banality of virtue." The common men and women who somehow dug greatness from within their souls—the people who sang to the children during the blitz, who joined the Resistance and said 'No' to tyranny, the people who hid the Jews and the dissidents, the people who became, for a moment, the repositories of all the courage of the West—from a child named Anne Frank to a hero named Wallenberg.

These names shine. They give us heart forever. And the glow from their beings, the glow of their memories, lit Europe in her darkest days.

Who can forget the days after the war? They were hard days, yes, but we can't help but look back and think: Life was so vivid then. There was the sense of purpose, the joy of shared effort, and, later, the impossible joy of our triumph. Those were the days when the West rolled up her sleeves and repaired the damage that had been done. Those were the days when Europe rose in glory from the ruins.

Together, we created and put into place the Marshall Plan to rebuild from the rubble. Together we created the Atlantic Alliance, the first alliance in the world which proceeded not from transient interests of state but from shared ideals. Together we created the North Atlantic Treaty Organization, a defense system aimed at seeing that the kind of tyrants who had tormented Europe would never torment her again. NATO was a triumph of organization and effort, but it was also something very new, very different. For NATO derived its strength directly from the moral values of the people it represented. It was infused with their high ideals, their love of liberty, their commitment to peace.

But perhaps the greatest triumph of all was not in the realm of a sound defense or material achievement. No, the greatest triumph of Europe after the war is that in spite of all the chaos, poverty, sickness, and misfortune that plagued this continent—in spite of all that, the people of Europe resisted the call of new tyrants and the lure of their seductive philosophies. Europe did not become the breeding ground for new extremist philosophies. Europe resisted the totalitarian temptation. Instead, the people of Europe embraced democracy, the strongest dream, the dream the fascists could not kill. They chose freedom.

Today we celebrate the leaders who led the way—Churchill and de Gaulle, Adenauer and Schuman, de Gasperi and Spaak, Truman and Marshall. And we celebrate, too, the free political parties that contributed their share to greatness: the Liberals and the Christian Democrats, the Social Democrats and Labour and the Conservatives. Together they tugged at the same oar; and the great and mighty ship of Europe moved on.

If any doubt their success, let them look at you. In this room are the sons and daughters of soldiers who fought on opposite sides 40 years ago. Now you govern together and lead Europe democratically. You buried animosity and hatred in the rubble. There is no greater testament to reconciliation and to the peaceful unity of Europe than the men and women in this room.

In the decades after the war, Europe knew great growth and power. You enjoyed amazing vitality in every area of life, from fine arts to fashion, from manufacturing to science to the world of ideas. Europe was robust and alive, and none of this was an accident. It was the natural result of freedom, the natural fruit of the democratic ideal. We in America looked at Europe and called her what she was: an Economic Miracle.

But in time, in Europe and also in America, prosperity brought a changing political climate. The West turned to a new, and understandable preoccupation: security. Economic security, which we looked for from the state. And security from war, which we looked for from varying sources. Some of us began to question the ideals and philosophies that had guided the West for centuries. We questioned our partnerships. In time, some of us even questioned the moral and intellectual worth of the West.

I wish to speak to that questioning today. I speak as a friend and admirer of the people of Europe, but I am disturbed by what is reported to me about trends in Europe that I have also seen in America.

I pick up your magazines and newspapers, I talk to your leaders and citizens, and behind the words I hear a sound like a bell tolling softly in the night. They tell me that Europe has lost her way. They say that Europe has somehow lost her will. I read of what you yourselves are calling "Europessimism," "Europaralysis." *I am told that the new generation lacks faith and the belief that they can influence events.*

And it is right to address these questions in Strasbourg—where Goethe studied, where Pasteur taught, and Hugo first knew inspiration. *Here clamorous armies fought for centuries over the soil on which this building stands. Here one of the great parliaments of man began. This city of torn history has known the highest and saddest of the European experience, so there is no better place to speak of what Europe was and is.*

For a quarter century after the war, Europe was the economic leader of the world. As late as the late 1970s, Europe was the locomotive of the world economy, pulling the West along. Members of the Community employed 108 million people, and unemployment was only 5.5 percent of the civilian labor force.

But now unemployment is twice what it was twenty years ago, no new jobs have been added, and growth has virtually disappeared. I suspect you anticipate my feelings, but I assert today that Europe's recent decline is traceable to a departure from the philosophy that guided and galvanized the Economic Miracle of the 1950s and 1960s.

I believe that we in the West—all of us, to varying degrees—have been so preoccupied with providing economic security that we have inadvertently engaged in policies that have reduced economic opportunity. We know what those policies are: massive growth in public expenditure, both in volume and as a percentage of GNP—and a bias against individual freedom—and where there is no freedom, prosperity perishes.

Have we forgotten some bracing truths? The free enterprise system, from freedom of invention to freedom of investment, is the one system designed by man that succeeds in raising up the poor. When men and women are encouraged and allowed to start their own businesses, and create wealth and jobs, they not only add to the sum total of happiness in their communities—they add to the sum total of economic energy in their country, and sum total of economic strength in the West.

We are at a unique time in the world's history in that we both know what to do and have the means to do it. Now is the time to realize that all economic policies must be judged by their effects on economic growth. I believe that now is the time to strengthen incentives and remove the impediments to growth—to lower tax rates on our people, restrain government spending, eliminate regulatory burdens, and reduce tariff barriers.

And I would like to note here that all of us in the West should honor the entrepreneur for his—and her—contributions to the common good, the common welfare. To invest one's time and money in an enterprise is a profoundly faithful act, for it is a declaration of faith in the future. Entrepreneurs take risks that benefit us all—and they deserve rewards.

My friends, pro-growth policies in one country enhance the economic well-being of all the world's citizens, for when we increase the supply and the demand for goods and services in one country, all the markets of the world are enhanced. And I believe we must realize that if our young people feel powerless, part of the solution is returning to them a chance at economic power.

Europe's economic growth will require further development of European unity. Tomorrow will mark the 35th anniversary of the European Coal and Steel Community, the first block in the creation of a united Europe. It ensured that never again would Europe have to fight over resources, and it was a huge step toward peace—the kind of step only democracies could succeed at. It was the child of Robert Schuman's genius—and if he were here today I believe he would say: We have only just begun!

I am here to tell you America remains, as she was forty years ago, dedicated to the unity of Europe. We continue to see a strong and unified Europe not as a rival but as an even stronger partner. We favor the expansion of the European Community; we welcome the entrance of Spain and Portugal into that Community, for their presence makes for a stronger Europe, and a stronger Europe is a stronger West.

The economic summit we have just concluded in Bonn has reaffirmed once again the importance of Western economic cooperation. And it reaffirmed the importance of the commitment we all share to liberalize trade and resist protectionist pressures. I believe a key step to ensuring continued growth is to launch a new round of multilateral trade negotiations next year. And so I welcome the idea, given new impetus at Bonn, of a "Brussels Round."

If reality is on the side of capitalism, morality is surely on the side of democracy. But I wonder, too, if all of us still have faith in this fact. It seems to me the dilemma is both political and perceptual. Forty years ago, the vast majority of the good people of Europe knew who their adversaries were and why.

But some in the West today seem confused about what is right and what is wrong, what is a decent system and what is not, which philosophies should be resisted by man and which encouraged.

This terrible moral confusion is reflected even in our language. We speak of "East-West" tensions as if the West and the East were equally responsible for the threat to world peace today. We speak of "The Superpowers" as if they are moral equals—two huge predators composed in equal parts of virtue and of vice. We speak of the "senseless spiral of the arms race" as if the West and the East are equally consumed by the ambition to dominate the world. We speak as if the world were morally neutral—when in our hearts, most of us know it is not.

Let us look at the world as it is. There is a destabilizing force in the world—and it is not the democracies of the West. There is a political entity which, through its enormous military power, means to spread its rule—and it is not the democracies of the West. There is a political system that sees as its enemy the free peoples of the world—and it is not the democracies of the West.

The central cause of the tensions of our time is the conflict between totalitarianism and democracy. The evidence of this is all around us, all around you. Europe is split in two. One side is free, democratic, non-expansionist, non-threatening and peace-loving. The other side is populated by subjugated peoples who, against their will, are suffering under the dictatorship of an implacably expansionist power.

In 1961, in Berlin, a city half free and half communist, 50,000 people a week were fleeing from one side to the other. I would ask the young people of Europe: which side were these people fleeing from, and why? And which regime had to build a wall and imprison the people within so they would not flee?

In the late 1970s, in Indochina, the boat people fled communism. In Afghanistan they flee communism. In Central America they flee communism. In Eastern Europe, 40 years after she was subsumed by the Soviet State, they still flee from communism.

It is communism that is the destabilizing influence in the world today, and it is the acquisitive impulses of communism against which we are forced to defend ourselves. And knowing this, admitting this, is not "unhelpful" or "reactionary." Knowing this is the beginning of wisdom and security for the West. For without this knowledge we cannot maintain the strength that maintains our peace.

Over the past decade, we have witnessed a massive and sustained military build-up by the Soviet Union. There is no justification for this build-up—and the Soviets know it. In 1979, we in the NATO countries were forced to deploy a limited number of long-range I.N.F. missiles to offset the Soviet build-up of SS-20 missiles—a build-up that had led to an enormous and widening gap. It was not an easy decision and it was not made without political cost. Many of the leaders of Europe were as brave as the great leaders of the World War II in resisting pressures to stop deployment. And on this day I thank them.

Now new talks have begun between the United States and the Soviet Union in Geneva, and we are hopeful that they will yield fair and verifiable agreements that could lead to significant reductions in the size of their nuclear arsenal and ours. We will meet with the Soviet Union in good faith. We pray that the Soviets, having decided to rejoin us at the negotiating table, will adopt the same attitude. We will make it clear, as we have in the past, that the United States continues to have peaceful intentions—and only peaceful intentions—toward the Soviet Union.

We do not go to the bargaining table expecting the Soviets to suddenly change their system or their intentions in a magnanimous gesture of good will. But we hope to encourage the Soviets to see that it is in their own interests to stop trying to achieve a destabilizing superiority over the West—for the cost of their effort is great, and it is doomed to failure because we will not allow it to succeed.

There is one area of our defense that I want to speak about today because it is misunderstood by some of our friends. Ever since the Soviet Union came into possession of the secrets of nuclear technology, we in the West have had no choice but to rely upon the so-called "balance of terror" in order to deter war. Deterrence has worked for 40 years now, but we have long hoped for a better way. I believe we may have found it in emerging new technologies aimed at enhancing our safety through defensive means—non-nuclear means. The United States has begun to investigate these new technologies in a research program we call the Strategic Defense Initiative—or S.D.I.

This space shield is the most hopeful development of our time. With it comes the possibility that if a nuclear weapon is ever launched at you or at us we won't have to launch a missile in response—we will be able to knock the incoming missile right out of the sky.

Can the potential benefits of this technology be any clearer? Certainly not to the Soviets, for they are doing the same kind of research. And we do not fear this—we welcome it.

S.D.I. is not an attempt to achieve nuclear superiority—it is an attempt to achieve security. It is not an attempt to abrogate existing arms control treaties— S.D.I. would be carried out in full compliance with such treaties. S.D.I. is not destabilizing—in fact, as the Soviets may well soon have such a system, it will be destabilizing if the West does not. S.D.I. will not "decouple" America from Europe—S.D.I. is part of the security system that will protect all of the West.

We all want peace; we all want to protect the world. But we have a better chance of preserving the peace if we in the West see the world as it is and deal honestly with its hard realities. The peace movements of the West call for disarmament, a thoroughly laudable and understandable desire. But I cannot help note that it is the West, usually the United States, that they see as the chief aggressor in the so-called arms race. And it is the West, and only the West, to which they make their appeal. There is pathos in this, and a strange, hidden tribute. Pathos because their decision not to confront the creator of the arms race, the chief aggressor of our time, dooms their movement to failure. And a hidden tribute because they obviously feel that at least we, the reasonable people of the West, will give them a hearing.

But I wonder if this one-way communication does not contribute to the confusions of the modern age. I would ask the members of the peace movement in Europe: does it make you feel safer to know that the peace activists of the Soviet Union are in the Gulag? Does it make you feel safer to know that the Russians who truly desire peace with the West are in psychiatric hospitals?

I would ask the members of the peace movement: Is it really arms control you desire—or only the signing ceremonies? I ask this because if you really care about arms control you must care about compliance in arms control agreements. And I do not hear about compliance from you. I think it is important that you show some interest in this matter, for arms control means nothing unless both sides comply. And I would ask if it is not reasonable to state the following: that anyone who talks arms control, but never about compliance is, wittingly or unwittingly, really working not for peace but for the unilateral disarmament of the West. And we cannot have that, because if the West and only the West is disarmed, then we will wind up back in 1939—and the tanks of the totalitarians will roll again.

History has taught a lesson we must never forget: Totalitarians do not stop—they must be stopped. And how? What is the West to do?

I believe we must remember first of all that we are not powerless before history. The answer to the dilemma of the West resides within the heart of the West; it resides in the knowledge that "the history of the world begins anew with every man, and ends with him."

We have much to do—and we must do it together.

We must always remember that the road to peace does not run through Munich. We must remain unified in the face of attempts to divide us. We must remain strong in spite of attempts to weaken us. And we must remember that our unity and our strength are not a mere impulse of like-minded allies, not a mere geopolitical calculation. Our unity is the natural result of our shared love of liberty.

I am here today to reaffirm to the people of Europe the constancy of the American purpose. We were at your side through two great wars; we have been at your side through 40 years of a sometimes painful peace; and we are at your side today. It is not mere sentiment that dictates this, though sentiment we feel. We are here because, like you, we have not veered from the ideals of the West—the ideals of freedom, liberty, and peace. Let no one—no one—doubt our purpose.

I am here today to ask for your help and support in the greatest moral challenge of our time; I am here to ask your help in encouraging freedom movements throughout the world. All of us in this room want to preserve and protect our own democratic liberties—but don't we have a responsibility to foster *and encourage democracy throughout the world? And not because democracy is "our" form of government but because we have learned that democracy is, in the last analysis, the only peaceful form of government. It is, in fact, the greatest Conflict Resolution Mechanism ever devised by man. For only in its atmosphere can man peacefully resolve his differences through the ballot, through a free press, through free speech and free political parties and the right to redress injustice.*

Throughout the world Freedom Fighters cry out for our help—in Afghanistan, in Asia, in Africa and Central America, in all the faraway places that are really so close. And the most heartening thing, the most inspiring thing about these movements is that they are dominated by the young. It is freedom that is new again, democracy that is the new idea; and we know why, because their newness is eternal. All the other systems—all the isms—reek with feebleness and age.

We in the United States are attempting, as you know, to give aid and assistance to the democratic resistance of Nicaragua. And I know this has garnered some criticism from those who have labeled our policy hostile, unhelpful, and dangerous. Well, all I can say is that Churchill was not being "hostile" when he tried to protect Europe from the totalitarians—de Gaulle was not being unhelpful when he fought for freedom—and the members of the French Underground were not encouraging tension when they risked their lives to root out the source of Europe's tensions. We in the West must not stop being ashamed of supporting the only political system ever devised by man to let the full freedom of God's gifts flourish. And I wanted very much to address this point in the city of Strasbourg, because, as you know, it was the people of this city who 200 years ago sent a whole regiment of young soldiers to help the fight for independence in a faraway place called America. And we will never forget.

And we in the West must, finally, remember those who have, for now, lost out in the long fight for freedom—but only for now. On this 40th anniversary of the liberation of the victims of yesterday, I wish to speak to the victims of today. The people of the communist countries, the people who live in slavery and oppression. I wish to speak to the people of the Soviet Union, the people of the nations of Eastern Europe, the people of the fallen nations of Asia. I wish to speak to those who live in the slave labor camps and the psychiatric hospitals, the people behind the walls, and the barbed wire, and the secret police border guards.

To them I say: We will not forsake you nor forget you. We are your spiritual allies. We are with you as you suffer. We know what you have been told to confuse you, but please understand that we in the West want only peace, true peace, for you and for ourselves.

To the people of the Free World, I say: we have great challenges, great goals ahead of us, great missions inspired by great love. There are some who say the West lacks energy—the moral and spiritual energy to carry forth these great hopes and plans. But that is not true. Remember what Churchill said: We have not come this far because we are made of sugar candy.

I cannot believe that the people of Europe are these days paralyzed and pessimistic. But if this is so, then all I can say as an objective friend who has observed you for 74 years is:

Europe, beloved Europe, you are greater than you know. You are the treasury of centuries of Western thought and Western culture, you are the father of Western ideals and the mother of Western faith.

Europe, you have been the power and the glory of the West, and you are a moral success. In fact, in the horrors after World War II, when you rejected totalitarianism, when you rejected the lure of a new "Superman," and a "New Communist Man," you proved that you were—and are—a moral triumph.

You are a Europe without illusions, a Europe firmly grounded in the ideals and traditions that made her greatness, a Europe unbound and unfettered by communism or fascism. You are, today, a New Europe on the brink of a New Century—a democratic continent with much to be proud of.

Throughout your hard history people have told you you're finished. Seventy years ago, at the beginning of World War I, a British diplomat looked out his window and said, "The lights are going out all over Europe." Well, I have been here many times in recent years, and let me tell you, you are incandescent still.

There is great work ahead, work that is not unlike the building of a great cathedral. The work is slow, complicated, and painstaking. It is passed on with pride from generation to generation. It is the work not only of leaders but of ordinary people. The cathedral evolves as it is created, with each generation adding its own vision—but the initial spark of vision remains constant, and the faith that drives the vision persists. The results may be slow to see, but our children and their children will trace in the air the emerging arches and spires and know the faith and dedication and love that produced them. My friends, Europe is the Cathedral, and it is illuminated still.

And if you doubt your will, and your spirit, and your strength to stand for something, think of those people 40 years ago—who wept in the rubble, who laughed in the streets, who paraded across Europe, who cheered Churchill with love and devotion, and who sang the "Marseillaise" down the boulevards. May I tell you: spirit like that does not disappear; it cannot perish; it will not go away. There's too much left unsung within it.

Thank you, all of you, for your graciousness on this great day. Thank you, and God bless you all.

Notes

Notes to Introduction

1. James MacGregor Burns, *Leadership* (New York: Harper and Row, 1979): 5; and Robert Frost, "How Hard It Is to Keep from Being King When It's in You and in the Situation," in *In the Clearing* (New York: Holt, Rinehart and Winston, 1962): 79.

2. The political scientist James Ceaser has pointed out the uniqueness of the Reagan presidency: "Reagan's goals have been . . . a matter of changing how people *think* about the role of government and about the mission of the United States in the world" (italics in the original). James W. Ceaser, "The Reagan Presidency and American Public Opinion," in Charles O. Jones, ed., *The Reagan Legacy: Promise and Performance* (Chatham, N.J.: Chatham House, 1988): 173. See also John Kenneth White, *The New Politics of Old Values* (Hanover, N.H.: University Press of New England, 1988).

3. See Reagan's "Remarks at the St. Ann's Festival in Hoboken, New Jersey," July 26, 1984, *PP84*:2:1100.

Notes to Part One: "Ronald Reagan's Bully Pulpit"

1. Anthony King and David Sanders, "The View from Europe," in Charles O. Jones, ed., *The Reagan Legacy: Promise and Performance* (Chatham, N.J.: Chatham House, 1988): 266.

2. David A. Stockman, *The Triumph of Politics: How the Reagan Revolution Failed* (New York: Harper and Row, 1986); Garry Wills, *Reagan's America: Innocents at Home* (Garden City, N.Y.: Doubleday, 1987); Lou Cannon, *Reagan* (New York: G.P. Putnam's Sons, 1982).

3. Stockman, *The Triumph of Politics*, 129, 140, 109.

4. Ibid., 13, 235, 296, 354, 297.

5. Wills, *Reagan's America*, 320.

6. Cannon, *Reagan*, 372.

7. The columnist Nicholas von Hoffman once called Reagan an "unlettered, self-assured bumpkin," as quoted in James W. Ceaser, "The Reagan Presidency and American Public Opinion," in Charles O. Jones, ed., *The Reagan Legacy: Promise and Performance* (Chatham, N.J.: Chatham House, 1988): 179. The article by Ceaser is instructive and extremely perceptive.

8. Stockman, *The Triumph of Politics*, 344, 190, 214.

9. Ibid., 375.

10. Wills, *Reagan's America*, 375–77, 369. See also Cannon, *Reagan*, 414.

11. Stockman, *The Triumph of Politics*, 11.

12. Wills, *Reagan's America*, 322.

13. Cannon, *Reagan*, 410. The British observer Nigel Bowles was struck by the energy Reagan devoted to congressional liaison while seeming to have done it effortlessly: "For those to whom they were directed, Reagan's personal efforts at persuasion appeared warmly unhurried." See Bowles, *The White House and Capitol Hill: The Politics of Presidential Persuasion* (Oxford: Oxford/ Clarendon, 1987): 238.

14. One of Governor Reagan's principal opponents in California, Assembly Speaker Bob Moretti, emphasized Reagan's purposefulness: "[Reagan] had a philosophy he was willing to pursue, to enunciate, that he was willing to attempt to push. Even if you disagreed with that philosophy, the fact that he had one and that he stood up for it was something. And he was a strong personality. . . . He had an enduring desire to leave something behind that was really material which he could point to as a change. He wanted to improve where he had been." Cannon, *Reagan*, 186.

15. Ibid., 375. Cf. Wills, *Reagan's America*, 312: "Reagan [accepted responsibility] for the less glamourous task of governing California. And govern it he did, competently, popularly, routinely. . . . Reagan was able to accomplish this through an extraordinarily efficient team."

16. Cannon, *Reagan*, 372, 115, 376.

17. Ibid., 415.

18. Wills, *Reagan's America*, 324.

19. Stockman, *The Triumph of Politics*, 9.

20. Cannon, *Reagan*, 408, 410, 186 (speaking there of Reagan's California gubernatorial experience. Cannon's chapter on "The Delegated Presidency" maintains the same point; see *Reagan*, 382.

21. See Part Three, Figures 1 and 2.

Notes to Chapter One

1. Unemployment and inflation had both been high in 1980 (7.1 and 13.5 percent, respectively), a condition economists dubbed "stagflation." See *Statistical Abstract of the United States, 1987*, 107th ed. (Washington, D.C.: Department of Commerce, 1986): Tables 665 and 764.

2. On reciprocity and its benign effects on political behavior, see William K. Muir, Jr., *Legislature: California's School for Politics* (Chicago: University of Chicago Press, 1982).

3. One example of the capacity for empathy is the fact that in 1987 Americans donated a record $97.1 billion to nonprofit charitable and educational organizations; U.S. Bureau of the Census, *Statistical Abstract of the United States, 1989*, 109th ed. (Washington, D.C.: U.S. Government Printing Office, 1989): 317, Table 615. See Part Three herein.

4. See President Reagan's "Remarks at Naturalization Ceremonies for New United States Citizens in Detroit, Michigan," October 1, 1984, *PP84*:2:1395, where he warned an audience of 1,500 new citizens, "You've joined a country that has been called 'The least exclusive club in the world—with the highest dues.'"

5. Rushworth M. Kidder, "Soviets' Lesson at Andover," *Christian Science Monitor*, February 24, 1986, 21.

6. Tocqueville, on the basis of his observations of nineteenth-century America, credited democracy, and not technology, with the fact "that our sensibility is extended to many more objects." Alexis de Tocqueville, *Democracy in America*, trans. Henry Reeve, ed. Phillips Bradley, rev. Francis Bowen (New York: Random House, 1954): 2:175.

7. Ibid., 115.

8. Hannah Arendt, "The Crisis of Education," in *Between Past and Future* (New York: Viking Press, 1961): 192: "Because the world is made by mortals it wears out; and because it constantly changes its inhabitants it runs the risk of becoming as mortal as they. To preserve the world against the mortality of its creators and inhabitants it must be constantly set right anew."

9. Joan Didion, *Slouching towards Bethlehem* (New York: Simon and Schuster, 1979): 122–23.

10. "Address to the Nation," July 15, 1979, in *Weekly Compilation of Presidential Documents*, vol. 15 (Washington, D.C.: Government Printing Office, 1979): 1237.

11. Tocqueville, *Democracy in America*, 2:21.

12. Ronald Reagan to James W. Baker, February 1, 1985, in *WC85*:21:118–19.

Notes to Chapter Two

1. Martin Anderson, *Revolution* (San Diego: Harcourt Brace Jovanovich, 1988): 209.

2. Alexander Hamilton, *The Federalist Papers*, No. 79.

3. George E. Reedy, *The Twilight of the Presidency: From Johnson to Reagan*, rev. ed. (New York: New American Library, 1987): 179.

4. Alexis de Tocqueville, *Democracy in America*, trans. Henry Reeve, ed. Phillips Bradley, rev. Francis Bowen (New York: Random House, 1954): 1:60.

5. Principal deputy press secretary Larry Speakes depicted his relationship with journalists in chapter 14 ("Beat the Press") of a memoir he wrote with Robert Pack, *Speaking Out: The Reagan Presidency from Inside the White House* (New York: Charles Scribner's Sons, 1988): 216–45.

6. The best-known use of radio was President Franklin Delano Roosevelt's Fireside Chats (which averaged two a year from 1933 to 1936). With them, Roosevelt would teach his radio audience about subjects as diverse as domestic banking and foreign affairs, even once asking the public to open up their family atlases and follow his discussion of global events. According to Larry Speakes, "Reagan's Saturday radio broadcasts, which started in April 1982, at the suggestion of long-time Reagan aide Joe Holmes, were one of our most effective public relations instruments." *Speaking Out*, 239.

7. American presidents are not alone in the assistance airplanes have given moral leaders in the modern world; see Paul Johnson's description of the world tours of Pope John Paul II: "He used the new combination of the jet and the helicopter to make global travel a routine part of the pontificate. During his first three years as pope he visited large parts of South and Central America, Africa,

North America, parts of Europe, South East Asia, the Middle and Far East. These appearances attracted some of the biggest crowds in history. Over 100 million attended his services." Paul Johnson, *Modern Times: The World from the Twenties to the Eighties* (New York: Harper and Row, 1983): 700.

8. "Reagan . . . averaged a month away from Washington in each of his first three years" in domestic political travel, according to Samuel Kernell, *Going Public: New Strategies of Presidential Leadership* (Washington, D.C.: CQ Press, 1986): 96–97.

9. Like all things, speechwriting in the White House had its seasons—1984–1985 were summer years. In contrast, 1986 brought discord between the Speechwriting Department and the president's chief of staff, Donald Regan, who would dismiss Elliott, the chief of the department, and provoke the departure of Noonan. The demoralization that resulted was soon compounded by the furor dubbed "Irangate": the public disclosure of secret arms sales to Iran and covert funding of the democratic resistance in Nicaragua.

10. Bently T. Elliott, interview with the author, June 10, 1985, Washington, D.C.

11. Peggy Noonan, interviews with the author, December 7 and 14, 1984, Washington, D.C.

12. "Remarks at a Ceremony Commemorating the 40th Anniversary of the Normandy Invasion, D-Day," June 6, 1984, *PP84*:1:817–18.

13. In fact, there was an adjunct member of the Speechwriting Department, Ken Khachigian, who was not on the White House staff, but was called in to help write several major speeches. Principal deputy press secretary Larry Speakes called him "Reagan's best speechwriter." Larry Speakes, with Robert Pack, *Speaking Out*, 88.

14. Anthony Dolan, interview with the author, December 3, 1984, Washington, D.C.

15. Al Meyer, interview with author, November 30, 1984, Washington, D.C.

16. In 1987 Rohrabacher was elected to Congress from Southern California. In 1986 he set out what he called "my view of the Reagan team world view" in "The Goals and Ideals of the Reagan Administration," a chapter in B. B. Kymlicka and Jean V. Matthews, eds., *The Reagan Revolution?* (Chicago: Dorsey, 1988): 25–41.

17. Peter Robinson, interview with the author, August 27, 1984, Washington, D.C.

Notes to Chapter Three

1. Dana Rohrabacher, interview with the author, December 11, 1984, Washington, D.C.

2. Dana Rohrabacher, speech to a journalism class, University of Florida, Gainesville, December 4, 1984.

3. Dana Rohrabacher, interview with the author, December 11, 1984, Washington, D.C. All further Rohrabacher quotations in this chapter are taken from this interview.

4. Peter Robinson, interview with the author, August 27, 1984, Washington, D.C.

5. Al Meyer, interview with the author, November 30, 1984, Washington, D.C.

6. Peggy Noonan, interview with the author, December 7, 1984, Washington, D.C. All further Noonan quotations in this chapter are taken from this interview.

7. See Noonan's later account of the incident in Peggy Noonan, "Confessions of a White House Speechwriter," *New York Times* Magazine, October 15, 1989, 24ff., 73.

8. Al Meyer, interview with the author, November 1984. All further Meyer quotations in this chapter are taken from this interview.

9. In President Reagan's farewell remarks to his longtime conservative political supporters, he was to put Meyer's point in this picturesque way:

We knew that the future of the Republican party at the national level did not lie in running a light beer campaign, offering people everything our opponents did, but less. No, it lay in offering the American people more—more jobs, more income, more opportunity, and more freedom. It was much more than our opponents could conceive of and far more than they could hope to match, because our opponents could only offer the people things that they had taken from them while we could offer the American people far more than they ever had: the full fruits of their own abundant creativity. ("Remarks at a Dinner Honoring Representative Jack F. Kemp of New York," December 1, 1988, *WC88*:24:1577)

10. "Remarks at the Annual Conference of the National League of Cities," March 5, 1984, *PP84*:1:300–302.

11. Anthony R. Dolan, interview with the author, December 3, 1984, Washington, D.C.

Notes to Chapter Four

1. Peggy Noonan, interview with the author, December 7, 1984, Washington, D.C.

2. Peter Robinson, interview with the author, August 27, 1984, Washington, D.C.

3. Peggy Noonan, interview with the author, December 14, 1984, Washington, D.C.

4. Puzzlingly, I could not discover whether Roosevelt ever really spoke or wrote the term. No biographer appeared to make specific reference to "the bully pulpit." Moreover, the phrase is missing altogether from the *Theodore Roosevelt Cyclopedia*, ed. Albert Bushnell Hart and Herbert Ronald Ferleger (New York: Roosevelt Memorial Association, 1941), a comprehensive cataloguing of Roosevelt's views and coinages.

5. Similar criticism of Theodore Roosevelt's prepresidential rhetoric was expressed by one of his recent biographers: "He preached the gospel of Americanism, ad nauseam, at every public or private opportunity. Ninety-nine percent of the millions of words he thus poured out are sterile, banal, and so droningly repetitive as to defeat the most dedicated researcher. There is no doubt that on this subject Theodore Roosevelt was one of the bores of all ages; the wonder is that during his lifetime so many men, women, and children worshipfully pondered every platitude." Edmund Morris, *The Rise of Theodore Roosevelt* (New York: Coward, McCann and Geoghegan, 1979): 467.

6. Theodore Roosevelt, "Address at the laying of the cornerstone of the office building of the House of Representatives, Washington, April 14, 1906,"

in Willis Fletcher Johnson, ed., *Addresses and Papers of Theodore Roosevelt* (New York: Unit Book Publishing, 1909): 310–11.

7. "Campaign Address at Chicago, Illinois," October 14, 1936, *The Public Papers and Addresses of Franklin D. Roosevelt*, ed. Samuel I. Rosenman (New York: Random House, 1938): 5:487–88.

8. "Inaugural Address," March 4, 1933, ibid., 2:11.

9. John F. Kennedy, "Inaugural Address," January 20, 1961, *Public Papers of the Presidents of the United States: John F. Kennedy* (Washington, D.C.: Government Printing Office, 1962): 1–3.

10. Peggy Noonan, interview with the author, December 7, 1984, Washington, D.C. See also Carter speechwriter, James Fallows's appraisal of his former boss: "One explanation [of his ineffectiveness] is that Carter had not given us an idea to follow. . . . Carter believes fifty things, but no one thing. . . . Whenever he edited a speech, he did so to cut out the explanatory portions and add 'meat' in the form of a list of topics." James Fallows, "The Passionless Presidency," *Atlantic* 243, no. 5 (May 1979): 42.

11. Peter Robinson, interview with the author, August 27, 1984, Washington, D.C.

12. "Second Inaugural Address," March 4, 1865, *Abraham Lincoln: Speeches and Writings 1859–1865*, ed. Don E. Fehrenbacher (New York: Library of America, 1989): 687.

13. Sometimes Lincoln's imagery was so good that the Reagan writers more than a century later felt shameless about borrowing it. Consider the image at the close of Lincoln's first inaugural as he urged South and North to reconcile before the start of war in 1861:

> We are not enemies but friends. We must not be enemies. Though passion may have strained, it must not break our bonds of affection.
> The mystic chords of memory, stretching from every battlefield and patriot grave to every living heart and hearthstone all over this broad land, will yet swell the chorus of the Union, when again touched, as surely they will be, by the better angels of our nature. (First Inaugural Address," March 4, 1861, *Abraham Lincoln*, 224)

The "mystic chords of memory," to "swell the chorus of the Union"—this musical motif would appear in the public rhetoric of the Reagan presidency.

Even in informal conversation the speechwriters would use Lincoln's phrases. For example, Noonan said that Reagan's philosophical speeches attempted to "touch the larger mystic chord of memory: they speak to why we are here." Peggy Noonan, interview with the author, December 14, 1984, Washington, D.C.

Notes to Part Two: "The Ideas of Freedom"

1. See Herbert McClosky and John Zaller, *The American Ethos: Public Attitudes toward Capitalism and Democracy* (Cambridge, Mass.: Harvard University Press, 1984). McClosky and Zaller characterize the conflict between liberty and equality as one between the values of "capitalism and democracy." On the basis of extensive surveys of American attitudes *before* the Reagan presidency, they conclude (p. 302):

Our argument, then, can be summarized as follows: conflicts between capitalism and democracy remain a recurrent feature of American life; when these conflicts surface, they are likely to be resolved in ways predominantly favorable to the democratic tradition; and some type of welfare capitalism is the institutional form this resolution is likely to take.

2. Alexis de Tocqueville, *Democracy in America*, trans. Henry Reeve, ed. Phillips Bradley, rev. Francis Bowen (New York: Random House, 1954): 1:56.
3. Ibid., 2:21.

Notes to Chapter Five

1. Peggy Noonan, interview with the author, December 7, 1984, Washington, D.C.
2. "Commencement at Howard University: 'To Fulfill These Rights,'" June 4, 1965, in *Public Papers of the Presidents of the United States: Lyndon B. Johnson, 1965* (Washington, D.C.: Government Printing Office, 1966): 636. For a provocative and influential exposition of the footrace metaphor, see John H. Schaar, "Equality of Opportunity, and Beyond," in his *Legitimacy in the Modern State* (New Brunswick, N.J.: Transaction Books, 1981): 193–209, 197.
3. *Public Papers of the Presidents of the United States: Lyndon B. Johnson, 1965*, 636.
4. The most familiar New Testament reference to the image of humankind's passage through life is Paul's farewell to Timothy, written from his prison cell in Rome just before he was executed: "For I am now ready to be offered, and the time of my departure is at hand. I have fought a good fight, I have finished my course, I have kept the faith" (2 Tim. 4:6–7). Paul's "course," however, was less like a race track than a highway, for it led somewhere—to the "heavenly kingdom"; the finishing time was irrelevant for "the Lord stood with me, and strengthened me" at all times; the prize for finishing, "a crown of righteousness," was awarded "not to me only, but unto all them also that love his appearing" (2 Tim. 4:18, 17, 8). A heavenly destination, the insignificance of time as a competitive factor, and the abundance of prizes distinguish Paul's course from President Johnson's footrace.

Abraham Lincoln, in his talks to Union regiments when they were being mustered out of service, likened life to a race. But to Lincoln the race was not a savagely competitive one, but a race "with all its desirable human aspirations." In part, he said, "I beg you to remember this, not merely for my sake, but for yours. I happen temporarily to occupy this big White House. I am a living witness that any one of your children may look to come here as my father's child has. It is in order that each of you may have through this free government which we have enjoyed, an open field and a fair chance for your industry, enterprise, and intelligence; that you may all have equal privileges in the race of life, with all its desirable human aspirations. It is for this the struggle should be maintained, that we may not lose our birthright." In Abraham Lincoln, *Selected Speeches, Messages, and Letters*, ed. T. Harry Williams (New York: Holt, Rinehart and Winston, 1957): 271.
5. As a matter of fact, four justices of the U.S. Supreme Court once said as much. See the opinion of Justices William J. Brennan, Jr., Byron R. White,

Thurgood Marshall, and Harry A. Blackmun in *Board of Regents of the University of California* v. *Bakke*, 438 U.S. 265, at 365–66 (1978), where it is written:

> If it was reasonable to conclude—as we hold that it was—that the failure of minorities to qualify for admission at Davis [a University of California medical school] under regular procedures was due principally to the effects of past discrimination, then there is a reasonable likelihood that, but for pervasive racial discrimination, respondent [Bakke] would have failed to qualify for admission in the absence of Davis's special admissions program.

That is, had completely fair rules historically been in place in the United States, neither Bakke nor the class of white male individuals he represented would have had a "reasonable likelihood" of winning the race of life (that is, of becoming a doctor). This interesting (and perverse) observation never obtained a majority on the Court, however.

6. Karl Marx and Friedrich Engels, *The Communist Manifesto* (New York and London: Modern Reader Paperbacks, 1968): 23, 62.

7. Garry Wills, *Nixon Agonistes: The Crisis of the Self-Made Man* (Boston: Houghton Mifflin, 1970): 238. "For where, when one gets down to it, is the starting line? Does a man begin the race at birth? Or when he enters school? When he enters the work force? When he attempts to open a business of his own? Or is the starting line at each of these points? And if so, then why not all the intermediate points as well? And how does one correlate this man's starting line (or lines) with the staggered endlessly multiplied starting lines of every other individual? How do we manage the endless *stopping* of the race involved in *starting* it so often? One second after the gun has sounded, new athletes pop up all over the field, the field itself changes shape, and we must call everybody in, to line them up once more. We never even get to surmise where, in this science-fiction world of starting and racing, the finish line might be. Or, rather, the staggered, infinite finishing lines for each runner. The metaphor is a mess."

8. Where did the metaphor of partnership come from? One thing is clear. It evolved after President Reagan took office in 1981. At the first inaugural, Reagan spoke of "the new beginning," but one looks in vain for any allusion to partnership in it, either by name or in concept. The New York City Partnership, an association of 100 business and civic leaders, which found summer jobs for disadvantaged youth, may well have been the immediate inspiration for the application of the partnership metaphor to the Reagan policy of voluntarism. See "Remarks at the Annual Meeting of the National Alliance of Business," October 5, 1981, *PP81*:884.

Other presidents had sporadically used the notion of partnership: for example, President Jimmy Carter spoke of a "public-private partnership" in 1979 before the annual convention of the National Conference of Catholic Charities, Kansas City, Missouri, October 15, 1979, *Public Papers of the Presidents of the United States: Jimmy Carter, 1979* (Washington, D.C.: Government Printing Office, 1980): 2:1979. No president before Reagan ever stressed the metaphor and developed it as elaborately as he did.

9. To quote one typical message, "Farm and city people have long been partners in economic and social progress. Without farms to provide food and fiber, cities would be barren; without the products and services of cities, farms would be primitive." "Proclamation 4881—National Farm-City Week," October 29, 1981, *PP81*:999.

10. "Address before the Japanese Diet in Tokyo," November 11, 1983, *PP83*:2:1578. The president used the metaphor of the mountaineers more than once; see, for example, "Remarks at the Annual Meeting of the Boards of Governors of the International Monetary Fund and World Bank Group," September 25, 1984, *PP84*:2:1369–70.

11. "Toasts of the President and Prime Minister Zenko Suzuki of Japan at the State Dinner," May 7, 1981, *PP81*:411.

12. "Radio Address to the Nation on the Canadian National Parliamentary Elections and Free Trade," November 26, 1988, *WC88*:24:1569.

13. This conception of reciprocity as the necessary basis of a perpetually peaceful and prospering world underlay Walter Lippmann's brilliant *The Good Society*, perhaps the twentieth century's finest defense of liberalism. See Lippmann, *The Good Society* (New York: Grosset and Dunlap, 1943):193, where Lippmann said of economic freedom and the revolution it effected in the eighteenth and nineteenth centuries: "For the first time in human history men had come upon a way of producing wealth in which the good fortune of others multiplied their own." The president quoted this very passage in his first address to the nation on his economic program, "Address to the Nation on the Economy," February 5, 1981, *PP81*:82.

14. Alexander Hamilton, *The Federalist*, No. 6.

15. George Bush in his remarks accepting the Republican Party's 1988 presidential nomination, *New York Times*, August 19, 1988, A14. Little wonder that when a team of sociologists talked with some highly educated Americans in the generation that had taken the footrace metaphor most seriously—the college students of the 1960s—it reported widespread ignorance of America's vast voluntary sector. The vision of that generation had been distorted by a metaphor that made charitable habits odd. See Robert N. Bellah, Richard Madsen, William M. Sullivan, Ann Swidler, and Steven M. Tipton, *Habits of the Heart: Individualism and Commitment in American Life* (Berkeley and Los Angeles: University of California Press, 1985): 1–8.

16. Mark Benedick, Jr., and Phyllis M. Levinson reported, "During his first thirty-two months in office, Mr. Reagan featured the subject of private-sector initiatives in more than eighty-four separate speeches, public appearances, proclamations, or similar events, an average rate of nearly one per week." See their "Private-Sector Initiatives or Public-Private Partnerships?" in Lester M. Salamon and Michard S. Lund, eds., *The Reagan Presidency and the Governing of America* (Washington, D.C.: Urban Institute Press, 1985): 457. See also Renee A. Berger, "Private-Sector Initiatives in the Reagan Era: New Actors Reword an Old Theme," in *The Reagan Presidency and the Governing of America*, 181–218. Prior presidents had also made efforts to stimulate voluntarism, but their attempts floundered. See, for example, Richard P. Nathan, *The Plot That Failed: Nixon and the Administrative Presidency* (New York: John Wiley & Sons, 1975): 28–29.

17. "Remarks at the Annual Meeting of the National Alliance of Business," October 5, 1981, *PP81*:883, 886.

18. Ibid., 886–87.

19. "Remarks at a Breakfast Meeting With Representatives From the Private Sector Engaged in Volunteer Work," September 21, 1981, *PP81*:816.

20. "Remarks in New Orleans, Louisiana, at the Annual Meeting of the International Association of Chiefs of Police," September 28, 1981, *PP81*:845.

21. Ibid., 817.

22. The term "public charity" was coined by Alexis de Tocqueville in a short "Memoir on Pauperism" he wrote in 1835. The "Memoir," republished in

Tocqueville and Beaumont on Social Reform (New York: Harper and Row, 1968):1–27, elaborates brilliantly on the different moral effects of public and private charity. In turn, the insight of the "Memoir" is applied to present-day America by Charles Murray, *Losing Ground: American Social Policy 1950–1980* (New York: Basic Books, 1984).

23. Anthony Dolan, interview with the author, December 3, 1984, Washington, D.C.

24. Alexis de Tocqueville, *Democracy in America*, trans. Henry Reeve, ed. Phillips Bradley, rev. Francis Bowen (New York: Random House, 1954), 1:198–99. The president frequently paraphrased this passage. For example,

> That often-quoted-by-afterdinner-speakers Frenchman, De Tocqueville, who came to this country so long ago to find out what was the secret of our greatness and all—there was one line in his book, when he went back and wrote a book for his fellow citizens, in which he said, "You know, there's something strange in the United States." He said, "Some individual sees a problem." And he said, "They walk across the street to a friend or a neighbor and they tell them of the problem, and they talk about it. And pretty soon, a committee is formed. And the next thing you know, they are solving the problem." And you won't believe this. He wrote, "But not a single bureaucrat was involved." ("Remarks at a Breakfast Meeting with Representatives from the Private Sector Engaged in Volunteer Work," September 17, 1981, *PP81*:815–16)

25. Tocqueville, *Democracy in America*, 2:114–15.

26. Ibid., 2:324–26.

27. Ibid., 2:116, 118.

28. Bently T. Elliott, interview with the author, June 10, 1985, Washington, D.C.

29. "Remarks at the Annual Dinner of the Knights of Malta in New York City," January 13, 1989, *WC89*:25, 69.

30. "Address before a Joint Session of the Congress on the State of the Union," January 25, 1988, *WC88*:24, 85.

Notes to Chapter Six

1. Richard Reeves, *American Journey: Travelling with Tocqueville in Search of "Democracy in America"* (New York: Simon and Schuster, 1982): 197.

2. Ibid., 198, 199.

3. Tocqueville thought that people living in democratic ages (in contrast to those living in aristocratic times) would be tempted to accept deterministic explanations of their condition: "Historians who live in democratic ages, then, not only deny that the few have any power of acting upon the destiny of a people, but deprive the people themselves of the power of modifying their own condition, and they subject them either to an inflexible Providence or to some blind necessity. . . . To their minds it is not enough to show what events have occurred: they wish to show that events could not have occurred otherwise." Alexis de Tocqueville, *Democracy in America*, trans. Henry Reeve, ed. Phillips Bradley, rev. Francis Bowen (New York: Random House, 1954) 2:92–93.

4. Sigmund Freud, *New Introductory Lectures on Psycho-Analysis,* trans. W. J. H. Sprott, in *The Works of Sigmund Freud,* ed. Robert Maynard Hutchins (Chicago: Encyclopaedia Britannica, 1952).

5. The terms "evangelical" and "evangelist" derive from the Greek word *euangelion,* meaning good news. Paul's last letter to Timothy encouraged him, "[D]o the work of an evangelist, make full proof of thy ministry," 2 Tim. 4:5. Many people associate present-day American evangelicals with Fundamentalists and think the two constitute the traditional wing of the Protestant denominations. In fact, however, there are evangelicals in virtually every Protestant denomination. The characteristic that separates those who call themselves evangelical from those who don't is less doctrinal than behavioral. Evangelicals emphasize the church's role as missionaries to non-Christians. They are aggressive promoters of Christianity, the Reverends Billy Graham and Pat Robertson being their prototypes. They seem to be most prominent among the Methodists (that is, the adherents of the greatest American evangelist, John Wesley), Baptists, Mormons, and Presbyterians and virtually absent from the more passive sects, such as the Quakers, Christian Scientists, and Episcopalians. George Marsden calls them "a transdenominational movement." See his "The Evangelical Denomination," in Richard John Neuhaus and Michael Cromartie, eds., *Piety and Politics: Evangelicals and Fundamentalists Confront the World* (Washington, D.C.: Ethics and Public Policy Center, 1987): 65. Their political preferences run the whole gamut, from extremely conservative to radical left. See, for example, "Devout Dissidents: Radical Evangelicals Are Gaining Influence Protesting U.S. Policy," *Wall Street Journal,* May 24, 1985, 1.

6. "Remarks at the Annual Convention of the National Association of Evangelicals in Orlando, Florida," March 8, 1983, *PP83*:1:362, 363–64.

7. The reference to C. S. Lewis highlights Lewis's remarkable role in Anglo-American Protestant and Catholic life today. In Chapter Eleven we will return to his role, but consider political scientist Michael Nelson's appraisal: "The popularity of C. S. Lewis, known for his apologetic and imaginative works of Christian literature, refuses to wane. Indeed, the opposite is more nearly true. His books now sell around two million copies each year in his native Britain and in America—six times the number sold during his lifetime." Nelson goes on to point out that Lewis's Christianity was "orthodox, not liberal, and supernaturalist, not modern" and that Lewis felt his mission was to explain to his unbelieving neighbors and defend "the belief that has been common to nearly all Christians at all times." In other words, "What Lewis did, by shedding light on the historic teachings of the church, was to help Christians understand what they already realize is important, even if most of their leaders have forgotten." In doing so, he has kept alive the traditional doctrines of sin, the resurrection, and the afterlife, whereas the modern church leaders offer sermons and publications "prepared mainly by academic seminaries, where avant garde theology, radical biblical criticism, and social and political relevancy are the reigning gods." See Michael Nelson, "C. S. Lewis, Gone but Hardly Forgotten," *New York Times,* November 22, 1988, A15 (Pacific Coast edition).

8. "Address at Commencement Exercises at Eureka College in Illinois," May 9, 1982, *PP82*:1:582.

9. "Address to Members of the British Parliament," June 8, 1982, *PP82*:1:744.

10. Anthony R. Dolan, interview with the author, December 3, 1984, Washington, D.C. All of the following quotations of Dolan are from this interview.

11. Ronald Reagan's best-known nonpresidential speech is reprinted in the Appendix. He wrote and gave it over a period of years in the late 1950s and

early 1960s, when he worked for General Electric as a corporate after-dinner speaker. Sometimes called "A Time for Choosing," often just referred to as "The Speech," it dealt largely with fiscal and social policies of the federal government, but it did refer to the Soviet Union as "the most evil enemy mankind has known in his long climb from the swamp to the stars."

12. See, for example, "Address before the Japanese Diet in Tokyo," November 11, 1983, *PP83*:2:1575.

13. James Madison, *The Federalist*, No. 51.

14. "Jacobinism" is the name Walter Lippmann gave to the notion of perfectible human nature. See his brilliant indictment of Jacobinism in *Essays in the Public Philosophy* (New York: New American Library, Mentor, 1955), chap. 7.

15. Archibald MacLeish, "Riders on Earth Together, Brothers in Eternal Cold," *New York Times*, December 25, 1968, 1, republished in Archibald MacLeish, *Riders on the Earth* (Boston: Houghton Mifflin Company, 1978): xiii–xiv.

Notes to Chapter Seven

1. Alexis de Tocqueville, *Democracy in America*, trans. Henry Reeve, ed. Phillips Bradley, rev. Francis Bowen (New York: Random House, 1954): 2:3.

2. Dewey is silent, however, on the question of assigning ethical value to efforts that fail to produce results. *Theory of Valuation* (Chicago: University of Chicago Press, 1939).

3. See, for example, Joseph Wambaugh's *The Onion Field* (New York: Delacorte, 1973). This is the true story of the assassination of a Los Angeles policeman that depicts an ethos within the Police Department based on the assumption that every injury is avoidable. As a result, the policemen in the story were blamed for events over which they clearly had no control, and a policeman whose heroism was plain to see was dishonored.

4. Max Weber, "Politics as a Vocation," in *From Max Weber: Essays in Sociology*, ed. and trans. Hans Gerth and C. Wright Mills (New York: Oxford University Press, 1946): 123.

5. This is not to say that pragmatists as thoughtful and humane as William James did not worry about the spiritual side of life. See William James, "What Makes a Life Significant," in *The Writings of William James*, ed. John J. McDermott (Chicago: University of Chicago Press, 1977): 645–60. His very "unpragmatic" answer was, "The solid meaning of life is always the same eternal thing,—the marriage, namely, of some unhabitual ideal, however special, with some fidelity, courage, and endurance; with some man's or woman's pains" (659).

6. "Remarks at a White House Ceremony Commemorating the Day of Remembrance of Victims of the Holocaust," April 20, 1982, *PP82*:1:496.

7. The political realist will object that the president used his rhetorical powers on such occasions merely to deflect criticism from politically embarrassing events. The realist typically will cite as evidence of presidential motive a random remark made by a young White House staff assistant to that effect. To this I reply, "Perhaps, but . . ." and argue that the purposes of men are complex, never *merely* one thing or another, and the range of motivations is likely to change as men grow older. A president who has lived a full seven decades may see very different reasons for discussing failure than a staff assistant who has not yet lived two score years.

8. Peter Robinson, interview with the author, April 6, 1984, Washington, D.C.

9. Typically, the president's introductory remarks, in forewarning the audience of his unusual topic, restated first principles: "I'm not going to talk to you about some of the things we've talked about before and some of the things we've tried to accomplish and that we haven't yet. With regard to that, I will only say let us all heed the words of an old Scotch ballad, 'For those defeats that we've had so far, we are hurt; we are not slain. We'll lie us down and rest a bit, and then we'll fight again.' " ("Remarks at the Baptist Fundamentalism Annual Convention," April 13, 1984, *PP84*:1:530)

10. Ibid., 533–34.

11. Peggy Noonan, interview with the author, December 14, 1984. Other Noonan remarks quoted in this chapter come from this interview.

12. Tocqueville, *Democracy in America*, 2:4.

13. Compare the notion of "communities of memory" in Robert N. Bellah, Richard Madsen, William M. Sullivan, Ann Swidler, and Steven M. Tipton, *Habits of the Heart: Individualism and Commitment in American Life* (Berkeley and Los Angeles: University of California Press, 1985).

14. See "Personal Satisfaction Rises in U.S., Poll Shows," *New York Times* (Pacific edition), December 25, 1988, 10. To the question, "Are you satisfied with the way things are going in your personal life?," 87 percent of the respondents to a Gallup poll said Yes (compared with 72 percent in 1979). To a parallel question about their feelings toward their country ("Are you satisfied with the way things are going in the United States?"), the changes wrought during the Reagan presidency were especially striking. Where only 12 percent had responded positively in 1979, 58 percent felt satisfaction at the end of September 1988.

15. Tocqueville, *Democracy in America*, 2:142.

16. "Text of Governor Cuomo's Keynote Address," *Congressional Quarterly*, July 21, 1984, 1781–84.

17. Tocqueville, *Democracy in America*, 2:336.

18. "Address before the 43rd Session of the United Nations General Assembly," September 26, 1988, *WC88*:24:1211–12.

Notes to Chapter Eight

1. Anthony R. Dolan, interview with the author, December 3, 1984, Washington, D.C. All of the following quotations of Dolan are from this interview.

2. Richard Neustadt focuses on this important role of the president in *Presidential Power* (New York: John Wiley and Sons, 1960). See Chapter Fifteen.

3. Donald T. Regan, *For the Record: From Wall Street to Washington* (New York: Harcourt Brace Jovanovich, 1988): 257.

4. Peggy Noonan's own account of the drafting of the European Parliament speech appears in her funny and wise book, *What I Saw at the Revolution: A Political Life in the Reagan Era* (New York: Random House, 1990): chap. 11, 219–33, a chapter she entitled *"Ich Bin ein* Pain in the Neck."

5. All of the following quotations from the Noonan draft come from the Peggy Noonan and Bently Elliott draft of "Presidential Address: To European Parliament, Strasbourg, France," in White House Staffing Memorandum, April 23, 1985, 10. See the Appendix.

6. *WC85*:21:605.

7. Ibid.

8. Ibid., 608.

9. Ibid., 605–6.
10. "Remarks and Question-and-Answer Session with Students and Guests of the University of Virginia in Charlottesville, Virginia," December 16, 1988, *WC88*:24:1632.

Note to Part Three: "Moral Institutions"

1. "Address to the Nation," July 15, 1979, in *Weekly Compilation of Presidential Documents*, vol. 15 (Washington, D.C.: Government Printing Office, 1979), 1237.

Notes to Chapter Nine

1. In the literature of social psychology, I have found the most accessible account of "ideas" to be by Milton J. Rosenberg et al., *Attitude Organization and Change* (New Haven, Conn.: Yale University Press, 1960).
2. "Remarks at Fudan University in Shanghai, China," April 30, 1984, *PP84*:1:607.
3. "Remarks at the Bicentennial Observance of the Battle of Yorktown in Virginia," October 19, 1981, *PP81*:968.
4. "Remarks at the Republican National Convention in New Orleans," August 15, 1988, *WC88*:24:1067.
5. "Remarks to the Passikivi Society and the League of Finnish American Societies in Helsinki, Finland," May 17, 1988, *WC88*:24, 680.
6. Alexis de Tocqueville, *Democracy in America*, trans. Henry Reeve, ed. Phillips Bradley, rev. Francis Bowen (New York: Random House, 1987): 2:14.
7. W. H. Auden and Louis Kronenberger, *The Viking Book of Aphorisms: A Personal Selection* (New York: Viking, 1962): 354.
8. Robert Frost, "The Silken Tent" (1942), in Edward Connery Lathem, ed., *The Poetry of Robert Frost* (New York: Holt, Rinehart and Winston, 1968): 331–32.
9. "A state without the means of some change is without the means of its conservation." Edmund Burke, *Reflections on the Revolution in France* (Garden City, N.Y.: Doubleday, 1961): 33.

Notes to Chapter Ten

1. Richard Reeves, *American Journey: Travelling with Tocqueville in Search of "Democracy in America"* (New York: Simon and Schuster, 1982): 20–22.
2. See William K. Muir, Jr., *Law and Attitude Change: Prayer in the Public Schools* (Chicago: University of Chicago Press, 1974): chap. 7, "The Force of Law." It depicts the moral effectiveness of a lawyer sitting down with his fellow school board members to help them reconcile their religious beliefs with the Supreme Court's ban on public school prayer.
3. Alexis de Tocqueville, *Democracy in America*, trans. Henry Reeve, ed. Philipps Bradley, rev. Francis Bowen (New York: Random House, 1954): 1:376, 259.
4. Ibid., 1:290. The passage was preceded by one of Tocqueville's most frequently quoted observations:

Scarcely any political question arises in the United States that is not resolved, sooner or later, into a judicial question. Hence all parties are obliged to borrow, in their daily controversies, the ideas, and even the language, peculiar to judicial proceedings. As most public men are or have been legal practitioners, they introduce the customs and technicalities of their profession into the management of public affairs. The jury extends this habit to all classes.

5. Ibid., 1:288.

6. Ibid., 1:106, 290, 105 ("As it is the first of laws, it cannot be modified by a law"), 104.

7. Ibid., 1:288.

8. Legal historians are inclined to date the founding of the first American law school, at Litchfield, Connecticut, at 1837. When Tocqueville spoke of law schools, he was undoubtedly referring to the more informal, academy-like arrangements made by a number of would-be lawyers with a single notable legal scholar (like Virginia's George Mason).

9. Ibid., 1:286, 287.

10. Ibid., 1:106. Also see Tocqueville's discussion of how the gradual pace with which the judiciary proceeded diminished the social resistance to it, ibid., 1:106.

11. Ibid., 1:287.

12. Ibid., 1:288.

13. The estimate for 1984 was 649,000 lawyers; Barbara A. Curran, "American Lawyers in the 1980's: A Profession in Transition," *Law & Society Review* 20 (1986): 20.

14. Herbert McClosky and Alida Brill, *Dimensions of Tolerance: What Americans Believe about Civil Liberties* (New York: Russell Sage Foundation, 1983): 245–47.

15. Judicial opinions are full of personal and political philosophy, which are taught as "law" to law students. For example, in the famous flag-salute case, *West Virginia State Board of Education* v. *Barnette*, 319 U.S. 624, at 639–40 (1943), which dealt with schools and religious freedom, Justice Jackson redefined "liberalism" as a philosophy of the activist state, reversing its former laissez-faire connotation. He wrote (and thousands of students read):

These [liberal] principles [of the eighteenth century] grew in soil which also produced a philosophy that the individual was the center of society, that his liberty was attainable through the mere absence of governmental restraints, and that government should be entrusted with few controls and only the mildest supervision of men's affairs. We must transplant these rights to a soil in which the *laissez-faire* concept or principle of non-interference has withered at least as to economic affairs, and social advancements are increasingly sought through closer integration of society and through expanded and strengthened governmental controls.

16. *Steward Machine Co.* v. *Davis*, 301 U.S. 548 (1937).

17. "Federal judgeships are . . . certain to have great political significance and priority in presidential politics after the Reagan era," said David M. O'Brien, "The Reagan Judges: His Most Enduring Legacy?" in Charles O. Jones, ed., *The Reagan Legacy: Promise and Performance* (Chatham, N.J.: Chatham House, 1988): 97.

18. The notion of moral institutions is best elaborated by two books, one theoretical, the other empirical: Chester I. Barnard, *The Functions of the Executive* (Cambridge, Mass.: Harvard University Press, 1938); and Herbert Kaufman, *The Forest Ranger* (Baltimore: Johns Hopkins University Press, 1960).

Notes to Chapter Eleven

1. Wartime was the obvious exception to that rule, for as commander-in-chief the president headed the military, a moral organization of great effectiveness and size when galvanized by crisis. No doubt much of Lincoln's moral ascendancy stemmed from that fact, as did Franklin Roosevelt's. For example, Lincoln spoke to regiments that were being mustered out of service so that he might express the purposes for which they fought in the Civil War.

2. At last count there were 321,627 clergy with a congregation; *Statistical Abstract of the United States: 1987* (Washington, D.C.: Government Printing Office): Table 74.

3. In these latter decades of the twentieth century, the leaders of several mainline religious groups have not been able to persuade the congregations to accept certain nontraditional theological and political interpretations. It was the hierarchies in the Christian denominations, and not the local clergy and parishioners, who tended to stray from the traditional notion of original sin, deemphasize an afterlife, and point the finger at society for mankind's problems. They were the ones who blamed the marketplace for cultivating selfishness, supported active government, and railed against bourgeois materialism. In contrast, the laypersons in the local congregations (and their pastors) tended to hold to the traditions of man's imperfectibility, the importance of self-reliance, and the inevitability of personal tragedy. As a result, they dismissed notions of warring social classes, conceived the family and voluntary association as the matrix of civilization, and appreciated the marketplace as a source of heightened morals. See Michael Nelson, "C. S. Lewis, Gone but Hardly Forgotten," *New York Times* (Pacific Coast edition), November 22, 1988, A15.

> The lives of people in the modern church typically have seemed almost schizophrenic. The sermons they hear and the denominational publications they read are prepared mainly by church leaders trained in liberal academic seminaries, where avant garde theology, radical biblical criticism, and social and political relevance are the reigning gods. These leaders have little to say about sin, resurrection, the afterlife or other traditional doctrines.
>
> But the liturgies of worship and the memories of worshippers are filled with prayers, hymns, Scripture and creeds that embody orthodoxy and keep it alive, if uncomprehended, in the minds of the laity. What [C. S.] Lewis did, by shedding light on the historic teachings of the church, was to help Christians to understand what they already realize is important, even if most of their leaders have forgotten.

4. Religious division (and competition) was an old story in America. Most commentators have felt it was a good thing. See, for example, Max Lerner, *America as a Civilization: Life and Thought in the United States* (New York: Simon and Schuster, 1957): 710: "[Sectarian competition] is closely linked with religious freedom which,

as Madison put it at the Virginia Convention of 1788, 'rises from the multiplicity of sects which pervades America and which is the best and only security for religious liberty in any society.' The competition of creeds has prevented Americans from erecting intolerance into a principle of government."

5. This consideration, for example, disqualified a relatively well-established moral institution, the Freudian network. Freudianism, like the law, had a text, principally Freud's *A General Introduction to Psycho-Analysis* and *The Interpretation of Dreams*. The American Psychoanalytic Association, with its several regional institutes, its hierarchy of training analysts, and its separateness from the medical profession, constituted the "final say," the teaching academy, and the disciplinary mechanism. Scholarly journals and a vast popular psychology media connected the community and provided a ready means for commentary. And the initiation rites to the profession, plus the uniqueness of the Freudian vocabulary and the often counterintuitive nature of its doctrines identified its disciples to themselves and set them apart from others. See Janet Malcolm, *Psychoanalysis: The Impossible Profession* (New York: Vintage Books, 1982).

6. Peter Robinson, interview with the author, August 27, 1984, Washington, D.C.

7. Peggy Noonan, interview with the author, December 7, 1984, Washington, D.C.

8. Anthony R. Dolan, interview with the author, December 3, 1984, Washington, D.C.

9. "Annual Convention of the National Conference of Catholic Charities, Kansas City, Missouri," October 15, 1979, *Public Papers of the Presidents of the United States: Jimmy Carter, 1979* (Washington, D.C.: Government Printing Office, 1980): 2:1927.

10. "National Prayer Breakfast," January 18, 1979, ibid., 1:58–61.

11. "Remarks on Presenting the Robert F. Kennedy Medal to Mrs. Ethel Kennedy," June 5, 1981, *PP81*:488.

12. "Remarks on Presenting the Presidential Medal of Freedom to the Family of the Late Senator Henry M. Jackson of Washington," June 26, 1984, *PP84*:1:913, 914.

13. "Remarks at the Presentation of the Congressional Gold Medal Honoring Hubert H. Humphrey," September 11, 1984, *PP84*:2:1267.

14. "Remarks at the Annual Convention of the National Religious Broadcasters," February 9, 1982, *PP82*:1:158. All remaining quotations from his remarks to this meeting of the religious broadcasters come from 157–60.

15. "Remarks at the Annual Convention of the National Religious Broadcasters," January 31, 1983, *PP83*:1:153–54. All remaining quotations from his remarks to this meeting of the religious broadcasters come from 151–54.

16. "Remarks at the Annual Convention of the National Religious Broadcasters," January 30, 1984, *PP84*:1:121. All remaining quotations from his remarks to this meeting of the religious broadcasters come from 117–21.

17. Of course, the president was nurturing these ideas before lay audiences all the while. For example, Kansas State University invited him to extend his thoughts about a free society and the role of government. On that occasion he noted that government had several important functions: to exercise the police power ("to ensure that liberty does not become license to prey on each other") and to cultivate morality (to see that people develop "standards of right and wrong" and take satisfaction in "liv[ing] up to" them. But those standards, said the president, can only be crystallized by good deeds based upon them—deeds "renewing our spirit of friendship, community service, and caring for the needy."

When the government exceeds its policing and moral function, when it acts beyond its proper sphere, it denies individuals the chance to reinforce their personal morality with the pride of personal accomplishment: "This Federal government of ours, by trying to do too much, has undercut the ability of individual people, of communities, churches, and businesses to meet the real needs of society as Americans have always met them in the past."

But if government was limited, who would do the things the individual is too small to accomplish? The president introduced the notion of intermediate powers in language virtually the same as he would later use before the religious broadcasters: "Look around you: There's so much more to America than government on the one hand and individuals with nowhere to turn for help but to government on the other. Between the government and the individual, there are a great number of natural, voluntary organizations which people form for themselves—like the family, the church, the neighborhood, and the work place, where people learn, grow, help, and prosper." "Remarks at Kansas State University at the Alfred M. Landon Lecture Series on Public Issues," September 9, 1982, *PP83*:2:1121.

18. "Remarks at the Conservative Political Action Conference Dinner," March 20, 1981, *PP81*:276–78.

19. "Remarks at a Conservative Political Action Conference Dinner," February 26, 1982, *PP82*:1:228, 229.

20. "Remarks at the Annual Convention of the National Association of Evangelicals in Orlando, Florida," March 8, 1963, *PP83*:1:360–64.

21. "Remarks at the Annual Convention of the National Association of Evangelicals in Columbus, Ohio," March 6, 1984, *PP84*:1:305–7.

22. "Remarks at an Ecumenical Prayer Breakfast in Dallas, Texas, August 23, 1984, *PP84*:2:1165–68.

23. Peter Robinson, interview with the author, August 27, 1984, Washington, D.C.

24. The inaugural issue of the *Notre Dame Journal of Law, Ethics and Public Policy*, vol. 1, no. 1 (1985): 7–11, for example, reprinted the president's ecumenical prayer breakfast remarks in their entirety as its lead article,

25. The renowned Polish philosopher, Leszek Kolokowski, for example, was selected in 1984 to give the 15th Annual Jefferson Lecture by the government-supported (and presidentially appointed) National Endowment for the Humanities. His address, later published as "The Idolatry of Politics," sounded many of the same themes as the president: the fact of personal responsibility, the overreliance on government, and the problem of personal meaning in a relativistic moral world.

26. The American Roman Catholic Church, for example, hosted throughout the Reagan presidency an extraordinary debate on the moral consequences of economic freedom, a debate turning on the preparation and publication of a "Pastoral Letter on Catholic Social Teaching and the U.S. Economy" (first draft, November 11, 1984). See *National Catholic Reporter*, November 23, 1984, 9–30. Among its public defenders was Governor Mario Cuomo of New York; among its more vocal detractors was a group of Catholic laymen (headed by former secretary of the Treasury William Simon and writer Michael Novak), which prepared a counterdocument called, "Toward the Future: Catholic Social Thought and the U.S. Economy."

Notes to Chapter Twelve

1. "Remarks on the Caribbean Basin Initiative at a White House Briefing for Chief Executive Officers of United States Corporations," April 28, 1982, *PP82*:1:528.

2. "Remarks at a White House Briefing on the State of Small Business," March 1, 1982, *PP82*:1, 237.

3. "Inaugural Address," March 4, 1933, *The Public Papers and Addresses of Franklin D. Roosevelt*, ed. Samuel I. Rosenman (New York: Random House, 1938): 2:11.

4. "Campaign Address at Chicago, Illinois," October 14, 1936, ibid., 5:482.

5. "Address at the Jackson Day Dinner," January 8, 1936, ibid., 5:43.

6. "Annual Message to the Congress, 1936," January 3, 1936, ibid., 5:13–14.

7. Ibid. "The wealthy criminal class," the "lunatic fringe," "battle," and the admonition to "drive some people from power"—this was the language of incitement, aggression, and virtual annihilation. It was most certainly not the measured cadences of reason and conciliation. This was a challenge of class warfare, of good against evil, of benevolent central government against selfish and unscrupulous exploiters.

8. In 1989, for example, the columnist Henry Fairlie concluded his *New Republic* criticism of President George Bush's first inaugural address by invoking FDR's inaugural diatribe:

> Bush did not refer to today's money changers who stand indicted in the courts of law—some of them having contributed more than $100,000 to Bush's campaign. "The money changers have fled from the high seats in the temple of our civilization. We may now restore the temple to the ancient truths," said FDR. Bush's appeal to old values offered no such challenge. He sought to make no enemies, and such a man cannot lead. You cannot address a nation in short pants. (Henry Fairlie, "Go Fly a Kite: Bush's Windy Inaugural Address," *New Republic*, vol. 200, no. 7 [February 13, 1989]: 16)

9. That was Speaker of the House O'Neill's term of opprobrium for President Reagan. See "'Tip' and His Democrats: Where Now?" *U.S. News & World Report*," November 26, 1984, 28. It was the influential economist, John Maynard Keynes, who wrote: "In the field of economics and political philosophy there are not many who are influenced by new theories after they are twenty-five or thirty years of age, so the ideas which civil servants, and politicians, apply to current events are not likely to be the newest. But, soon or late, it is ideas, not vested interests, which are dangerous for good or evil." John Maynard Keynes, *The General Theory of Employment, Interest, and Money* (New York: Harcourt, Brace, 1936): 183–84. If ever one looked for illustration of the enduring power of anachronistic ideas in "the field of economics and politics," one could hardly find a better example than Speaker O'Neill.

10. "Inaugural Address," January 20, 1981, *PP81*:2.

11. See Chapter Five and the discussion of the foot race metaphor of President Lyndon Johnson [Commencement address at Howard University], June

242   *Notes to pages 151–155*

4, 1965, *Public Papers of the Presidents of the United States: Lyndon B. Johnson, 1965* (Washington, D.C.: Government Printing Office, 1967), 636.

12. "Inaugural Address," January 20, 1981, *PP81*:1.

13. The exact language was vague at best, however: "this administration's objective will be a healthy, vigorous, growing economy. . . . With the idealism and fair play which are the core of our system and our strength, we can have a strong and prosperous America." Ibid., 2.

14. "Address to the Nation on the Economy," February 5, 1981, *PP81*:80–81.

15. Ibid., 80: "We're victims of language. The very word 'inflation' leads us to think of it as just high prices. Then, of course, we resent the person who puts on the price tags, forgetting that he or she is also a victim of inflation. Inflation is not just high prices; it's a reduction in the value of our money."

16. See Keynes, *The General Theory of Employment*, 383–84: "Practical men, who believe themselves to be quite exempt from any intellectual influences, are usually the slaves of some defunct economist. Madmen in authority, who hear voices in the air, are distilling the frenzy from some academic scribbler of a few years back."

17. See Alexis de Tocqueville, *Democracy in America*, trans. Henry Reeve, ed. Phillips Bradley, rev. Francis Bowen (New York: Random House, 1954): 1:201ff.: "In America the citizens who form the minority associate in order, first, to show their numerical strength and so to diminish the moral power of the majority; and, secondly, to stimulate competition and thus to discover those arguments that are most fitted to act upon the majority; for they always entertain hopes of drawing over the majority to their side."

18. "Remarks at a White House Briefing on the State of Small Business," March 1, 1982, *PP82*:1:235. Unless otherwise noted, all subsequent Reagan quotations are taken from these remarks, *PP82*:1:235–38.

19. Ibid., 237. Later he would develop the notion that taxes were the "prices" that government exacted to maintain itself:

> Tax rates are prices—prices for working, saving, and investing. And when you raise the price of those productive activities, you get less of them and more activity in the underground economy—tax shelters and leisure pursuits. You in small business understand that you can't force people to buy merchandise that isn't selling by raising your price. But too many in Washington and across the country still believe that we can raise more revenues from the economy by making it more expensive to work, save, and invest in the economy.
>
> We can't repeal human nature. ("Remarks at the National Conference of the National Federation of Independent Business," June 22, 1983, *PP83*:1:900–901)

20. Particularly instructive were the president's "Remarks at the National Conference of the National Federation of Business," June 22, 1983, *PP83*:1:896–901, and "Remarks at the Annual Convention of the Concrete and Aggregates Industries Association in Chicago, Illinois," January 31, 1984, *PP84*:1:125–29.

21. "Radio Address to the Nation on Small Business," May 14, 1983, *PP83*:1:705.

22. George Gilder, *Wealth and Poverty* (New York: Basic Books, 1981). Next to Tocqueville, Gilder may well have been the most frequently cited author in

Reagan's speeches. Gilder's cousin, Josh Gilder, joined the Speechwriting Department in 1985, but he was not alone in his admiration for *Wealth and Poverty*. Moreover, the president liked George Gilder's penchant for telling exemplary tales of entrepreneurial success. See, for example, George Gilder, *The Spirit of Enterprise* (New York: Simon and Schuster, 1984).

23. *Adkins* v. *Children's Hospital*, 261 U.S. 525, at 561 (1923).

24. "Radio Campaign Address to Dinners of Businessmen, Held throughout the Nation," October 23, 1936, *The Public Papers and Addresses of Franklin D. Roosevelt*, 5:535.

25. *Lochner* v. *New York*, 198 U.S. 45, at 75–76 (1905).

26. Joseph A. Schumpeter, *Capitalism, Socialism and Democracy*, 3rd ed. (New York: Harper & Brothers, 1950): 61, 161.

27. Schumpeter's despair about the "bourgeoisie" not really caring eerily echoed Joan Didion's observations of the parents of the flower children of the 1960s: "At some point . . . we had somehow neglected to tell these children the rules of the game we happened to be playing. Maybe we had stopped believing in the rules ourselves." See Chapter One.

28. At a Republican party fund-raiser in the spring of 1984 Reagan talked of the good Mariotta was doing—"providing jobs and training for the hardcore unemployed of the South Bronx" and after experiencing all the ups and downs of entrepreneurship helping "hundreds of people who would otherwise be condemned to menial jobs or a life on the dole"—through WedTech, the company he had built. "Remarks at a New York Republican Party Fundraising Dinner," March 6, 1984, *PP84*:1:313.

29. See Chester I. Barnard's brilliant *The Functions of the Executive* (Cambridge, Mass.: Harvard University Press, 1938): c.17. Barnard himself was a phone company executive.

30. Fareed Zakaria, "Ethics for Greedheads," *New Republic*, October 19, 1987, 20.

31. The professional business schools avoided such moral and intellectual discipline. The Haas School of Business Administration at the University of California, Berkeley, was (I think) typical of such schools throughout the 1980s. Although it offered more than 150 courses, none dealt systematically with what Peter L. Berger called "a theory of capitalism"—a comprehensive account of the connection between capitalism and morals, political structure, values, culture, and innovation. Peter L. Berger, *The Capitalist Revolution: Fifty Propositions about Prosperity, Equality, and Liberty* (New York: Basic Books, 1986).

32. See David Vogel, *Fluctuating Fortunes: The Political Power of Business in America* (New York: Basic Books, 1989), which insightfully touches on the ineffectiveness of the business community as a moral institution. See, especially, p. 227, where he discusses the intellectual justification for capitalism presented by George Gilder in *Wealth and Poverty* and Michael Novak in *The Spirit of Democratic Capitalism*. Although their works were widely discussed, neither Gilder nor Novak found a place in courses within business school and economics department curricula: the moral questions they raised never seemed to have a niche to fit in. Thus, although Vogel remarks, "By the early 1980's, 'capitalism' had once again become a reputable term in American political and intellectual discourse," the commentary community was too weak to sustain the debate for long and the word was never amplified with the force with which the religious community debated the nature of man.

Notes to Chapter Thirteen

1. "Interview With Steven R. Weisman and Francis X. Clines of the New York Times on Foreign and Domestic Issues," March 28, 1984, *PP84*:1:427.

2. "Annual Dinner of the White House Correspondents Association," April 21, 1988, *WC88*:24:512:

A President may like members of the press personally, and I do . . . but a President institutionally seeks to wield power to accomplish his goals for the people. The press complicates the wielding of that power by using its own great power, and that makes for friction. Every President will try to use the press to his best advantage and to avoid those situations that aren't to his advantage. To do otherwise results in a diminution of his leadership powers. The press is not a weak sister that needs bracing. It has more freedom, more influence, than ever in our history. The press can take care of itself quite nicely. So, what I hope my epitaph will be with the White House correspondents, what every President's epitaph should be with the press is this: He gave as good as he got. And that I think will make for a healthy press and a healthy Presidency.

3. "Inaugural Address," March 4, 1933, *The Public Papers and Addresses of Franklin D. Roosevelt*, ed. Samuel I. Rosenman (New York: Random House, 1938): 2:14.

4. Responding to a question whether Jews should pay taxes to their Roman rulers, Christ pointed to the profile of Caesar on the currency of the day and said, "Whose is this image and superscription? . . . Render therefore unto Caesar the things which are Caesar's; and unto God the things that are God's," Matt. 22:17–21. It would be hard to find a better epigraph for the New Deal than Saint Paul's admonition to the Romans, "We then that are strong ought to bear the infirmities of the weak, and not to please ourselves," Rom. 15:1.

5. "Address before the Federal Council of Churches in Christ," December 6, 1933, *The Public Papers and Addresses of Franklin D. Roosevelt*, 2:517–19.

6. Here, in its entirety, was that letter:

Your high calling brings you into intimate daily contact not only with your own parishioners, but with people generally in your community. I am sure you see the problems of your people with wise and sympathetic understanding.

Because of the grave responsibilities of my office, I am turning to representative clergymen for counsel and advice, feeling confident that no group can give more accurate or unbiased views.

I am particularly anxious that the new social security legislation just enacted, for which we have worked so long, providing for old-age pensions, aid for crippled children and unemployment insurance, shall be carried out in keeping with the high purposes with which this law was enacted. It is also vitally important that the works program shall be administered to provide employment at useful work, and that our unemployed as well as the Nation as a whole may derive the greatest possible benefits.

I shall deem it a favor if you will write me about conditions in your community. Tell me where you feel our Government can better serve our people. We can solve our many problems, but no one man or single group can do it. We shall have to work together for the common end of better spiritual and material conditions for the American people.

May I have your counsel and your help? I am leaving on a short vacation, but will be back in Washington in a few weeks and I will deeply appreciate your writing to me.

Very sincerely yours,
Franklin Delano Roosevelt

("The President Asks for the Counsel and Help of the Clergy of America," September 23, 1935, ibid., 4:370)

7. "Note" to "The First Press Conference," March 8, 1933, ibid., 2:38–40.

8. Ibid., 2:41, 45, quoting Theodore G. Joslin, *Sunday Star* of Washington, D.C., March 4, 1934.

9. "The Two Hundred Sixtieth Press Conference, Held for Faculty Members of Several Schools of Journalism," December 27, 1935, *The Public Papers and Addresses of Franklin D. Roosevelt*, 4:508.

10. "The First Press Conference," March 8, 1933, ibid., 2:31.

11. *United States* v. *Schecter*, 295 U.S. 495 (1935).

12. Ibid., 553.

13. The quotations from this press conference are from "The Two Hundred Ninth Press Conference," May 31, 1935, *The Public Papers and Addresses of Franklin D. Roosevelt*, 4:200–201, 205, 232, 324, 215–16, 218–19, 221–222.

14. See the questions asked of President Reagan by reporters at "The President's News Conferences" of June 16, March 6, and November 10, 1981, and by Walter Cronkite in "Excerpts from an Interview with Walter Cronkite of CBS News," March 3, 1981, *PP81*:526, 209, 1031, and 194.

15. Compare the vision of the presidency likely to be held by the Washington press corps with that reflected in Tony Dolan's remarks:

> Progress in our nation is what the people do, not what the government does for them. . . . The president is convinced that the presidency is not, and should not be, that important. . . . There was a story of the Malta shopkeeper—in Malta there is a government with Marxist-Leninist notions—who said, "We never used to care who was the Minister of This or the Minister of That. Now, we are constantly reminded of who he is." Remember the definition of Hell which C. S. Lewis gave us in *The Screwtape Letters*? Hell is bureaucracy. (Anthony R. Dolan, interview with the author, December 3, 1984, Washington, D.C.)

16. Some advisers had direct experience as journalists themselves to support such expectations: for example, chief speechwriter Elliott. His experiences at CBS convinced him that "a lot of reporters and producers had this certain view of the world that I did not share: that the [Vietnam] war was a force for instability in the world; that our own society was riddled with corruption; that we were basically a dishonest society; that Americans and American business people prey on one another; that people were victims and not able to control their own

destinies; that if there was a problem, it was someone else's fault." Bently Elliott, interview with the author, June 10, 1985, Washington, D.C.

17. Charlotte Saikowski, informal interview with author, summer 1984, Washington, D.C. Reagan and his speechwriters appreciated the limitations imposed on journalists by this definition of newsworthiness. In speaking to the Knights of Columbus, the Roman Catholic lay service arm of the church, he spoke of the necessity of reporters looking at events in the short range:

> Now, in pointing out this tendency of some commentators to focus on only the immediate or the political, I don't mean to sound too critical. Actually, the American press does a remarkable job of piecing together quite clearly, and sometimes in a matter of hours or minutes, the dizzying events of the modern world. Yet I think the very speed of this process can oftentimes cloud the understanding and serve as an obstacle to good judgment and historical perspective. . . .
>
> It would have been hard, for example, for any reporter covering those first meetings of the Knights of Columbus in St. Mary's basement to have sensed the potential importance of Father McGivney and his small band of Catholic laymen. But as the history of the Knights of Columbus has proven, discussions of our basic values are a vital part of our national political dialogue, for it's only in these values, only in the faith that sees beyond the here and now, that we find rationale for our own daring notions about the inalienable rights of free men and women. (*PP82*:2:1009–10.)

18. "The President's News Conference," December 8, 1988, *WC88*:24:1603.

Notes to Chapter Fourteen

1. In the past presidents have been deserted by their principal moral supporters. Because of Vietnam War developments, for example, President Lyndon Johnson was abandoned by the two institutional collaborators on which his original moral efforts had depended, the church and the academic community.

2. See William K. Muir, Jr., *Police: Streetcorner Politicians* (Chicago: University of Chicago Press, 1976): 252–57, which discusses a police chief who built up his police academy program and then participated heavily in instruction.

3. Ronald Reagan, "A Time for Choosing," October 27, 1964, in *Ronald Reagan Talks to America*, intro. Richard M. Scaife (Old Greenwich, Conn.: Devin Adair, 1983): 3–18. See the Appendix for the text of "The Speech."

4. Ibid.

5. Al Meyer, interview with the author, November 30, 1984, Washington, D.C.

6. The information for most of this chapter comes from interviews, in Washington, D.C., with individuals performing the speechwriting function in eleven executive agencies: Agriculture (Eugene Hemphill, April 8, 1985); Commerce (B. J. Cooper, November 28, 1984); HUD (Jayne W. Gallagher, June 14, 1985); Interior (Bob Walker, September 6, 1984); Justice (Terry Eastland, June 26, 1985); Labor (Don Smyth, June 18, 1985); Office of Management and Budget (Ed Dale, June 21, 1985); State (Peter Rodman, December 27, 1984); Office of the Trade

Representative (David Demarest, October 31, 1984); Transportation (Joe Dugan, April 9, 1985); and Treasury (Terry Bresnahan, December 20, 1984).

7. Richard Fenno wrote of the cabinet in earlier years: "Agriculture, Commerce, and Labor were created in part by a specialized clientele, and the close relationships established then have been strengthened since. These departments have, from the beginning, been subjected to lines of influence which often pull them away from the president. Their position is quite different from the Secretary of State who came into being without any group support." Richard Fenno, *The President's Cabinet: An Analysis in the Period from Wilson to Eisenhower* (Cambridge, Mass.: Harvard University Press, 1959): 24. See also his "President-Cabinet Relations: A Pattern and a Case Study," *American Political Science Review* 52 (June 1958): 388–405.

8. James Q. Wilson, *American Government: Institutions and Policies*, 4th ed. (Lexington, Mass.: D.C. Heath, 1989): 332–33. See also Richard P. Nathan, *The Plot That Failed: Nixon and the Administrative Presidency* (New York: John Wiley and Sons, 1975): chap. 3. Nathan quotes Nixon's domestic policy chief John Ehrlichman: "After the Administration appointed key officials to high posts and they had their picture taken with the President, 'We only see them at the annual White House Christmas Party; they go off and marry the natives'" (40).

9. Martin Anderson, *Revolution* (San Diego and New York: Harcourt Brace Jovanovich, 1988): 224. Chapter 19 of that book is the best description thus far of how cabinet councils functioned to harmonize relations between senior White House staff and the cabinet. The subject areas of the cabinet councils were economic affairs, natural resources and environment, commerce and trade, human resources, food and agriculture, legal policy, and management and administration.

10. William A. Niskanen, *Reaganomics: An Insider's Account of the Policies and the People* (New York: Oxford University Press, 1988): 305. Niskanen, member and one-time acting chair of the Council of Economic Advisers, thought the cabinet council system "very valuable" from a policy-making standpoint (304–6).

11. Both Fenno and Wilson found in earlier presidencies that the cabinet secretaries were not "especially interested" in discussing policies outside their particular agencies' domains. See Wilson, *American Government*, 323; and Fenno, *The President's Cabinet*, 137. If such was once the case, things were different in the Reagan cabinet. Secretary of Commerce Malcolm Baldrige, for example, "through the Cabinet and Cabinet Councils, . . . essentially has really gotten involved in policy making." Commerce Department speechwriter B. J. Cooper, interview with the author, November 28, 1984, Washington, D.C.

12. "Remarks at the Swearing-In Ceremony for George P. Shultz," July 16, 1982, *PP82*:2:930.

13. The "use of routinized cabinet-level committees inculcated a highly legitimated collective esprit among appointees [and] maintained a sense of teamwork among cabinet secretaries," wrote Colin Campbell, *Managing the Presidency: Carter, Reagan, and the Search for Executive Harmony* (Pittsburgh, Pa.: University of Pittsburgh Press, 1986): 273.

14. For example, the agriculture secretary addressed such groups as the Meat Institute, the National Corngrowers Association, and the Western States Dairy Conference; the interior secretary would speak to the American Mining Conference, the American Water Resources Association, and the Ranchers Association; the labor secretary to the NAACP, the Commonwealth Club of San Francisco, and the East Bay Labor Council; the transportation secretary to the Pittsburgh Traffic Club; the attorney general to the American Bar Association; the secretary of state to the Trilateral Commission; and so on.

15. Public presentation consumed a large part of the time of cabinet secretaries. Getting used to this rhetorical task did not always come easy. Agriculture Department speechwriter Eugene Hemphill told of his boss's initial resistance to its demands:

> The Secretary [of Agriculture Jack Block] did not like giving speeches repeatedly, but then he got tired of learning a new speech every time. He speaks so much, maybe three or four times a week, and there is very little blending of audiences; so you can repeat the same speech many times. . . . Block was first like old Earl Butz [President Eisenhower's Agriculture Secretary], who would put his written remarks in his pocket and never refer to them. To overcome that, we evolved a procedure which has worked really well. Every week, maybe every other week, we will go into the Secretary's office and for half an hour to an hour, we will talk about issues. We will have a tape recorder on, and the Secretary talks his mind. We have improved the way we write for him as a result. We pick up the way he talks, his pet phrases, like "I will have to admit that . . . " and "I am worried . . . "—lots of ellipsis, lots of dashes. It doesn't look good on paper, but it sounds good. And we hear Block's humor: it is good humor. We also taped every speech Block made. And as a result the Secretary gradually became involved. (Agriculture Department Speechwriter Eugene Hemphill, interview with the author, April 8, 1985, Washington, D.C.)

16. Those conservative journals included *Public Interest, Commentary, Conservative Digest, National Review, Human Events,* the *Wall Street Journal,* and (irony of ironies) the once archliberal *New Republic.*

17. "The Times Turns 5, Defies Odds, Confounds Critics," *Washington Times,* May 18, 1987, 1A. The publication's stated objective was "to give the conservative option a clear and quality voice in the information mix" (9B).

18. Alexis de Tocqueville, *Democracy in America,* trans. Henry Reeve, ed. Phillips Bradley, rev. Francis Bowen (New York: Random House, 1954): 2:119–20.

19. "Remarks to Members of the Empire and Canadian Clubs in Toronto," June 21, 1988, *WC88:24:838.*

Notes to Chapter Fifteen

1. Richard E. Neustadt, *Presidential Power: The Politics of Leadership* (New York: John Wiley and Sons, 1960): 10.

2. Ibid., 2.

3. Ibid., 2, 44, 38, 52. Neustadt pointed out that important administration officials would resist their president's reasoned arguments, not because the reasoning was faulty, but because they had to judge it on the basis of where they sat: "They will be bound to judge it [the president's command] by the standard of their own responsibilities, not his" (43). In Neustadt's conception, could a president ever affect "the standards of [his officials'] own responsibilities"? Could he take steps to discipline them to see "all things through the same glasses" (44)? According to *Presidential Power,* the answer was no. President Truman (the president whom Neustadt observed directly) never was able to take effective steps to establish a common outlook. Neustadt made no mention of Truman

using presidential rhetoric to infuse a sense of teamwork and common purpose in his administration. In the end Neustadt maintained that a president could do little more than induce others "to believe that what he wants of them is what their own appraisal of their own responsibilities requires them to do in their interest, not his" (46).

4. Ibid., 35, 39, 52.

5. Ibid., 86.

6. The members of the Washington community were the centerpiece of Neustadt's book—the "incestuous" insiders in Congress and on congressional staffs, executive officials, the press and other "president-watchers." A president "must concern himself with what they think," Neustadt said, about the president, about *his* capacity and will to threaten or help the Washington insiders, about *his* "tenacity," *his* political skill, "his professional reputation as a governor" (60, 62). When Neustadt said "what they think," he alluded not to personal and political philosophy, but to petty gossip, columnist talk, inside dopesterisms— the "vivid demonstrations of tenacity and skill," political shoptalk about the personal "consequences of ignoring what he wants," and assurances of executive support "if they [the insiders] support him" (63,64).

Oratory had only one purpose, to move the national government to greater activity. When the president made a public broadcast, it was to justify "action taken" (18), explain decisions made, announce to the nation a command given (19). The point of talking publicly was to publicize—to disclose the fact that an order had been given to someone, thus exposing anyone contemplating resistance to the spotlight of public scrutiny. Publicity was "a means to raise the cost of defiance," to embarrass the recalcitrant, to discourage resistance. The role of the public was instrumental: "to watch the response" of officials, to hold public servants accountable, to make "the other men involved in governing the country" do what the president wanted them to do (22). Animating the public to do things for itself was not a presidential objective Neustadt much cared about.

7. Ibid., 192.

8. Ibid., 2. Neustadt did not entirely ignore the potential importance of presidential rhetoric in shaping public opinion. He remarked, for example, that a president's words could educate the public, as long as they could be embroidered on deeds. But they were of minimal significance. Consider his estimate of Franklin Roosevelt's reassuring words in his first inaugural, "We have nothing to fear but fear itself": "Had there not been One Hundred Days, and work relief, and a degree of real recovery, the lesson of those words would have been bitter for the country and his phrase would be remembered now with mockery not cheers" (104). Neustadt did not credit the possibility that Roosevelt's instructive words might have been critical in bringing about economic recovery. Rather, he felt that Roosevelt's lesson about courage and fear was merely embroidery, an aftermath of the real recovery that governmental action had brought about.

9. James W. Ceaser, "The Reagan Presidency and American Public Opinion," in Charles O. Jones, ed., *The Reagan Legacy: Promise and Performance* (Chatham, N.J.: Chatham House, 1988): 175, 201.

10. In speaking to the business community during these months of travail he attempted to promote an "economic bill of rights," a mishmash of minor policies incoherently justified. The idea turned out to be a nonstarter, and his campaign for it stopped as soon as the Iran-Contra scandal disappeared from public sensitivity.

11. "Conservative Political Action Conference," February 20, 1987, *WC87*:23:176.

12. Jeffrey K. Tulis has argued that a "rhetorical presidency," in rallying public opinion with careless references to crises, endangers thoughtful governmental consideration of public policy. *The Rhetorical Presidency* (Princeton, N.J.: Princeton University Press, 1987): chap. 6. I think his general warning is well taken; I think, also, that in making Reagan a noteworthy exception, he is right, as well: "Reagan and his advisers have been sensitive to some of the pitfalls of the rhetorical presidency that I have mentioned. This administration has given considerable attention to the structure of speeches, crafting them not just for the immediate presentation but as written documents as well [in order to] contribute to the deliberative process" by making an ordered argument (191–92).

13. "White House Meeting with Members of the National Governors' Association," February 22, 1988, *WC88*:24:240.

Notes to Part Four: "Epilogue"

1. Ronald Reagan, interview with the author, August 11, 1989, Los Angeles, California.

2. Lou Cannon, *Reagan* (New York: G. P. Putnam's Sons, 1982): 94: "He learned how to listen to a live audience. He paid attention to the response of his listeners, making mental notes about which jokes succeeded and which statistics served to make his points. Politicians and performers love to please their audiences by saying what they think those audiences would like to hear, and Reagan is good both at politics and at performing. The audiences of Reagan's GE tours usually were of the service club or corporate variety, and the questions thrown at him often focused on inflation or government regulation. In the process of answering these questions in a manner pleasing to the questioners, Reagan became a defender of corporations and a critic of the government that the corporate leaders thought was strangling them. The process was gradual, but pervasive. Reagan believes in what he says, and he wound up believing what he was saying. More than anything, it is his GE experience that changed Reagan from an adversary of big business into one of its most ardent spokesmen."

3. See Garry Wills, *Reagan's America: Innocents at Home* (Garden City, N.Y.: Doubleday, 1987): 282: "He accepted [GE's] censorship of his own speeches about TVA [the Tennessee Valley Authority, a government agency customer of GE]." Cannon (*Reagan*, 95), however, contradicts Wills and accepts Reagan's version of the incident, namely, that GE, as "a matter of principle," did not censor Reagan's criticisms of TVA and that Reagan, after inadvertently discovering GE's discomfort with them, removed the troublesome paragraph voluntarily.

4. Paul Gavaghan, a GE publicity director who conducted Reagan on one of his New England tours, told Garry Wills about Reagan's sense of craftsmanship as writer and speaker at that time: "His speech was always the same, he had it polished to perfection . . . always lively, with entertaining stories. . . . He was a professional." Garry Wills, *Reagan's America*, 283.

5. See Cannon, *Reagan*, 106: "Reagan's decision to run was now widely known, but he left himself an escape hatch in case neither money nor support materialized."

6. See ibid., 113: "Late in 1965, under the auspices of Friends of Ronald Reagan, Reagan made a number of speaking trips around the state to give short talks and answer questions. The speeches were Spencer's idea, developed as an advance rebuttal to anticipated criticism that Reagan was simply an actor repeating lines others had written for him."

7. See R. A. Bauer, "The Communicator and the Audience," *Journal of Conflict Resolution* 2 (1958): 67–77: "A person might never formulate his impression . . . until he was in the position of having to communicate them to someone else. In this event, the first audience to whom he addressed himself would influence the way in which he would organize his information and the terms in which he would couch his conclusions. In this way the audience would influence what he would later remember and believe."

Index

About the Author

William Ker Muir, Jr., is professor of political science at the University of California, Berkeley. He served for two years in the Reagan administration as a speechwriter for Vice President George Bush. Among his previously published books is *Police: Streetcorner Politicians,* for which he won the Hadley B. Cantril Prize. Professor Muir is also a recipient of U.C. Berkeley's Distinguished Teaching Award.